Portfolio Construction and Risk Budgeting

Portfolio Construction and Risk Budgeting

Bernd Scherer

Published by Risk Books, a division of the Risk Waters Group.

Haymarket House
28–29 Haymarket
London SW1Y 4RX
Tel: +44 (0)20 7484 9700
Fax: +44 (0)20 7484 9758
E-mail: books@risk.co.uk
Sites: www.riskbooks.com, www.riskbooks.com,
        www.riskpublications.com

Every effort has been made to secure the permission of individual copyright
holders for inclusion.

© Risk Waters Group Ltd 2002

ISBN 1 899 332 44 8

British Library Cataloguing in Publication Data
A catalogue record for this book is available from the British Library

Risk Books Commissioning Editor: Sarah Jenkins
Desk Editor: Kathryn Roberts

Typeset by Special Edition

Printed and bound in Great Britain by Bookcraft (Bath) Ltd, Somerset

About the Author

Dr Bernd Scherer heads the Advanced Applications Group in Europe and the Middle East at Deutsche Bank's Asset Management division, offering cutting edge investment solutions to a sophisticated institutional client base. Before joining Deutsche Bank, Dr Scherer globally headed fixed-income portfolio research at Schroder Investment Management in London. During his 10-year career in asset management he has held various positions at Morgan Stanley, Oppenheim Investment Management and JP Morgan Investment Management. He publishes widely in relevant asset management industry journals and investment handbooks and is a regular speaker at investment conferences. Dr Scherer's current research interests focus on asset valuation, portfolio construction, strategic asset allocation and asset liability modelling. Dr Scherer holds MBA and MSc degrees from the University of Augsburg and the University of London, as well as a PhD in finance from the University of Giessen.

To Jana, Katharina and Sabiene

Contents

Introduction

OBJECTIVES AND CONTENT

This book aims to provide a comprehensive treatment of alternative portfolio construction techniques, ranging from traditional methods based on mean–variance and lower partial moments approaches, through Bayesian techniques, to more recent developments such as portfolio resampling and stochastic programming solutions using scenario optimisation.

Chapter 1 starts with a review of Markowitz-based solutions, with a particular focus on issues that are of concern to practitioners but are rarely treated in conventional textbooks. These include asset liability management, the use of cluster analysis to redefine the investment universe, the treatment of illiquid asset classes, life-cycle investing, time-varying covariance and implied return analysis.

Chapter 2 moves away from the classical model and introduces non-normality. It provides a toolkit that will enable the user to judge when non-normality is a problem and when it is not. Lower partial moments-based portfolio construction is carefully discussed, and the chapter covers all the mathematical tools needed to apply this important technique to real world portfolio problems.

Chapter 3 introduces estimation error and shows how to deal with it heuristically using portfolio resampling or constrained optimisation. Particular attention is given to the concept of resampled efficiency, which has recently appeared in the literature as an increasing number of investors become interested in this approach to estimation error.

Chapter 4 deals with estimation error from a more conventional angle, reviewing various Bayesian techniques. Close attention is paid to problems with data, particularly time series of different lengths and how to deal them with as they represent one of the main data problems faced by practitioners.

Chapter 5, on scenario optimisation, is a natural extension of the four previous chapters. It describes the most general form of portfolio optimisation that can simultaneously deal with data problems (estimation error, time series of different lengths) and with non-linear instruments, non-normal distributions and non-standard preferences.

Chapter 6 leaves the world of asset allocation and reviews key concepts in making benchmark-relative decisions. Again, the focus is on problems that are rarely handled in traditional textbooks, such as implicit funding assumptions and risk decomposition, optimisation against multiple benchmarks, and tracking error and its forecasting ability. The latter is considered through a comparison of the efficiency of the tracking error approach with that of mean–variance methods.

The book concludes with Chapter 7 on budgeting active manager risk. This provides the mathematical tools to address such questions as how much of a fund to have actively managed, where to be active, and whether core–satellite investing is superior to enhanced indexing.

TARGET AUDIENCE

Anyone developing, managing or selling financial products – whether on the buy or the sell side – needs to know how his or her financial products fit into an investor's portfolio and how much the investor might find optimal. Hence, an understanding of how a scarce risk budget is optimally allocated is essential.

This book has been written primarily for practitioners, including portfolio managers, consultants, strategists, marketers and quantitative analysts. It is largely self-contained, and so could also prove useful to final-year undergraduates and MBAs who wish to extend their knowledge beyond the narrow world of mean–variance-based solutions typically taught at business schools.

Great care has been taken to illustrate theoretical concepts with simple examples that can be reproduced by readers to check their understanding of the methodology involved. This should allow practitioners to apply the algorithms discussed in the text to everyday problems with the minimum difficulty. The book is intended to be accessible to the mathematically interested practitioner who has a basic understanding of calculus, matrix algebra and statistics. Some knowledge of financial economics will also prove helpful.

We think the book comes at the right time as it reviews all the major portfolio construction techniques at a time when portfolio construction is on everybody's radar screen.[1]

IMPORTANCE OF PORTFOLIO CONSTRUCTION

Portfolio construction – meaning the optimal implementation of a set of "signals" generated by strategists, asset allocators, analysts and the like – is at the centre of any modern investment process.[2] This has not always been the case, and cynics might argue that the increased interest in risk management techniques in the asset management arena is in large part a response to the significant underperformance of many investment houses along with its unpleasant consequences, such as legal actions, compensa-

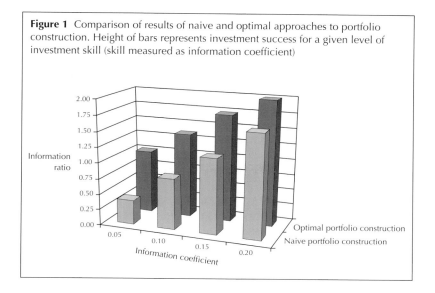

Figure 1 Comparison of results of naive and optimal approaches to portfolio construction. Height of bars represents investment success for a given level of investment skill (skill measured as information coefficient)

tion and/or a shift to passive management. Although that might not apply in all cases, the asset management industry as a whole is undergoing a more realistic assessment of its performance-generating skills.

At this point it is worth drawing the reader's attention to a finding that goes some way to explaining the asset management industry's focus on portfolio construction. For different skill levels we compared the outcome of *naive* portfolio construction (equally overweight/underweight assets with the best/worst signals) with *optimal* portfolio construction (optimally over/underweight assets depending on signal strength as well as risk contributions). Skill levels were measured as an information coefficient, ie, the correlation between forecast returns and actual returns. Performance was measured as the information ratio, which is the active return divided by the active risk – ie, tracking error. The results are summarised in Figure 1.[3]

At realistic levels of investment skill (information coefficient of 0.05), optimal portfolio construction does make a difference, giving an information ratio about four times higher than that of the the naive method. As the skill level rises (moving to the right in the graph), the gap narrows considerably, confirming the intuition that you don't need risk management if you have good forecasts. However, investment skill has to be tripled, from 0.05 to 0.15, to arrive at the same risk-adjusted performance as optimal portfolio construction. Given that an information coefficient of 0.05 might be viewed as the level achieved by the average asset manager, Figure 1 suggests there is good reason for the increasing focus on portfolio construction methods with a sound analytical basis.

PORTFOLIO CONSTRUCTION VERSUS RISK BUDGETING

Contrary to the belief of some, there is no difference between portfolio construction using various portfolio optimisation tools that attempt to trade off expected return against expected risk (return risk, estimation risk, modelling risk, etc) and risk budgeting. That is why this book has been titled "portfolio construction and risk budgeting". Investors have to trade off risk and return in an optimal way, ie, in a way that is both in accordance with their beliefs and preferences and which also ultimately optimises their portfolios. Practitioners may be confused as the result of the optimal portfolio construction exercise is an allocation either in nominal dollar terms or in percentage weights, whereas risk budgeting does not arrive at asset weights but at risk exposures expressed in terms of value-at-risk or percentage contributions to risk.

However, if risk budgets are optimally derived, this is just a presentational difference – one that certainly has educational value but with no investment value. Hence, the biggest advantage of the risk budgeting approach is that it becomes evident to investors that even small positions can carry large risks (a 5% departure from the benchmark allocation into emerging market debt for a portfolio benchmarked against government bonds will consume most of an investor's risk budget). The fact that portfolio optimisation reports results in terms of actual asset weights does not mean that a portfolio optimiser does not look at the risk contributions of different asset classes. Those who see risk budgeting simply as a way of enforcing diversification, and who diversify by assuming rather than deriving a solution, will fail – by over- or underdiversifying – to achieve the highest return per unit of risk and will therefore expose an investor to more risk than necessary.

ACKNOWLEDGEMENTS

I am indebted to Dean Barr (Global CIO at Deutsche Asset Management) and Christoph Bernard (CIO Europe at Deutsche Asset Management) for providing an intellectually stimulating work environment, and to Kenneth Yip (Global Head of Research at Deutsche Asset Management) and colleagues at the Global Research Centre in New York Greg van Invegen, Colm O-Cinnceneide, Ivillina Popova and Christopher Donohue for invaluable discussions. All errors, of course, remain mine.

Writing a book like this at the same time as holding a challenging job also needs the support of your editor. I want to thank the staff at Risk Books – in particular, Conrad Gardener for his enthusiasm to undertake the project and seeing its value from the beginning, Sarah Jenkins for her tireless efforts in coordinating the whole process, and Katy Roberts for her tactful insistence whenever it was needed. However, the biggest appreciation of all goes to my family, whose patience I have tried.

1   The author appreciates comments and ideas and can be contacted at drberndscherer @aol.com.

2   Although the terms "investment process" and "investment philosophy" are often used interchangeably, we believe that there is an important distinction to be made. An investment *philosophy* comprises, among other things, an investor's beliefs concerning how markets operate, where inefficiencies arise and how they can be exploited; in short, the value proposition. The investment *process* refers to the organisational structure and defines best practice on how to implement an existing investment philosophy most effectively. Portfolio construction and risk budgeting are, therefore, integral parts of an investment process but not of an investment philosophy. Investment philosophy is about signal generation, whereas the investment process concerns how a given set of signals is put to use.

3   Chapter 7 provides a more detailed explanation of the calculations behind Figure 1.

Philosophy
how to generate
    signals

Process
how to use
    signals

Traditional Portfolio Construction: Selected Issues

1.1 MEAN–VARIANCE-BASED PORTFOLIO CONSTRUCTION

The theory of mean–variance-based portfolio selection is a cornerstone of modern asset management.[1] It rests on the presumption that rational investors choose among risky assets purely on the basis of expected return and risk, with risk measured as variance. In this case a portfolio is considered mean–variance-efficient if it minimises the variance for a given expected mean return or if it maximises the expected mean return for a given variance. Mean–variance efficiency rests on firm theoretical grounds if either:

❏ investors exhibit quadratic utility – in which case they ignore non-normality in the data;[2] or
❏ returns are multivariate normal – in which case the utility function is irrelevant as all higher moments, such as skewness or kurtosis, can be expressed as a function of mean and variance and, hence, all optimal solutions satisfy the mean–variance criterion.[3]

Both assumptions will be relaxed in Chapters 2 to 5.

1.1.1 Mean–variance optimisation in an asset-only world

We start with the solution to the portfolio construction problem in a world without stochastic liabilities, ie, where liabilities come in the form of a fixed-hurdle rate (like cash).

Suppose we know the $k \times 1$ vector of expected returns, $\boldsymbol{\mu}$, where the ith element represents the expected return over cash, c,[4] and that we also know the $k \times k$ covariance matrix of returns, $\boldsymbol{\Omega}$.[5] We now want to find the $k \times 1$ vector of optimal portfolio weights, $\mathbf{w}^*$. The matrix and the two vectors can be written as

$$\boldsymbol{\Omega} = \begin{bmatrix} \sigma_{11} & \cdots & \sigma_{1k} \\ \vdots & \ddots & \vdots \\ \sigma_{k1} & \cdots & \sigma_{kk} \end{bmatrix}, \quad \mathbf{w} = \begin{bmatrix} w_1 \\ \vdots \\ w_k \end{bmatrix}, \quad \boldsymbol{\mu} = \begin{bmatrix} \mu_1 \\ \vdots \\ \mu_k \end{bmatrix} \quad (1.1)$$

where $\sigma_{ij} = \mathrm{cov}(R_i - c, R_j - c)$ and $\mu_i = \mathrm{E}(R_i - c)$, where R_i is the total return of the ith asset. Portfolio risk, σ_p^2, measured as variance, and portfolio return, μ_p, are calculated from[6]

$$\sigma_p = \begin{bmatrix} w_1 \\ \vdots \\ w_k \end{bmatrix}' \begin{bmatrix} \sigma_{11} & \cdots & \sigma_{1k} \\ \vdots & \ddots & \vdots \\ \sigma_{k1} & \cdots & \sigma_{kk} \end{bmatrix} \begin{bmatrix} w_1 \\ \vdots \\ w_k \end{bmatrix}, \quad \mu_p = \begin{bmatrix} w_1 \\ \vdots \\ w_k \end{bmatrix}' \begin{bmatrix} \mu_1 \\ \vdots \\ \mu_k \end{bmatrix} \qquad (1.2)$$

where primes indicate a transposed matrix. In practice we can either:

❏ minimise portfolio variance for all portfolios ranging from minimum return to maximum return to trace out an efficient frontier (the geometric location of all mean–variance-efficient portfolios, ie, of future investment opportunities); or
❏ construct optimal portfolios for different risk-tolerance parameters, λ, and, by varying λ, find the efficient frontier.

We follow the latter approach, which trades off risk against return by maximising

$$Utility \approx \mu_p - \frac{1}{2\lambda}\sigma_p^2 = \mathbf{w}'\boldsymbol{\mu} - \frac{1}{2\lambda}\mathbf{w}'\boldsymbol{\Omega}\mathbf{w} \qquad (1.3)$$

for various risk-tolerance parameters. *Utility* is a measure of happiness. The higher our risk tolerance, the less weight is given to the variance (penalty) term and the more aggressive our portfolios will become.[7]

The optimal solution[8] is found by taking the first derivative with respect to portfolio weights, setting the term to zero and solving for the optimal weight vector, $\mathbf{w}^*$:[9]

$$\frac{\mathrm{d}\,Utility}{\mathrm{d}\mathbf{w}} = \boldsymbol{\mu} - \frac{1}{2\lambda}2\boldsymbol{\Omega}\mathbf{w} = \boldsymbol{\mu} - \frac{1}{\lambda}\boldsymbol{\Omega}\mathbf{w} = 0$$

$$\mathbf{w}^* = \lambda\boldsymbol{\Omega}^{-1}\boldsymbol{\mu} \qquad (1.4)$$

Note that the portfolio in Equation (1.4) does not add up to 100%, but we can think of cash as the difference remaining because cash has a zero risk premium and no variance. The optimal allocation into risky assets rises with higher risk tolerance, higher return and diminishing uncertainty about the mean return (the inverse of a covariance matrix is a measure of the precision of mean returns).

1.1.2 Introducing constraints
To be more realistic, we introduce general (binding) linear constraints of the form $\mathbf{Aw} = \mathbf{b}$, where $\mathbf{A}$ denotes a matrix with k columns (equal to the number of assets) and m rows (equal to the number of equality

constraints) and where $\mathbf{b}$ is a $k \times 1$ vector of limits.[10] We maximise

$$Utility \approx \mathbf{w}'\boldsymbol{\mu} - \frac{1}{2\lambda}\mathbf{w}'\boldsymbol{\Omega}\mathbf{w} \quad \text{subject to } \mathbf{A}\mathbf{w} = \mathbf{b} \quad (1.5)$$

Forming the standard Lagrangian $L = \mathbf{w}'\boldsymbol{\mu} - \frac{1}{2\lambda}\mathbf{w}'\boldsymbol{\Omega}\mathbf{w} - \boldsymbol{\gamma}'(\mathbf{A}\mathbf{w} - \mathbf{b})$, where $\boldsymbol{\gamma}$ is the $m \times 1$ vector of Lagrangian multipliers (one for each constraint), and taking the first derivatives with respect to the optimal weight vector and the vector of multipliers yields

$$\frac{dL}{d\mathbf{w}} = \boldsymbol{\mu} - \frac{1}{\lambda}\boldsymbol{\Omega}\mathbf{w} - \boldsymbol{\gamma}'\mathbf{A} = 0, \quad \mathbf{w}^* = \lambda\boldsymbol{\Omega}^{-1}(\boldsymbol{\mu} - \boldsymbol{\gamma}'\mathbf{A}) \quad (1.6)$$

$$\frac{dL}{d\boldsymbol{\gamma}} = \mathbf{A}\mathbf{w} - \mathbf{b} = 0, \quad \mathbf{A}\mathbf{w} = \mathbf{b} \quad (1.7)$$

Inserting Equation (1.6) into Equation (1.7) and solving the resulting equation for the Lagrange multipliers, we arrive at

$$\lambda\mathbf{A}\boldsymbol{\Omega}^{-1}\boldsymbol{\mu} - \mathbf{b} = \lambda\mathbf{A}\boldsymbol{\Omega}^{-1}\mathbf{A}'\boldsymbol{\gamma}$$

$$\boldsymbol{\gamma} = \frac{\mathbf{A}\boldsymbol{\Omega}^{-1}\boldsymbol{\mu}}{\mathbf{A}\boldsymbol{\Omega}^{-1}\mathbf{A}'} - \frac{1}{\lambda}\frac{\mathbf{b}}{\mathbf{A}\boldsymbol{\Omega}^{-1}\mathbf{A}'} \quad (1.8)$$

Substituting Equation (1.8) into Equation (1.6), we finally get the optimal solution under linear equality constraints:

$$\mathbf{w}^* = \boldsymbol{\Omega}^{-1}\mathbf{A}'(\mathbf{A}\boldsymbol{\Omega}^{-1}\mathbf{A}')\mathbf{b} + \lambda\boldsymbol{\Omega}^{-1}\left(\boldsymbol{\mu} - \mathbf{A}'(\mathbf{A}\boldsymbol{\Omega}^{-1}\mathbf{A}')^{-1}\mathbf{A}\boldsymbol{\Omega}^{-1}\boldsymbol{\mu}\right) \quad (1.9)$$

The optimal solution is split into a (constrained) minimum-variance portfolio and a speculative portfolio. This is known as "two-fund separation", and can be seen from Equation (1.9), where the first term depends neither on expected returns nor on risk tolerance – and is hence the minimum-risk solution – whereas the second term is sensitive to both inputs. Constrained optimisation reduces the efficiency of the solution as a constrained solution must be less optimal than an unconstrained solution. The loss in efficiency can be measured as the difference between a constrained and an unconstrained solution.[11]

However, it should be stressed that not every difference is for real, ie, statistically or economically significant.[12] We would, for example, expect optimising across sectors to yield better results than optimisation across countries simply because there are more sectors to choose from.

To test for significance, we use the Sharpe ratio, SR. Consider the simple case of running an unconstrained optimisation with k' assets and a constrained optimisation with only k assets ($k' > k$). Whether the better performance of the unconstrained portfolio is statistically significant can be calculated using[13]

$$\frac{(T-k')(k'-k)\left(SR'^2 - SR^2\right)}{\left(1+SR^2\right)} \sim F_{k',\ T-(k'+k+1)} \tag{1.10}$$

where T is the number of observations and SR' is the Sharpe ratio of the unconstrained strategy. The above statistic is F-distributed. However, as we will see in Chapter 3, this is not the only technique for testing whether the performance of two portfolios is significantly different.

1.1.3 Asset–liability management and the surplus-efficient frontier

A conceptual problem of the analysis so far has been that in practice we cannot isolate assets from liabilities. Investors without liabilities do not need assets. Asset–liability management[14] becomes imperative for every investor who seeks to define his or her potential liabilities carefully.[15] It focuses on managing the difference between assets and liabilities, also called "surplus". The change in surplus depends directly on the returns of the asset portfolio, R_p, as well as the liability returns (percentage changes in the value of outstanding liabilities), R_l:

$$\Delta Surplus = Assets \times R_p - Liabilities_t \times R_l \tag{1.11}$$

We will express surplus returns as change in surplus relative to assets:[16]

$$\frac{\Delta Surplus}{Assets} = R_p - \frac{Liabilities}{Assets} R_l$$

$$= R_p - fR_l \tag{1.12}$$

where f is the ratio of liabilities to assets. If we set $f = 1$ and $R_l = c$, we are back in a world without liabilities (alternatively we could think of liabilities as cash). Surplus volatility, $\sigma^2_{surplus}$, can now be incorporated into the well-known framework of Equation (1.2) by including a short position in liabilities:[17]

$$\sigma^2_{surplus} = \begin{bmatrix} w_1 \\ \vdots \\ w_1 \\ -f \end{bmatrix}' \begin{bmatrix} \sigma_{11} & \cdots & \sigma_{1k} & \sigma_{1l} \\ \vdots & \ddots & \vdots & \vdots \\ \sigma_{k1} & \cdots & \sigma_{kk} & \sigma_{kl} \\ \sigma_{l1} & \cdots & \sigma_{lk} & \sigma_{ll} \end{bmatrix} \begin{bmatrix} w_1 \\ \vdots \\ w_1 \\ -f \end{bmatrix} \tag{1.13}$$

We assume that liabilities can be summarised as one single asset, l, whereas, for example, σ_{kl} summarises the covariance of the kth asset with our liabilities.[18] If assets equal liabilities, we arrive at a traditional active optimisation where liabilities directly play the role of a benchmark asset. How, then, can we transform the asset–liability management problem into the well-known portfolio optimisation so that we need not change portfolio optimisation algorithms and can still search for the optimal solution in terms of assets only? All we have to do is to express the covariance matrix in terms of surplus risk, ie, as the volatility of return differences between assets and liabilities (very much like any other active optimisation problem). The covariance matrix of assets and liabilities is transformed via a matrix of long–short positions into the covariance matrix of surplus returns:

$$
\mathbf{\Omega}_{\text{surplus}} =
\begin{bmatrix}
1 & 0 & \cdots & 0 & -f \\
0 & 1 & & & -f \\
\vdots & & \ddots & & \vdots \\
0 & 0 & \cdots & 1 & -f
\end{bmatrix}
\begin{bmatrix}
\sigma_{11} & \cdots & \sigma_{1k} & \sigma_{1l} \\
\vdots & \ddots & & \vdots \\
\sigma_{k1} & & \sigma_{kk} & \sigma_{kl} \\
\sigma_{l1} & \cdots & \sigma_{lk} & \sigma_{ll}
\end{bmatrix}
\begin{bmatrix}
1 & 0 & \cdots & 0 & -f \\
0 & 1 & & & -f \\
\vdots & & \ddots & & \vdots \\
0 & 0 & \cdots & 1 & -f
\end{bmatrix}'
$$

$$(1.14)$$

As well as offering the convenience of using the same portfolio optimisation algorithm, writing the covariance matrix in terms of surplus variance will lead to a much better understanding of risk in an asset–liability framework. While cash, for example, is a very conservative asset in an asset-only framework, in an asset–liability framework it becomes one of the most risky assets as it has no covariation with liabilities (often similar to long bonds) and therefore cannot serve as a liability-hedging asset.[19] To remain consistent, we manipulate the expected returns to reflect the relative return of assets versus liabilities:

$$
\mathbf{\mu}_{\text{surplus}} =
\begin{bmatrix}
\mu_1 - f\mu_l \\
\vdots \\
\mu_k - f\mu_l
\end{bmatrix}
+ c\,(1-f)
\tag{1.15}
$$

As with Equation (1.5), we maximise $\textit{Utility} \approx \mu_{\text{surplus}} - \frac{1}{2\lambda}\sigma_{\text{surplus}}$ subject to $\mathbf{Aw} = \mathbf{b}$, which yields[20]

$$
\mathbf{w}^* = \mathbf{\Omega}_{\text{surplus}}^{-1}\,\mathbf{A}'\left(\mathbf{A}\mathbf{\Omega}_{\text{surplus}}^{-1}\mathbf{A}'\right)^{-1}\mathbf{b} \;+
$$

$$
\lambda\,\mathbf{\Omega}_{\text{surplus}}^{-1}\left(\mathbf{\mu}_{\text{surplus}} - \mathbf{A}'\left(\mathbf{A}\mathbf{\Omega}_{\text{surplus}}^{-1}\mathbf{A}'\right)^{-1}\mathbf{A}\mathbf{\Omega}_{\text{surplus}}^{-1}\,\mathbf{\mu}_{\text{surplus}}\right) \tag{1.16}
$$

Varying the risk-tolerance parameter λ, we can trace out the surplus-efficient frontier (the geometric location of surplus-efficient portfolios. Unconstrained (asset-only) efficient frontier and surplus-efficient frontier coincide if:

❑ liabilities are cash (or, equally, if assets have no covariation with liabilities);

❑ all assets have the same covariation with liabilities (it does not matter which asset is chosen);[21] or
❑ there exists a liability-mimicking asset and it lies on the efficient frontier (it is a general result in benchmark-relative optimisation that optimising relative to a mean–variance-inefficient benchmark (liabilities) will never give a mean–variance-efficient portfolio).[22]

We will illustrate the concepts outlined so far using a numerical example to show that asset-only and asset–liability solutions generally differ. Suppose that the funding ratio of a pension fund is one (assets equal liabilities) and that we have the following information:[23]

$$\boldsymbol{\Omega} = \begin{bmatrix} 0.04 & 0.024 & 0.0028 \\ 0.024 & 0.0225 & 0.0021 \\ 0.0028 & 0.0021 & 0.0049 \end{bmatrix}, \ \boldsymbol{\Gamma} = \begin{bmatrix} 0.015 \\ 0.01125 \\ 0.00525 \end{bmatrix}, \ \boldsymbol{\mu} = \begin{bmatrix} 4\% \\ 3\% \\ 1.5\% \\ 2\% \end{bmatrix}, \ \sigma_{ll} = 0.0025$$

where $\boldsymbol{\Gamma}$ expresses the covariance between asset and liability returns. We can now directly calculate surplus volatility according to Equation (1.13):

$$\sigma^2_{surplus} = \begin{bmatrix} w_1 \\ w_2 \\ w_3 \\ -1 \end{bmatrix}' \begin{bmatrix} \boldsymbol{\Omega} & \boldsymbol{\Gamma} \\ \boldsymbol{\Gamma}' & \sigma_{ll} \end{bmatrix} \begin{bmatrix} w_1 \\ \vdots \\ w_1 \\ -1 \end{bmatrix}$$

Armed with these assumptions, we can now solve for both the unconstrained (Section 1.1.1) and the constrained (Section 1.1.2) efficient frontier as well as for the surplus-efficient frontier (Section 1.1.3) to confirm the points made above.

As shown in Figure 1.1, the surplus-efficient frontier is dominated by both (asset-) efficient frontiers, which offer a lower level of risk for the same level of expected return. This is not surprising as a different objective – optimising versus liabilities rather than cash – has been pursued; if we plotted the asset-efficient frontier in a surplus risk and return diagram, the opposite would be true. In a totally unconstrained optimisation the efficient frontier effectively becomes a straight line from the beginning as every portfolio can be leveraged without limit.[24] Asymptotically, the constrained frontiers also become nearly straight lines as the weights from the minimum-variance portfolio in Equation (1.9) have less and less influence.

We have seen in this section that asset-only and asset–liability management problems can be solved with the same analytical framework, applying essentially the same algorithms. All that is needed is a transformation of the original covariance matrix.

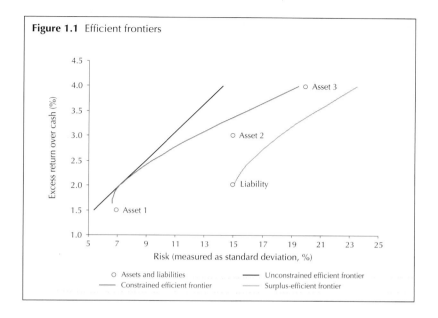

Figure 1.1 Efficient frontiers

1.2 HOW WELL DOES MEAN–VARIANCE INVESTING WORK?

In reality, returns are not multivariate normal-distributed (see Chapter 2); investors do not exhibit quadratic utility and they do not live in a one-period world – ie, they have an investment horizon that lasts longer than one period and they are able to take corrective actions within that period.[25] In fact, they have multiperiod objectives and will revise their decisions at the end of each period. How serious are these limitations on the practical use of mean–variance-based portfolio construction? Here we will concentrate on two important questions:

1. How well does the mean–variance framework approximate reality, where investors might have different utility functions and returns might not be normally distributed?
2. How well does the one-period solution approximate multiperiod optimality?

1.2.1 How well does the mean–variance framework approximate reality?

Suppose that an investor maximises a utility function, $u(R)$, that is a function of end-of-period wealth. Normalising start-of-period wealth to one, we can write utility as a function of end-of-period return, R. We can now expand the utility function around this expected end-of-period wealth and take expectations to arrive at an approximation of expected utility, $E[u(R)]$:[26]

$$E[u(R)] \approx u(\overline{R}) + \frac{1}{2}\frac{d^2 u(\overline{R})}{dR^2}\sigma^2 + \underbrace{\sum_{n=3}^{\infty}\frac{1}{n!}\frac{d^n u(\overline{R})}{dR^n}\sigma^n}_{\text{Higher-order terms}} \qquad (1.17)$$

$$\underbrace{\phantom{E[u(R)] \approx u(\overline{R}) + \frac{1}{2}\frac{d^2 u(\overline{R})}{dR^2}\sigma^2}}_{\text{Quadratic approximation}}$$

where $d^n u(\overline{R})/dR^n$ is the nth derivative, σ^n is the nth moment of the distribution of returns, R, and $\overline{R}$ is the centre of this distribution. If we limit ourselves to a quadratic approximation, we see that mean–variance analysis can be regarded as a second-order Taylor approximation of expected utility.[27] Alternatively, we could solve the "true" decision problem

$$E[u(R)] = \frac{1}{T}\sum_{t=1}^{T} u(R_t) \qquad (1.18)$$

where we calculate expected utility by adding up the utilities of end-of-period wealth in T equally likely scenarios, R_t (ie, the empirical return distribution).

The question now becomes: how well does Equation (1.17) approximate Equation (1.18)? This depends on several factors:

❏ *Specification of the utility function* The utility of highly risk-averse investors is heavily influenced by a few extremely negative returns; hence, the approximation will perform badly for large risk-aversions.

❏ *Distribution of returns* If returns are very non-normally distributed, the mean and variance no longer adequately describe the return distribution, so Equation (1.18) might assign different rankings to investment alternatives. It is also not clear that higher-order approximations do better as they only do better locally. In fact, as many returns are not infinitesimal, these approximations might even do worse. In these cases scenario optimisation (see Chapter 5) might be the only viable alternative. However, as long as portfolios are diversified, we can rely on the central limit theorem (see Chapter 2) to ensure that higher moments in excess of those of the normal distribution are close to zero.

❏ *Volatility* The greater the volatility of a return series (or, alternatively, the longer the time horizon), the less appropriate the Taylor approximation becomes.

In practice, the suitability of a mean–variance approximation is judged by ranking assets on the basis of Equation (1.18) and the mean–variance approximation of Equation (1.17). Then rank correlations between the two measures are calculated to see whether both place assets in the same order. Empirical results on the applicability of mean–variance-based approximation sometimes conflict as they seem to be time period-dependent.[28] The practical applicability of mean–variance-based investing should become an empirical issue of whether the data confirm the assumptions rather than a battle between dogmatic views.

1.2.2 How well does the one-period solution approximate multiperiod optimality?

The second area where the facts may differ in practice relates to the ability of the mean–variance framework to deal with multiperiod (ie, long-term) investment decisions. Recall that the Markowitz framework is used by institutional investors who have very long-term horizons. We will divide this problem into three separate questions:

1. Does the mean–variance frontier change as the investment horizon lengthens?
2. Should all long-term investors maximise geometric return?
3. Does repeatedly investing in myopic (one-period-efficient) portfolios result in multiperiod-efficient portfolios?

Note that the first two questions assume that investors cannot rebalance within the investment period, so a sequence of investment periods actually becomes one very long period, while the third question allows rebalancing.

The first question is easy enough to answer. Assuming non-time-varying, uncorrelated and normally distributed returns, expected portfolio excess returns and variance are scaled up by the number of periods, T. However, this leaves the curvature of the efficient frontier (trading off return against variance) unchanged, so all investors will choose the same portfolio irrespective of the scaling (ie, time horizon), T. It is true that Sharpe ratios (average return relative to standard deviation) rise with investment horizon as standard deviation rises only as the square root of T. However, it is equally true that Sharpe ratios must be compared between assets for a given time horizon and not between time horizons for a given asset. Risk does not diversify across time.

[margin note: Risk does NOT diversify across time.]

To answer the second question, an often-quoted example (which seems to affirm the suggestion underlying the question) can be used. Suppose that an investment starts at a value of 100, falls to 50 and rises again to 100. Although the average return is 25% ((−50 + 100)/2), the geometric return is zero. In fact, repeatedly investing in this portfolio would leave the expected average return constant at 25%, while the geometric return would eventually become negative. For a start, we see that geometric returns also have a risk dimension. *Ceteris paribus* (same average return), the higher the volatility (the less diversified a portfolio), the lower the geometric return on the portfolio will be and, hence, the lower the expected median wealth. (Equally, the same average return will produce a less diversified portfolio.) However, as the geometric mean return, g_p, can be approximated by $g_p \approx \mu_p - \frac{1}{2}\sigma_p^2$, where μ_p is portfolio return, we know that the portfolio that maximises geometric mean is merely a particular frontier portfolio.[29] It is represented by the point on the efficient frontier where the risk-tolerance parameter, λ, equals one and reflects a fairly aggressive investor. More aggressive portfolios, as well as less aggressive portfolios, would result in a lower geometric return. Investors who are concerned that mean–variance-efficient portfolios might reduce the long-term geometric returns are often recommended to ignore allocations lying to the right of this point. We now know that not every investor will maximise geometric returns, but what type of investor would? Suppose we engage in an investment where we either win 100% in T_{win} out of T cases (periods) or lose 100% in the remaining cases. Suppose that our initial wealth is one. How much would we bet in each draw to maximise the geometric return (assuming that $T_{win}/T > 0.5$)? Betting everything in every period would almost surely result in a total loss, while betting too little might not let our capital grow fast enough. The geometric return for the problem described so far can be written as

$$g = (W_T)^{\frac{1}{T}} = (1+b)^{\frac{T_{win}}{T}} (1-b)^{\frac{T - T_{win}}{T}} \qquad (1.19)$$

where W_T is end-of-period wealth at time T and b is the bet size (how much is invested per period). Taking logarithms, we see that Equation (1.17) becomes the expected utility maximisation for a log-utility investor:

$$\log(W_T)^{\frac{1}{T}} = \frac{T_{win}}{T} \log(1+b) + \frac{T - T_{win}}{T} \log(1-b) = \mathrm{E}[u(W)] \qquad (1.20)$$

Maximising Equation (1.18) with respect to the optimal bet size, b^*, results in[30]

$$b^* = 2\frac{T_{win}}{T} - 1 \qquad (1.21)$$

Choosing a higher bet size is called "over-betting" (as seen in more aggressive portfolios), and it would reduce geometric return and, hence, expected median wealth. If there is a 55% probability of winning in a single run we would, according to Equation (1.21), find it optimal to invest 10% per period. Rather than making geometric return maximisation a general objective, it is confined to log-utility investors.

Turning to the third question: suppose now that, in all future periods, we could readjust our optimal allocations at the start of each period. Under what circumstances would that affect today's decisions? Under fairly strict assumptions it has been shown that repeatedly investing in myopic (one-period-efficient) portfolios will also result in multiperiod-efficient portfolios if:[31]

❑ investors have constant relative risk-aversion (wealth level does not change optimal allocations) and only possess financial wealth;
❑ asset returns are not autocorrelated (investment opportunities are not time-varying) – ie, period returns are not forecastable;[32]

❑ portfolio returns are not path-dependent due to intermediate cash-flows (no cash infusion and/or withdrawals); and
❑ there are no transaction costs (which make optimal allocations path-dependent as rebalancing now depends on the size of returns).

The last two requirements, however, are unrealistic as investment opportunities are time time-varying (see Appendix B of Chapter 4) and transaction costs are unavoidable. However, a fifth condition has only recently been been added to the above list:

❑ there is no uncertainty about estimated parameters.

If investors face parameter uncertainty in relation to mean returns, they might actually reduce the optimal holding of risky assets as the time horizon lengthens (see Chapter 4). However, if investors learn to update their beliefs as they observe further return realisations, they might start to increase their holdings again.[33]

   As many of the implementation problems – such as estimation error (see next section) or the ability to specify a utility function – are likely to be worse in a multiperiod framework, and given the technicality of the subject, our analysis of multiperiod models will end here.[34]

1.3 CLUSTERING TECHNIQUES AND THE INVESTMENT UNIVERSE

Few investors are aware that the definition of the investment universe itself has a considerable impact on the outcome of portfolio construction. If, for example, the investment universe is constrained to government bonds and emerging market bonds, it is obvious that all combinations are efficient and investors are likely to place a considerable allocation in emerging market bonds. However, as soon as high-yield bonds and emerging market equities are introduced, this situation might change due to the correlation between these assets.

   To increase the transparency of the asset allocation process as well as to avoid the accumulation of estimation errors, portfolio optimisation should be limited to groups of assets that have high intragroup and low intergroup correlations.[35] The benefit of this correlation-guided asset class definition is a weakened sensitivity of the optimal portfolio solution with respect to mean return estimates (which carry the highest estimation error, as can be seen from Appendix A). Again, we start from the definition of optimal portfolio weights, $\mathbf{w}^*$, applied to the two-asset case:

$$\mathbf{w}^* = \begin{bmatrix} w_1^* \\ w_2^* \end{bmatrix} = \lambda \begin{bmatrix} \Omega_{11}^{-1} & \Omega_{12}^{-1} \\ \Omega_{21}^{-1} & \Omega_{22}^{-1} \end{bmatrix} \begin{bmatrix} \mu_1 \\ \mu_2 \end{bmatrix} \quad (1.22)$$

where Ω_{11}^{-1} denotes element $(1, 1)$ of Ω^{-1}. Taking the first derivative with respect to the expected mean of the first asset, μ_1, and applying the rules for the inverse of a partitioned matrix, we get [36]

$$\frac{dw_1^*}{d\mu_1} = \lambda\,\Omega_{11}^{-1} = \lambda\,\frac{\sigma_{22}}{\sigma_{11}\sigma_{22} - \sigma_{12}\sigma_{21}} = \lambda\,\frac{1}{\sigma_{11} - \rho^2\sigma_{11}} \qquad (1.23)$$

where ρ is the correlation between the two assets. As ρ approaches one, portfolio weights will react very sensitively to changes in means; as assets become more similar, any extra return becomes increasingly important for the allocation decision. Portfolio optimisation with highly correlated assets will almost certainly lead to extreme and undiversified results.

To avoid the accumulation of estimation errors mentioned above, we need to identify groups, or "clusters", of assets on the basis of the correlation between individual assets. The technique for doing this is cluster analysis.[37] Clustering methods can be divided into partitioning methods, which optimally separate the k assets into K ($K \le k$) distinct clusters, where K is given exogenously rather than derived within the analysis (producing a single partition), and hierarchical methods, which establish k partitions within one run. Hierarchical methods might appear to make partitioning methods obsolete as they determine all possible clusters in one run. However, this is achieved at the cost of less optimal clusters as hierarchical methods always look for the best add-on to an existing cluster and past add-ons are treated as fixed. We will focus here on hierarchical methods as they are not particularly computer-intensive and require less explanation. Readers wishing to arrive at a better grouping of the investment universe should experiment with partitioning methods (see note 37).

We start the grouping process with all assets still separate, each asset being viewed as a cluster of its own.[38] The first step is to merge the two "closest" assets, ie, those with the highest correlation. In clustering methodology this is also called the "minimum distance" and is measured as $1 - \text{Correlation}$.[39] We will explain the algorithm using the data for seven hedge fund sub-indices (monthly return data published by Hedge Fund Research, Inc, for the period January 1990 to March 2001).[40] The distance matrix is given in Table 1.1 and will allow the reader to follow through our example

The greatest distance is that between short sellers and all other hedge funds. The reason for this is the substantial negative correlation of this hedge fund style with other styles, as can be seen from the scatter plots in Figure 1.2. The scatter clouds of short sellers are negatively sloped. The smallest distance, though, is that between "event-driven strategies" and "distressed debt" (which, arguably, is also event-driven). How do we proceed from here? We compare the distances between all remaining clusters, including the cluster of event-driven strategies and distressed

Table 1.1 Distance (1 – Correlation) matrix for hedge fund data

	Arbitrage	Distressed debt	Long–short	Event-driven	Macro-investing	Market timing	Short sellers
Convertible arbitrage	0.00	0.33	0.49	0.35	0.60	0.63	1.38
Distressed debt	0.33	0.00	0.36	0.18	0.49	0.59	1.54
Long–short investing	0.49	0.36	0.00	0.22	0.37	0.29	1.85
Event-driven strategies	0.35	0.18	0.22	0.00	0.37	0.47	1.66
Macro-investing	0.60	0.49	0.37	0.37	0.00	0.45	1.46
Market timing	0.63	0.59	0.29	0.47	0.45	0.00	1.70
Short sellers	1.38	1.54	1.85	1.66	1.46	1.70	0.00

Figure 1.2 Bivariate scatter plots

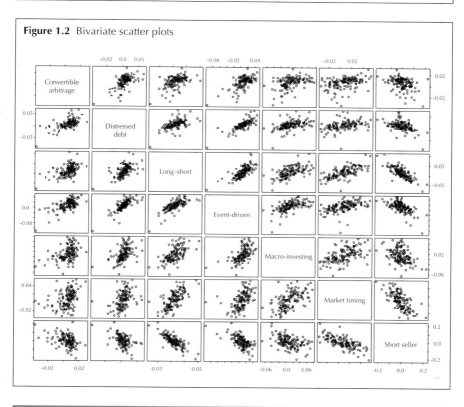

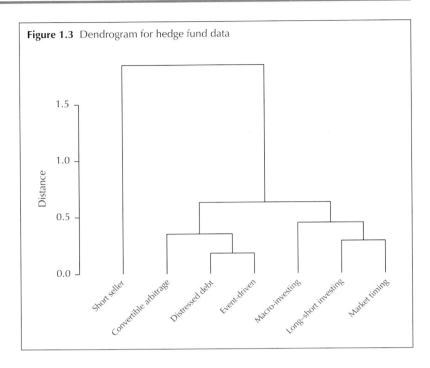

Figure 1.3 Dendrogram for hedge fund data

cluster
analysis

debt, and calculate, pairwise, the distances between this newly formed cluster, C_1, and the other assets (for notational convenience also called clusters) according to

$$\text{Distance}\left(C_1, C_2\right) = \frac{1}{\left|C_1\right|\left|C_2\right|} \sum_{\substack{i \in C_1 \\ j \in C_2}} \text{Distance}\left(i, j\right) \qquad (1.24)$$

where $\left|C_n\right|$ is the number of objects (assets) in cluster n, the distance between two clusters is the average distance between their individual elements, and distance is measured as 1 – Correlation. Casual inspection of Table 1.1 would tempt us to conclude that, after distressed debt (0.18), long–short investing is the closest (0.22) to event-driven strategies and, hence, that we should add it to cluster C_1. However, as we have to calculate the average distance between two clusters and the distance between long–short investing and distressed debt is relatively high (0.36), we find that the next closest assets are long–short investing and market timing (0.29), indicating that long–short investors still have considerable directional market exposure.

The complete picture is summarised in Figure 1.3, where the axis represents the distance between two clusters. With a bit of economic judgment we conclude that there are three clusters: strategies with directional market exposure (market timing, long–short investing and macro-investing); strategies with reverse market exposure (short sellers); and strategies that focus on company-specific events (convertible arbitrage, distressed debt and event-driven strategies). However, we should keep in mind that this partitioning is based on some marginal differences in the distance matrix, and in such cases an alternative algorithm may be desirable.[41]

1.4 ILLIQUID ASSETS: CORRECTING FOR AUTOCORRELATION

Some asset classes appear to show much less risk than practitioners commonly believe to be reasonable; for example, corporate high-yield indices exhibit much less volatility than their hybrid structure between equity and fixed income might otherwise suggest. For the period September 1986 to December 2000 the annualised volatility of the Merrill Lynch High Yield Master II Index was 5.6%.[42] The same problem arises with real estate, which shares the characteristics of fixed income (a steady stream of rental income) and equity (a claim on real assets) but, measured empirically, shows less than fixed-income volatility. Historical annualised volatility for UK real estate over the period January 1988 to October 2000 was 3.0% – hardly imaginable for an asset class that returned 10.3% per annum during the same period. Most prominently, hedge funds also appear to show little risk relative to traditional investments, which significantly boosts their Sharpe ratios.

If the risk of an asset class is underestimated, too much capital will be allocated to it and there will be a serious loss of portfolio efficiency. To avoid such problems we have to look at the causes behind what appear to be biases in risk. The volatility bias mentioned above – the very low volatility of UK real estate returns relative to the size of the returns – is due to the high positive autocorrelation of the period-by-period returns, ie, a positive return one month is likely to be followed by a positive return the next month. A series of such monthly returns shows less historical volatility than an uncorrelated series, where a positive return is more likely to be followed by a negative return. Equally, positively autocorrelated (or "trending") returns are inevitably accompanied by a greater level of risk as there is little diversification between period-by-period returns – as would be the case with uncorrelated returns – and end-of-period wealth becomes more dispersed and, hence, more risky.

But where does the autocorrelation in returns come from? Common to all illiquid asset classes is that most observed prices are not market prices due to infrequent trading in illiquid securities. This applies equally to real estate, small companies, and high-yield and hedge funds. Suppose that at time t only half of the securities in an index react to some bad news. This does not mean that the other assets are unaffected by the news; it may only mean that it is not reflected in their prices at time t as no trade in them has taken place. If these untraded assets are then traded at time $t + 1$, their prices will reflect the time-t information with a lag of one period and will therefore generate positive autocorrelation in the return series for the index as a whole. Apart from the resulting downward-biased volatility, we might also see too low a correlation with other asset classes. Hedge funds are an excellent example of an illiquid asset class where prices often reflect the valuation of traders rather than market prices.

mark-to-model vs. mark-to-market

1.4.1 A simple method

Most problems have many cures, so this book will focus on a method of checking and correcting for autocorrelation in return series that is easy to implement. Using a simple filter of the form[43]

$$r_t^* = \frac{1}{1 - a_1} r_t - \frac{a_1}{1 - a_1} r_{t-1} \qquad (1.25)$$

we can create a new transformed return series, r_t^*, using the returns, r, at times t and $t - 1$. The coefficient a_1 is estimated from an autoregressive first-order (AR(1)) model:

$$r_t = a_0 + a_1 r_{t-1} + \varepsilon_t \qquad (1.26)$$

where a_0 and a_1 are the regression coefficients and ε_t is the error term. The procedure is as follows:

1. Estimate the autoregressive model in Equation (1.26).
2. Use the returns at times t and $t - 1$ to calculate a new, filtered return for time t.
3. Repeat step 2 for all observations.[44]

1.4.2 Example

Returning to our hedge fund example, we will apply this methodology to return series for convertible arbitrage, distressed debt, event-driven strategies and macro-investing. The series we will use are monthly return data for the period January 1990 to December 2000, available, as before, from Hedge Fund Research.[45] The aim is to show how to arrive at more realistic beta estimates with respect to a core holding in US equities (here represented by a Morgan Stanley Capital International fund, MSCI USA). When data are non-synchronous (due to infrequent trading resulting from illiquidity), we are more likely to capture the real dynamics by running a regression of returns against both lagged and contemporaneous market returns:[46]

Table 1.2 Results for autocorrelation example – betas for selected hedge funds.

Type of hedge fund	a_1	β_0	β_0^*	$\beta_0 + \beta_1 + \beta_2 + \beta_3$
Convertible arbitrage	0.55 (7.66)	0.09	0.22	0.25
Distressed debt	0.52 (6.86)	0.18	0.44	0.49
Event-driven strategies	0.28 (3.56)	0.29	0.38	0.38
Macro-trading	0.18 (2.10)	0.29	0.37	0.52

Positive autocorrelation is indicated by the Student's t-values in parentheses; see text for explanation of other symbols.

$$r_{it} = \alpha + \beta_0 r_{mt} + \beta_1 r_{mt-1} + \cdots + \beta_l r_{mt-l} + \varepsilon_t \qquad (1.27)$$

where r denotes risk premia, β_0 is the contemporaneous beta and β_l is the regression coefficient on the lth lag of market returns, r_{mt-l}. An improved measure of beta can be found by adding the significant lags to the contemporaneous beta ($\beta_0 + \beta_1 + \cdots + \beta_l$). Alternatively, we could use the filter technique seen in Equation (1.25) to unsmooth the return series and calculate a standard regression beta from

$$r_{it}^* = \alpha + \beta_0^* r_{mt} + \varepsilon_t \qquad (1.28)$$

The results of this exercise are given in Table 1.2. All four hedge fund series show significant positive autocorrelation (as indicated by the t-values in brackets), while contemporaneous betas, β_0, are considerably smaller than those which include lagged betas (fifth column of table). As expected, we find that contemporaneous betas on filtered series (fourth column) are significantly higher than those from ordinary regressions and are, in most cases, close to betas derived from regressions using lagged market returns. The betas from ordinary return regressions appear to underestimate the true market exposure. This feature is particularly troublesome as it overstates the diversifying properties of hedge funds. It also casts doubt on the standard practice of "mapping" implicit hedge fund market exposure through a regression of hedge fund returns on underlying asset class returns. Hence it would be prudent to check assets that are suspected to be illiquid for auto-correlation and use the filtered estimates from Equation (1.28) for further analysis.

1.5 ANALYSIS OF IMPLIED RISK AND RETURN

1.5.1 Basic risk decomposition

For most investors a single risk number is not enough; they want to know the sources of risk and how well spread they are to enable them to judge whether a portfolio is diversified or not, and which assets are diversifying.[47] The starting point for the decomposition of total portfolio risk (sometimes also called the "risk budget") is the familiar formula for the standard deviation of portfolio returns:[48]

$$\sigma_p = \left(\mathbf{w}'\Omega\mathbf{w}\right)^{\frac{1}{2}} = \sum_i w_i^2 \sigma_{ii} + \sum_i \sum_{j \neq i} w_i w_j \sigma_{ij} \qquad (1.29)$$

The first question we want to address is: how would the portfolio risk change if we increased holdings in a particular asset? What we need is the "marginal contribution to risk" (MCTR), which can be calculated by taking the first derivative of Equation (1.29), giving

$$\mathbf{MCTR}_{k \times 1} = \frac{d\sigma_p}{d\mathbf{w}} = \frac{\Omega\mathbf{w}}{\sigma_p} \qquad (1.30)$$

where the ith element in this $k \times 1$ vector is given by

$$\frac{d\sigma_p}{dw_i} = \frac{w_i \sigma_{ii} + \sum_{j \neq i} w_j \sigma_{ij}}{\sigma_p} = \frac{\sigma_{ip}}{\sigma_p} = \beta_i \sigma_p \qquad (1.31)$$

The MCTR rises directly with asset weight, w_i, and asset riskiness, σ_{ii}. However, the net effect of an increase in weight can still be negative (falling risk) if the asset shows a sufficiently negative covariance, σ_{ij}, with the other assets.

Manipulation of Equation (1.31) shows that its numerator is equal to the covariance of asset i with portfolio p, which contains the asset:

$$\sigma_{ip} = \mathrm{cov}\left(r_i, r_p\right) = \mathrm{cov}\left(r_i, w_i r_i + \sum_{j \neq i} w_j r_j\right) = w_i \sigma_{ii} + \sum_{j \neq i} w_j \sigma_{ij} \qquad (1.32)$$

Adding up the weighted MCTRs yields the volatility of the portfolio:

$$\sum_i w_i \frac{d\sigma_p}{dw_i} = \sum_i w_i \frac{\sigma_{ip}}{\sigma_p} = \sigma_p \qquad (1.33)$$

Dividing Equation (1.32) by σ_p yields

$$\sum_i \frac{w_i}{\sigma_p} \frac{d\sigma_p}{dw_i} = \sum_i w_i \frac{\sigma_{ip}}{\sigma_p^2} = \sum_i w_i \beta_i = 1 \qquad (1.34)$$

which shows that the percentage contributions to risk (PCTR), which add up to 100%, are equal to the weighted betas. We can write this in matrix form as

Percentage Contribution to Risk

$$\mathbf{PCTR}_{k \times 1} = \frac{\mathbf{W}}{\sigma_p} \frac{d\sigma_p}{d\mathbf{w}} \qquad (1.35)$$

where $\mathbf{W}$ is a $k \times k$ matrix with portfolio weights on the main diagonal and zeros otherwise. An individual element of the vector of percentage risk contributions is given by

$$PCTR_i = \frac{w_i}{\sigma_p} \frac{d\sigma_p}{dw_i} = w_i \beta_i \qquad (1.36)$$

We can use Equations (1.29) to (1.36) to show that for the (unconstrained) minimum-variance portfolio all PCTRs have to equal the respective portfolio weights. For such a portfolio we know that all MCTRs have to be equal by definition, ie,

$$\frac{d\sigma_p}{dw_i} = \frac{d\sigma_p}{dw_j} = \frac{d\sigma_p}{dw}$$

If this were not so, we could always find a pair of assets where slightly increasing one holding while at the same time reducing the other would result in lowered risk. Using the fact that $\sum w_i = 1$, we can now show that, using Equation (1.32),

$$\sum_i w_i \frac{d\sigma_p}{dw_i} = \sigma_p = \frac{d\sigma_p}{dw}$$

$$\sum_i \frac{w_i}{\sigma_p} \frac{d\sigma_p}{dw} = \frac{w_i}{\sigma_p} \sigma_p = w_i \qquad (1.37)$$

PCTRs are also used as an indication of the level of diversification of a portfolio: for example, if 90% of the total risk comes from a few holdings, a portfolio is probably not very diversified. However, that does not reflect on the standard of the portfolio as diversification is not a value in itself.[49]

Table 1.3 Implied view analysis – assumptions

Asset	Weight (%)	Return (%)	Volatility (%)	Correlation						
Equity	40	11	18	1.0	0.0	0.5	0.5	0.3	0.3	0.0
Absolute return	15	12	8	0.0	1.0	0.0	0.0	0.0	0.0	0.0
Private equity	15	11	9	0.5	0.0	1.0	0.5	0.3	0.3	0.0
Real estate	5	10	14	0.5	0.0	0.5	1.0	0.5	0.3	0.0
US bonds	25	7	3	0.3	0.0	0.3	0.5	1.0	0.8	0.0
Non-US bonds	0	8	8	0.3	0.0	0.3	0.3	0.8	1.0	0.0
Cash	0	5	0	0.0	0.0	0.0	0.0	0.0	0.0	1.0

Column heads for correlation matrix read as items in "Asset" column – ie, from "Equity" (*left*) to "Cash" (*right*).

1.5.2 Implied view analysis – reverse optimisation

So far we have calculated optimal portfolio weights from given return expectations. Often, however, the only givens are portfolio weights. If investors have high return expectations for assets with high marginal risk contributions, how can we find out whether their portfolios truly reflect their views and whether what they invest in is really based on their opinions? As we all know, conviction is the natural enemy of diversification.

This can be done by "reverse optimisation" – a technique of mapping positions on to implicit return expectations. In an unconstrained portfolio optimisation, marginal risks (additional risks that arise through extending a position) are traded off against marginal returns (additional gains from extending a position). A portfolio is thus optimal when the relationship between marginal risks and marginal returns is the same for all assets in the portfolio. In this case, changing assets cannot generate a better risk–return relationship. However, as the Sharpe ratio of the portfolio also measures the relationship between incremental risk and return, we can express the relationship between marginal return and marginal risk as

$$\boldsymbol{\mu} = \left(\frac{\mu_P}{\sigma_P} \right) \frac{\boldsymbol{\Omega} \mathbf{w}}{\sigma_p} = \boldsymbol{\beta} \mu_P \qquad (1.38)$$

where $\boldsymbol{\beta} = \boldsymbol{\Omega}\boldsymbol{\beta}\sigma_p^{-1}$ denotes the $k \times 1$ vector of asset betas. Betas measure the sensitivity of an asset to movements of the portfolio. High-beta assets have to earn a high risk premium to justify the risk contribution to a particular portfolio. Note that Equation (1.38) follows from portfolio mathematics and not from an equilibrium condition. However, if the analysed portfolio were the market portfolio, we could give it an equilibrium interpretation. As the market portfolio is often conveniently proxied

Table 1.4 Implied view analysis – risk contributions and implied returns

Asset	$PCTR_i$ (%)	$MCTR_i$	Implied return (%)
Equity	79.1	0.174	9.84
Absolute return	1.9	0.011	0.62
Private equity	10.2	0.060	3.39
Real estate	4.8	0.085	4.80
US bonds	4.0	0.014	0.80
Non-US bonds	0.0	0.029	1.66
Cash	0.0	0.000	0.00

$PCTR_i$, percentage contribution to risk of ith asset; $MCTR_i$, marginal contribution to risk of ith asset. Implied return given by Equation (1.38).

by a capitalisation-weighted index of all publicly tracked assets, the implied returns would be the returns investors would need to hold the market portfolio. As capital market theory predicts that all investors hold the market portfolio, we could interpret these as equilibrium returns. This kind of analysis can be employed to show investors whether their return expectations are consistent with market realities, ie, whether they are over- or under-spending their risk budget in particular areas and whether they are investing in a way that is consistent with their views.

We will illustrate the reverse optimisation procedure with an example. Suppose that a US dollar-based investor has the views on the world set out in Table 1.3. The annual risk on this portfolio accumulates to 8.79% with an expected return of 10% (excess return of 5%) and a Sharpe ratio of 0.57. Risk contributions according to Equations (1.31) and (1.35) are given in Table 1.4.

What does a marginal risk contribution of 0.014 for US bonds mean? Suppose that instead of holding 25% (as in Table 1.3), we invested 26% in US bonds (we can assume that this extra 1% has been funded from cash – see also Chapter 6 on funding assumptions). Total portfolio risk would change from 8.7948 to 8.8089, a difference of 0.0141:[50]

$$\Delta \sigma_p = 8.8089 - 8.7948 = 0.0141 = \frac{d\sigma_p}{dw_{\text{US bonds}}} \Delta w_{\text{US bonds}}$$

The biggest increase in risk would come from equities (which already account for about 80% of the total risk budget), while the smallest increase would come from absolute return strategies, which are the most diversifying asset (under the set of assumptions given in Table 1.3). With these calculations in mind, we are now well equipped to analyse the implied views using Equation (1.38).

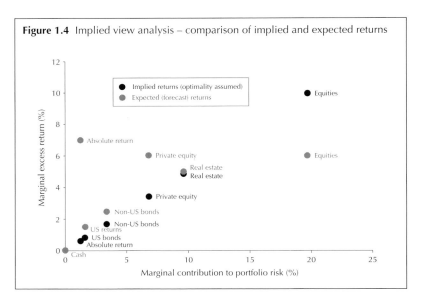

Figure 1.4 Implied view analysis – comparison of implied and expected returns

We see in Figure 1.4 that implied returns lie on a straight line with a slope equal to the portfolio Sharpe ratio. Return forecasts and actual allocations (risk allocations) in the figure are not consistent (if they were perfectly consistent they would overlap); the implied excess return for absolute return strategies (0.6%) is lower than forecast (7%). This means that the investor is underspending risk in this area. The opposite is true for equities, where the investor overspends risk (relative to the optimal allocation) for this asset class. A large allocation in a relatively undiversifying asset requires large implied returns to make the portfolio optimal. It also becomes apparent that the investor's implied return for equities (return required to make the position worthwhile) is higher than the historical experience.

Implied returns are often employed in what is called "view optimisation". This is not an optimisation but rather an iterative process of trial and error where an investor changes allocations (and sometimes forecasts) until implied and expected returns show a "reasonable" overlap. Implied returns could also be used to create a global firm view by optimally combining the views of regional model portfolio teams. However, this should be used with caution as implied views only show the view of an *unconstrained* investor. For example, if an investor is not allowed to hold more than 10% of a particular equity market, the implied views are also capped. This issue also applies to long-only constraints. Negative views on an asset with 2% index weight are capped as the maximum short position is 2% (ie, not owning this asset at all). If these issues are not addressed, mixing views and constraints contaminates the global firm view.

1.5.3 Applying investment information consistently across client portfolios

A final application of implied views is the so-called "portfolio-factory".[51] Typically, an asset manager has nearly as many benchmarks as clients. To complicate matters further, clients' guidelines differ. How can the asset manager ensure that all client portfolios are treated the same way, ie, that they are all based on the same investment information? When the global model portfolio has been specified, how can portfolio construction for each client be automated? One way (and probably the only way to achieve this in its purest meaning) is the following three-step procedure:

Step 1 Construct a totally unconstrained model portfolio (otherwise views are contaminated by constraints).

Step 2 Back out the implied returns (solve for the returns that make current weights optimal).

Step 3 Run a standardised portfolio optimisation with client-specific constraints for each client whereby the same implied returns are used for all clients.

Following this process, client portfolios would still differ in (active and total) weights but not in input information.

1.6 RISK BUDGETING VERSUS PORTFOLIO OPTIMISATION

Risk budgeting is an increasingly fashionable topic. The reason for this is clear: for a pension fund manager not to engage in risk budgeting would seem almost negligent. Also, as institutional investors are disappointed with the economic value that traditional portfolio optimisation methods have provided, they are more willing to embrace a budgeting framework that allows them to plan and spend risk budgets.

Many authors associate risk budgeting with value-at-risk (VAR) as a measure of investment risk.[52] In fact, supporters of risk budgeting transform monetary allocations into VAR (or marginal VAR). No additional economic insight is gained by this apart from the educational insight that even small monetary (weight) allocations can make a large contribution to total risk.

Promoters of risk budgeting would like to "separate risk budgeting and VAR measurement from classic investment risk practices, such as asset allocation",[53] while others argue that "we should regard risk budgeting as an extension of mean–variance optimisation that enables us to decouple a portfolio's allocation from fixed monetary values"[54] and, hence, that "VaR and the risk capital budgeting metaphor pour old wine into new casks".[55] With regard to the last two comments, it can additionally be argued that the merit of risk budgeting does not come from any increase in intellectual insight but rather from the more accessible way it provides of decomposing and presenting investment risks. That said, for the purposes of this book we will define risk budgeting as a process that reviews any assumption that is critical for the successful meeting of prespecified investment targets and thereby decides on the trade-off between the risks and returns associated with investment decisions. In a mean–variance world this defaults to Markowitz portfolio optimisation, where results are not only shown in terms of weights and monetary allocations but also in terms of risk contributions. Hence, as argued in the Introduction, risk budgeting should not be seen as a way of enforcing diversification. An isolated focus on risk is a meaningless exercise without trading off risk against return.

1.6.1 Equivalence of VAR-based risk budgeting

The equivalence of VAR-based measures and classic risk measures (as they have been known in portfolio theory for the last 40 years) is best shown by relating VAR to the analysis in Section 1.5. To do this we need only to transform VAR from its monetary form into a return VAR, R_p^*:[56]

$$VAR = \Delta P = PR_p^* = P\left(\mu_p + z_\alpha \sigma_p\right) \tag{1.39}$$

where ΔP denotes changes in portfolio value P and z_a is the critical value from a standard normal distribution. As in the previous section, we want to know marginal VAR, ie, we ask how VAR changes if we increase the holdings in the ith asset. Again, we take the first derivative of return VAR to arrive at marginal VAR:

$$\frac{dR_p^*}{dw_i} = z_\alpha \frac{d\sigma_p}{dw_i} = z_\alpha \beta_i \sigma_p = \beta_i R_p^* \tag{1.40}$$

As can be seen, the difference between the marginal contribution and risk in Equation (1.31) is merely the multiple z_a. The product of marginal VAR and portfolio VAR is called "component VAR" because the sum of the individual components adds up to total VAR:

$$\sum_i w_i \frac{dR_p^*}{dw_i} = \sum_i w_i \beta_i R_p^* = R_p^*$$

Again, this is just a multiple of Equation (1.33). Hence, in a normally distributed world, risk budgets are best derived by running a mean–variance optimisation first and subsequently transforming monetary allocations into VAR exposures.

1.6.2 Pitfalls: risk is not additive

The reverse approach, where investors first choose the VAR exposures of their activities (without trading off marginal risk and return) and then aggregate them to enforce diversification, suffers from various problems:

1. A bottom-up approach is not feasible as VAR is not additive (only being so in the case of perfectly correlated VARs). The sum of individual VARs will always be greater than portfolio VAR. It will therefore take many trials before a satisfactory answer is found to questions on how to spend the total risk (VAR) budget.

2. Without trading off marginal risks against marginal returns, the resulting solution is highly likely to be inefficient, ie, it carries too much risk per unit of return.

3. Individual VAR does not show the impact of a particular position on portfolio risk as correlations remain unaccounted for. Trial and error will not find trades that reduce portfolio risk in the best possible way as portfolio risk is best reduced by reducing the position of assets that have the highest marginal VAR rather than than those with the highest individual VAR.

4. Focusing on VAR as a risk measure might be the best option for some, but few would claim to be indifferent when faced with a choice between a loss that matches VAR and a loss that is 10 times VAR, which is the logic underlying VAR optimisation.

However, what about non-normality? VAR-based measures start to become preferable to mean–variance-based allocations if returns are significantly non-normal or if positions involve non-linearities. However, this does not mean that risk budgeting is different from portfolio optimisation. Risk budgeting still needs to find the optimal trade-off between risk and return (Chapters 2 and 6 show how non-normal returns can be incorporated into portfolio construction). Remarkably, proponents of risk budgeting describe in great detail how to calculate VAR and why this might be a good measure of risk, but they do not explain how to arrive at a risk budget.[57]

1.7 THE COVARIANCE MATRIX AND ITS PROPERTIES

The covariance matrix is a fundamental tool for risk estimation and one that investment professionals routinely use to calculate portfolio variance.[58] But what condition do we have to place on the covariance matrix to be sure that $\mathbf{w}'\boldsymbol{\Omega}\mathbf{w} \geq 0$ is always true? After all, variance cannot be negative.

Fortunately we can use some well-known results from matrix algebra.[59] A matrix, $\boldsymbol{\Omega}$, that satisfies $\mathbf{w}'\boldsymbol{\Omega}\mathbf{w} \geq 0$ for all $\mathbf{w}$ is referred to as "positive semi-definite". A necessary and sufficient condition for positive semi-definiteness (for symmetric matrices) is that all the eigenvalues of $\boldsymbol{\Omega}$ are positive or zero and at least one eigenvalue is greater than zero. This can be checked by obtaining the solutions to the eigenvalue equation $\boldsymbol{\Omega}\mathbf{x} = e\mathbf{x}$, where $\mathbf{x}$ is a $k \times 1$ vector ("eigenvector") and e is a scalar ("eigenvalue"). There are k solutions, $e_1, \ldots, e_k$ (eigenvalues), to this equation. If all the solutions (roots) are positive or zero, and at least one is positive, the matrix is said to be positive semi-definite.

Consider the following simple covariance matrix (to facilitate interpretation we will assume unit variances):

$$\Omega = \begin{bmatrix} 1 & 0.9 & 0.8 \\ 0.9 & 1 & 0.7 \\ 0.8 & 0.7 & 1 \end{bmatrix}$$

We calculate the following eigenvalues: $(e_1, e_2, e_3) = (2.6, 0.31, 0.08)$.[60] As none of them is negative, the above covariance matrix is positive semi-definite. However, if we construct an obviously contradictory case,

$$\Omega = \begin{bmatrix} 1 & 0.9 & -0.3 \\ 0.9 & 1 & 0.7 \\ -0.3 & 0.7 & 1 \end{bmatrix}$$

– where variables one and two as well as two and three are highly positively correlated but one and three are negatively correlated – we find that one of the eigenvalues, $(e_1, e_2, e_3) = (2, 1.28, -0.3)$, is negative. This situation typically arises if we fabricate numbers, if we generate estimates from time series of different lengths, or if the number of observations is smaller than the number of assets (risk factors).[61] So, what can we do to correct this problem with minimum damage to the input structure? The three-step process below is one possible method.[62]

1. Find the smallest eigenvalue (here e_3).
2. Create the minimum eigenvalue of zero by shifting the correlation matrix according to $\Omega^* = \Omega - e_3 I$, where I denotes the identity matrix.
3. Scale the resulting matrix by $1/(1 - e_3)$ to enforce for each variable a correlation with itself of one: $\Omega^{**} = \frac{1}{1-e_3} \Omega^*$.

The result is the new adjusted matrix

$$\Omega^{**} = \begin{bmatrix} 1 & 0.69 & -0.23 \\ 0.69 & 1 & 0.54 \\ -0.23 & 0.54 & 1 \end{bmatrix}$$

with eigenvalues $(e_1^{**}, e_2^{**}, e_3^{**}) = (1.77, 1.22, 0)$. Alternatively, we can obtain the same results as in the example above if we use the fact that $\Omega = XEX'$, where X is the $k \times k$ matrix of eigenvectors and E is a $k \times k$ diagonal matrix (eigenvalues on the main diagonal and all other terms being zero) of eigenvalues. If we set all negative eigenvalues to zero (E^*), we can calculate $\Omega^* = XE^*X'$. To ensure correlation values of one on the main diagonal, we calculate $\Omega^{**} = \frac{1}{\sqrt{D}} \Omega^* \frac{1}{\sqrt{D}}$, where D is a diagonal matrix containing the main diagonal of Ω^*.

1.7.1 Significance of inverse of the covariance matrix for portfolio construction

Now we have discussed conditions for the existence of a well-specified covariance matrix, we can throw further light on the economic interpretation of the inverse of the covariance matrix, Ω^{-1}, with regard to portfolio construction. From Section 1.1 we know the solution to the (unconstrained) portfolio optimisation problem $\mathbf{w} = \lambda \Omega^{-1} \boldsymbol{\mu}$. It has been shown that, after tedious manipulation, the inverse of the covariance matrix can also be expressed as[63]

$$\Omega^{-1} = \begin{bmatrix} \dfrac{1}{\sigma_{11}\left(1-R_1^2\right)} & -\dfrac{\beta_{12}}{\sigma_{11}\left(1-R_1^2\right)} & \cdots & -\dfrac{\beta_{1k}}{\sigma_{11}\left(1-R_1^2\right)} \\[2ex] -\dfrac{\beta_{21}}{\sigma_{22}\left(1-R_2^2\right)} & \dfrac{1}{\sigma_{22}\left(1-R_2^2\right)} & \cdots & -\dfrac{\beta_{2k}}{\sigma_{22}\left(1-R_2^2\right)} \\[2ex] \vdots & \vdots & \ddots & \vdots \\[2ex] -\dfrac{\beta_{k1}}{\sigma_{kk}\left(1-R_k^2\right)} & -\dfrac{\beta_{k2}}{\sigma_{kk}\left(1-R_k^2\right)} & \cdots & \dfrac{1}{\sigma_{kk}\left(1-R_k^2\right)} \end{bmatrix} \qquad (1.41)$$

Going through the above notation, we again write the variance of the ith asset as σ_{ii}, while the betas of a return regression of asset i against all other $k - 1$ assets are denoted as β_{ij}:

$$r_i = a + \sum_{j \neq i} \beta_{ij} r_j + \varepsilon_i \qquad (1.42)$$

The explanatory power of this regression is given as R_i^2. Inserting Equation (1.36) into the solution for optimal portfolio weights and expanding the terms, we obtain the optimal weight for the ith asset:

$$w_i^* = \lambda \left(\dfrac{\overbrace{\mu_i - \sum_j \beta_{ij}\mu_j}^{\substack{\text{Excess return after} \\ \text{regression hedging}}}}{\underbrace{\sigma_{ii}\left(1 - R_i^2\right)}_{\text{Non-hedgeable risk}}} \right) \qquad (1.43)$$

The numerator in Equation (1.43) shows the excess return after regression hedging – that is, the excess return after the reward for implicit exposure to other assets has been taken out – and is equivalent to a in Equation (1.42). As the total risk of an asset is given by σ_{ii}, the fraction of risk that cannot be hedged by other assets is $\sigma_{ii}(1 - R_i^2)$. In terms of Equation (1.42) this is the unexplained variance, which is the variance of the error term.

As the regression in Equation (1.42) tries to minimise the variance of the error term, Equation (1.43) will put maximum weight into those assets that are similar to all other assets but have a very small return advantage. It is this property that will lead to implausible results when estimation errors are taken into account (see Chapter 3).

1.8 COVARIANCE IN GOOD AND BAD TIMES

Unfortunately, in times of market meltdown, just when portfolio managers need them most, correlations within an asset class increase.[64] This section will not attempt to forecast the change in input parameters, but instead will discuss tools for evaluating the diversifying properties of different assets in unusual times.

Is the low correlation in a full-sample covariance matrix (one that uses all available data) just an artefact of reasonably positive correlation in normal times – ie, most of the time – but of highly negative correlation in unusual times? Or is it evidence of a truly diversifying asset? As regulators (and supervisory boards) become increasingly concerned about short-term performance, investors often do not have the luxury of betting on average correlation. This is certainly true for most pension funds. The average correlation between bonds and equities is positive (equity markets rise when yields fall and bond returns rise too), but in times of crisis it becomes negative – government bonds outperform as investors move into the safe haven of high-grade fixed income. This will raise the liabilities of pension funds while at the same time massively reducing the assets of equity-orientated schemes. Surplus risk-based measures (see Section 1.3) calculated from average covariances will fail to spot these risks.

1.8.1 A statistical definition of unusual times

To come up with correlation and volatility estimates for normal and unusual times, we must first define "unusual times". We will define them according to their statistical distance from the mean vector, as follows:[65]

$$\mathbf{d}_t = \left(\mathbf{r}_t - \hat{\boldsymbol{\mu}}_0\right)' \hat{\boldsymbol{\Omega}}_0^{-1} \left(\mathbf{r}_t - \hat{\boldsymbol{\mu}}_0\right) \tag{1.44}$$

where the distance vector $\mathbf{d}_t$ is a $k \times 1$ vector at time t, $\mathbf{r}_t$ is a vector of return observations for k assets at time t, $\hat{\boldsymbol{\mu}}_0$ is a $k \times 1$ vector of average returns and $\hat{\boldsymbol{\Omega}}_0$ is the unconditional covariance matrix (over all $t = 1, \ldots, T$ observations). We calculate Equation (1.44) for each cross-section of stock returns and compare the distance vector with the critical value of $\chi^2(k)$. If we define an unusual observation as the outer 10% of a distribution (it can also be called the "outlier") and we look at five return series, our cut-off distance is 9.23. In Equation (1.44) the return distance is weighted by the inverse of the covariance matrix. This means that we take into account asset volatilities (the same deviation from the mean might be significant for low-volatility series but not necessarily for high-volatility series) as well as correlations (return difference of the opposite sign for two highly correlated series might be more unusual than for a series with negative correlation). Hence, in theory, outliers are not necessarily associated with down markets (although they often are in practice).[66]

1.8.2 An application to real data

As before, an example should help us to understand the mechanics. We use Morgan Stanley Capital International (MSCI) data for US and Japanese equities, Salomon Brothers data for medium-term US bonds (World Government Bond Index (WGBI)), and Hedge Fund Research, Inc. (HFR), hedge fund series for market-neutral and market-timing hedge funds. All data are monthly returns in US dollars (September 1990–March 2001). Using the methodology explained above, we can split the data into two regimes (normal times and unusual times, where unusual times are defined as market movements that only happen in 90% of all cases) and calculate correlations as well as volatilities for both regimes.

The correlations are given in Table 1.5, which shows that market-neutral hedge funds have little correlation with equity markets in normal times (although the correlation indicates that some of the funds in the index universe use some market leverage to create their returns), but that they show increased dependency in unusual times. Conversely, market timers show a remarkable ability to decouple in unusual times. The table also confirms the crisis character of government bonds (negative correlation in times of crisis) as well as the stable–diversifying properties of Japanese equities.

Table 1.5 Correlation in normal and unusual times

	MSCI US	MSCI Japanese	SB WGBI	HFR neutral	HFR timing
Normal times					
MSCI US	1.00	0.35	0.34	0.25	0.69
MSCI Japanese	0.35	1.00	0.08	0.05	0.48
SB WGBI	0.34	0.08	1.00	0.23	0.22
HFR neutral	0.25	0.05	0.23	1.00	0.23
HFR timing	0.69	0.48	0.22	0.23	1.00
Unusual times					
MSCI US	1.00	0.41	−0.18	0.39	0.44
MSCI Japanese	0.41	1.00	−0.09	0.39	0.04
SB WGBI	−0.18	−0.09	1.00	−0.25	−0.10
HFR neutral	0.39	0.39	−0.25	1.00	0.46
HFR timing	0.44	0.04	−0.10	0.46	1.00

HFR, Hedge Fund Research, Inc (market-neutral investing and market timing); MSCI, Morgan Stanley Capital International (US and Japanese equities); SB, Salomon Brothers (World Government Bond Index).

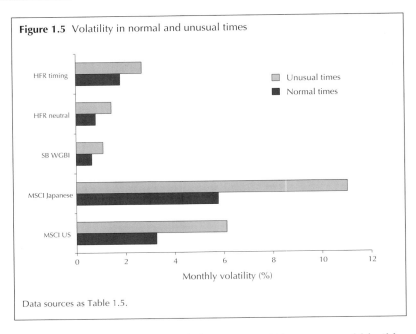

Figure 1.5 Volatility in normal and unusual times

Data sources as Table 1.5.

For those investors concerned about unusual times, we could build a new covariance matrix as a mixture of both covariance matrices with increasing weight put on the covariances in unusual times. To do so we need not only the objective probabilities from the correlation matrix for normal times, ie, 75% if we define outliers as those values that only occur in 25% of all cases) but also the relative risk-aversion to both regimes. It can be shown that the new combined covariance matrix is a mixture of covariances in good and bad times:

$$\Omega_{new} = p\lambda_{normal}\,\Omega_{normal} + \lambda_{unusual}(1-p)\,\Omega_{unusual} \qquad (1.45)$$

where p reflects the objective probabilities and λ_{normal} and $\lambda_{unusual}$ are rescaled risk-aversions such that their sum equals the actual risk-aversion of an investor.

Figure 1.5, which plots published volatility data for the investments in Table 1.5, confirms that the volatility for unusual observations is higher than for normal observations. Although the above analysis is useful as an exploratory tool, it should be noted that the results are sensitive to the inclusion of new assets, which might considerably change the properties of the already existing assets by changing previously normal periods to unusual periods and vice versa. This is why some researchers choose to define unusual periods in the narrow sense of down markets with particular reference to a prespecified core asset.[67]

1.9 A SIMPLE MODEL FOR LIFE-CYCLE INVESTING

So far we have assumed that investors possess only financial wealth, an assumption that was necessary to guarantee that the optimal equity allocation was independent of our time horizon. This assumption will now be relaxed.

Life-cycle investing refers to the evolution of asset classes in an investor's portfolio as he approaches retirement, and life-cycle concepts are becoming increasingly important as the asset management industry experiences a shift to defined-contribution plans. We know from Section 1.2 that if investors show constant relative risk-aversion, the proportion of their wealth invested in risky assets will stay the same independent of total wealth, and if investment opportunities are constant (equities are not a hedge against bad times), the optimal equity allocation will be independent of the investment horizon. In that case the optimal equity weight at time t, $w^*_{equity, t}$, becomes constant: $\overline{w}_{equity}$.[68]

Suppose, for expositionary convenience, that $\overline{w}_{equity} = 20\%$. How can we introduce life-cycle investing – ie, changes in the optimal bond–equity mix as time passes – into the conceptual framework above? The key is to recognise that investors possess both financial wealth, A, and human capital, H, defined as the present value of future savings.[69] (Slavery having been abolished, human capital is not tradable.) Suppose that an investor, a young investment banker, owns one monetary unit of financial wealth and four units of human capital. Since he, or she, owns only one unit of assets in which to physically invest (he cannot trade his human capital), he will put 100% of his assets into equities. This translates into 20% equities relative to his total wealth (financial assets plus human capital), assuming that human capital has the character of a bond. The optimal equity allocation, w^*_t, is then

$$w^*_t = \overline{w} + \overline{w}\,\frac{H_t}{A_t} = 20\% + 20\%\,\frac{4}{1} = 100\% \qquad (1.46)$$

In this equation the first 20% refers to the investor's optimal equity holding if his human capital were zero. The second part reflects the leverage necessary to arrive at 20% equity exposure on his total wealth (ie, five units of capital).

What about the nature of the human capital? Suppose that the investor's job carries risks related to the equity market, so he already owns (implicit) equity – say 5% – in his human capital. Would it still be optimal to invest 100% in equities? After taking into account the implicit equity risk, the optimal allocation in equities reduces to

$$w^*_t = \overline{w} + (\overline{w} - \omega_t)\,\frac{H_t}{A_t} = 20\% + (20\% - 5\%)\,\frac{4}{1} = 80\% \qquad (1.47)$$

The relationship between human and financial capital determines the way assets are allocated over the investor's lifetime. As he grows older, the investor's financial wealth will rise relative to his human capital (we assume that his financial wealth increases with age, which at the same time tends to reduce his human capital). At retirement, his human capital is zero and he owns 80% fixed income and 20% equities. With start- and end-points now known, it is interesting to see how the optimal asset allocation evolves over time. Taking two optimal allocations one period apart and subtracting the first from the second, we can write approximately

$$\Delta w^* \approx \frac{H}{A} \left[\underbrace{\overline{w} \times \left(R_H - R_p \right)}_{\substack{\text{Relative} \\ \text{performance}}} + \underbrace{\Delta \omega}_{\substack{\text{Change in} \\ \text{equity character}}} \right] \qquad (1.48)$$

where $R_H - R_p$ denotes the growth differential between human and financial (portfolio) capital. Changes in equity weights are expected to be negative (decreasing optimal equity allocation) as long as asset growth outperforms growth in human capital. This might not always be the case: if the investor is young and job changes lead to fast salary increases, human capital growth might outrun asset growth. This will result in rising equity allocations. However, as the investor approaches retirement, growth in human capital will eventually become negative as the time remaining in terms of professional life shortens. Changes in the equity character of human capital (typically negative, ie, decreasing equity character) will decelerate shifts into fixed income. Rebalancing within financial wealth will be contra-cyclical (equity will increase if financial wealth underperforms). The most sizeable shifts are likely to occur when investors are young as the ratio of human to financial capital is still large. Assuming no uncertainty in the character of equity, we get, by applying a variance operator to Equation (1.48):

$$\sigma^2 \left(\Delta w^* \right) \approx \left(\frac{H}{A} \left(\overline{w} - \varpi \right) \right)^2 \times \sigma^2 \left(R_H - R_p \right) \qquad (1.49)$$

The volatility of changes in the optimal allocation, $\sigma^2(\Delta w)$, is highest if H/A is large, ie, if investors are young. Time does not explicitly enter the equations for lifetime asset allocation, but it implicitly affects asset allocation through changes in human capital. Although the above model ignores everything that makes lifetime asset allocation a difficult problem to solve (we took consumption as exogenous, modelled uncertainty and the character of human capital in a very *ad hoc* way, did not account for elasticity in labour supply, etc), it provides a simple framework that requires little mathematical modelling apart from the calculation of present values and it gives answers that are very similar to much less manageable models.[70] The model shows that even young investors might find it optimal to invest most of their income in bonds if their human capital already exposes them to considerable equity risk. In general, it is not true that investors will always move along the efficient frontier from right to left. The rate at which they make their way along this frontier depends mainly on the relative performance of their human capital and, hence, is highly individual.

APPENDIX A: RELATIVE MAGNITUDE OF ESTIMATION ERRORS

We have already established that estimation error on mean returns is a critical factor in portfolio construction.[71] However, as estimation error applies equally to means and variances, we want to establish the relative magnitudes of the estimation errors calculated for them.

Suppose we have T years of data. This period is divided into n intervals of equal length ($n = T/\Delta t$). What can we do to reduce the estimation error for the mean return and the uncertainty about deviations from that mean? We can either try to extend the data period (ie, increase T), or we can concentrate on shorter frequencies (ie, increase n by reducing Δt). Although the first method is often neither feasible (some series might not have a longer history) nor recommendable (a reduction in sampling error often comes at the expense of an increase in non-stationarity, as discussed in Chapter 3), it is still a useful exercise to show how many data are needed to arrive at reasonably small estimation errors.

Suppose that a fairly typical calculation gives an estimated mean of 10% and a return volatility around that mean of about 20%. Tables A1 and A2 give the results of the relevant calculations. We can see from the first table that even with 50 years of data the confidence interval on the mean estimate (11%) is the same size as the mean estimate itself.[72]

It is apparent from Table A2 that the estimation error on the variance of returns is many times smaller than that on mean returns.[73] However, although the estimation error becomes smaller as we increase the sample

Table A1 Effect of sample period on estimation error for mean returns

Estimation period, T (years)	Estimation error (%)	95% confidence interval (%)
1	20	78
5	9	35
10	6	25
20	4	18
50	3	11

Table A2 Effect of sample period on estimation error for variance estimates (tabulated data are estimation errors (%))

Estimation period T (years)	Estimation frequency			
	Daily	Weekly	Monthly	Quarterly
1	0.35	0.79	1.71	3.27
5	0.16	0.35	0.74	1.30
10	0.11	0.25	0.52	0.91
20	0.08	0.18	0.37	0.64
50	0.05	0.11	0.23	0.40

frequency, this is not necessarily the best route to pursue as increasing the frequency leads to greater autocorrelation. Moreover, daily data will exhibit an artificially low correlation between assets of different time zones as only a small number of transactions contain the same information. However, the much smaller estimation error on variance relative to that on means is the justification for the standard practice of calculating risk estimates from historical figures.

Estimation errors on means and covariances often interact in a way that is difficult to understand. Estimation error in portfolio weights is therefore difficult to attribute to either or both. Although it is tempting to declare estimation error in means as uniquely important for all investors, it is worth noting that the importance of risk estimates increases with an investor's risk-aversion. This is equally true for passive investors who have to rely on risk estimates to find the best liability-mimicking portfolio. Chapter 3 deals with an interesting heuristic for visualising the uncertainty in portfolio weights created by the uncertainty in inputs.

APPENDIX B: ONE-STEP VERSUS TWO-STEP OPTIMISATION

When optimising a portfolio one often has to deal with a block structure, in that two or more blocks of assets – eg, equities and bonds, equities and currencies, or active managers and asset classes – must be optimally combined into one portfolio. Very often the correlation between blocks is ignored, or is conveniently set to zero, and the problem is solved either separately – the solution for the first block of assets ignoring that for the second, and vice versa – or in a two-step process in which one first finds the optimal asset allocation and then the optimal currency allocation. We will review the mathematics involved in this type of optimisation problem and illustrate the issues using a currency hedging example.

[handwritten margin notes:]
1. overlay (sep business)
1. partial
2. total

B1.1 Base model

Optimal currency hedging remains the subject of an ongoing debate between plan sponsors, asset managers and consultants.[74] In the terminology that follows we distinguish between *asset returns* (local return plus currency return minus domestic cash rate: $a_i = \Delta p_i/p_i + \Delta s_i/s_i - c_h$) and *currency returns* (local cash rate plus currency movement minus domestic cash rate: $e_i = \Delta s_i/s_i + c_i - c_h$). The covariance matrix of asset and currency returns is assumed to follow the block structure outlined below:

$$\Omega = \begin{bmatrix} \Omega_{aa} & \Omega_{ae} \\ \Omega_{ea} & \Omega_{ee} \end{bmatrix} \quad (B1)$$

where Ω_{aa} is the $k \times k$ covariance matrix of asset returns expressed in the home currency, Ω_{ee} is the $k \times k$ covariance matrix of currency returns (assuming that we have as many currencies as assets) and Ω_{ae} is the $k \times k$

covariance matrix between asset returns and currency returns.[75] Currency hedging takes place in the form of regression hedging, where we regress asset returns against all currency returns to allow for possible cross-correlation:

$$a_i = h_i + h_{i1}e_1 + h_{i2}e_2 + \cdots + h_{ik}e_k + \varepsilon_i \tag{B2}$$

Regression hedging can be expressed in matrix terms as $\mathbf{h} = \mathbf{\Omega}_{ae}\mathbf{\Omega}_{ee}^{-1}$, where the $k \times k$ matrix of regression hedges will contain the regression coefficients of Equation (B2):

$$\mathbf{h} = \begin{bmatrix} h_{11} & h_{12} & \cdots & h_{1k} \\ \vdots & \ddots & & \\ h_{k1} & & & h_{kk} \end{bmatrix} \tag{B3}$$

We can now define the variance in asset returns that remains unexplained by currency returns:

$$\mathbf{\Omega}_{a|e} = \mathbf{\Omega}_{aa} - \mathbf{h}'\mathbf{\Omega}_{ee}\mathbf{h} \tag{B4}$$

and rewrite the inverse of the covariance matrix of asset and currency returns as

$$\mathbf{\Omega}_{ae}^{-1} = \begin{bmatrix} \mathbf{\Omega}_{a|e}^{-1} & -\mathbf{\Omega}_{a|e}^{-1}\mathbf{h} \\ -\mathbf{h}\mathbf{\Omega}_{a|e}^{-1} & \mathbf{\Omega}_{ee}^{-1} + \mathbf{h}\mathbf{\Omega}_{a|e}^{-1}\mathbf{h}' \end{bmatrix}$$

where we use the results for the inverse of a partitioned matrix:

$$\begin{bmatrix} \mathbf{P}_{11} & \mathbf{P}_{12} \\ \mathbf{P}_{21} & \mathbf{P}_{22} \end{bmatrix}^{-1} = \begin{bmatrix} \mathbf{\Delta}^{-1} & -\mathbf{\Delta}^{-1}\mathbf{P}_{12}\mathbf{P}_{22}^{-1} \\ -\mathbf{P}_{22}^{-1}\mathbf{P}_{21}\mathbf{\Delta}^{-1} & \mathbf{P}_{22}^{-1} + \mathbf{P}_{22}^{-1}\mathbf{P}_{21}\mathbf{\Delta}^{-1}\mathbf{P}_{12}\mathbf{P}_{22}^{-1} \end{bmatrix}$$

$$\mathbf{\Delta} = \mathbf{P}_{11} - \mathbf{P}_{12}\mathbf{P}_{22}^{-1}\mathbf{P}_{21} \tag{B5}$$

We can, for example, check the value of the $\mathbf{\Delta}$:

$$\begin{aligned} \mathbf{P}_{11} - \mathbf{P}_{12}\mathbf{P}_{22}^{-1}\mathbf{P}_{12} &= \mathbf{\Omega}_{aa} - \mathbf{\Omega}_{ae}\mathbf{\Omega}_{ee}^{-1}\mathbf{\Omega}_{ae} \\ &= \mathbf{\Omega}_{aa} - \mathbf{\Omega}_{ae}\mathbf{\Omega}_{ee}^{-1}\mathbf{\Omega}_{ee}^{-1}\mathbf{\Omega}_{ee}^{-1}\mathbf{\Omega}_{ae} \\ &= \mathbf{\Omega}_{aa} - \left(\mathbf{\Omega}_{ee}^{-1}\mathbf{\Omega}_{ae}\right)\mathbf{\Omega}_{ee}^{-1}\left(\mathbf{\Omega}_{ee}^{-1}\mathbf{\Omega}_{ae}\right) \\ &= \mathbf{\Omega}_{aa} - \mathbf{h}\mathbf{\Omega}_{ee}^{-1}\mathbf{h} \\ &= \mathbf{\Omega}_{a|e} \end{aligned}$$

Before we can start to look at the differences between separate and simultaneous optimisation, we have to define the vector of optimal asset and currency weights, $\mathbf{w}' = [\mathbf{w}_a \ \mathbf{w}_e]$, as well as the vector of expected asset and currency returns, $\boldsymbol{\mu}' = \begin{bmatrix} \boldsymbol{\mu}_a & \boldsymbol{\mu}_e \end{bmatrix}$. We already know from Section 1.1 that the optimal (simultaneous) solution to an unconstrained currency hedging problem can be written as $\mathbf{w}_{\text{sim}}^* = \lambda \boldsymbol{\Omega}^{-1} \boldsymbol{\mu}$ (Equation 1.4). However, expanding this expression will generate additional insight.

B1.2 Simultaneous optimisation

We will start with the optimal solution (choosing optimal asset and currency positions simultaneously rather than using a two-step process) to the optimal hedging problem:

$$\mathbf{w}_{\text{sim}}^* = \begin{bmatrix} \mathbf{w}_{a,\,\text{sim}}^* \\ \mathbf{w}_{e,\,\text{sim}}^* \end{bmatrix} = \begin{bmatrix} \lambda \left(\boldsymbol{\Omega}_{a|e}^{-1} \boldsymbol{\mu}_a - \boldsymbol{\Omega}_{a|e}^{-1} \mathbf{h}' \boldsymbol{\mu}_e \right) \\ \lambda \boldsymbol{\Omega}_{ee}^{-1} \boldsymbol{\mu}_e - \mathbf{h} \mathbf{w}_{a,\,\text{sim}}^* \end{bmatrix} \quad \text{(B6)}$$

The optimal currency position in a simultaneous optimisation involves a speculative as well as a hedging demand:

$$\mathbf{w}_{e,\,\text{sim}}^* = \underbrace{\lambda \boldsymbol{\Omega}_{ee}^{-1} \boldsymbol{\mu}_e}_{\substack{\text{Speculative} \\ \text{demand}}} - \underbrace{\mathbf{h} \mathbf{w}_{a,\,\text{sim}}^*}_{\substack{\text{Hedge} \\ \text{demand}}} \quad \text{(B7)}$$

If currencies carry a positive risk premium (the currency return is, on average, larger than the interest rate differential), currencies will be included in the optimal portfolio because the first term in Equation (B7) will be positive. Let us instead focus on the case, often assumed by practitioners, that currencies do not offer a significant risk premium. In this case Equation (B6) becomes

$$\begin{bmatrix} \mathbf{w}_{a,\,\text{sim}}^* \\ \mathbf{w}_{e,\,\text{sim}}^* \end{bmatrix} = \begin{bmatrix} \lambda \boldsymbol{\Omega}_{a|e}^{-1} \boldsymbol{\mu}_a \\ -\mathbf{h} \mathbf{w}_{a,\,\text{sim}}^* \end{bmatrix} \quad \text{(B8)}$$

Suppose that local asset returns are uncorrelated with currency returns. In that case, taking on currency risk does not help to reduce (hedge) asset risk and, as currency risk always comes as an add-on to asset risk, we would intuitively find unitary hedging optimal – currencies only add noise to a portfolio.[76] How does this intuition carry over to Equation (B8)? If local returns, $\Delta P_i / P$, for the ith asset are not correlated with currency movements, $\Delta S_i / S_i$, we must find that the covariance between currency returns and foreign asset returns in home currency units contains solely the covariance between currencies:[77]

$$\text{cov}\left(\Delta P_i / P + \Delta S_i / S_i, \ \Delta S_j / S_j \right)$$

$$= \text{cov}\left(\Delta P_i / P, \ \Delta S_i / S_i \right) + \text{cov}\left(\Delta S_i / S_i, \ \Delta S_j / S_j \right)$$

$$= \text{cov}\left(\Delta S_i / S_i, \ \Delta S_j / S_j \right) \quad \text{(B9)}$$

In matrix terms this becomes $\mathbf{\Omega}_{ea} = \mathbf{\Omega}_{ee}$ and $\mathbf{h} = \mathbf{\Omega}_{ea}\mathbf{\Omega}_{ee}^{-1} = \mathbf{1}$, and hence the currency positions will completely hedge out the currency risk that arises from the unhedged asset positions:

$$\begin{bmatrix} \mathbf{w}_{a,\,\text{sim}}^{*} \\ \mathbf{w}_{e,\,\text{sim}}^{*} \end{bmatrix} = \begin{bmatrix} \lambda\,\mathbf{\Omega}_{a|e}^{-1}\,\mathbf{\mu}_{a} \\ -\,\mathbf{w}_{a,\,\text{sim}}^{*} \end{bmatrix} \tag{B10}$$

Now suppose the opposite – that foreign asset returns (in home currency units) and currency returns are not correlated. This scenario is very unlikely as, for example, it would be rare for Japanese equity returns in US dollars not to be positively correlated with the US dollar.

Hedging currency risk would now increase total risk as the negative correlation between local returns and currency returns would no longer affect portfolio risk. The optimal hedge ratio becomes zero and positions are given in Equation (B11):

$$\begin{bmatrix} \mathbf{w}_{a,\,\text{sim}}^{*} \\ \mathbf{w}_{e,\,\text{sim}}^{*} \end{bmatrix} = \begin{bmatrix} \lambda\,\mathbf{\Omega}_{aa}^{-1}\,\mathbf{\mu}_{a} \\ 0 \end{bmatrix} \tag{B11}$$

This follows from $\mathbf{\Omega}_{ea} = \mathbf{0}$, so $\mathbf{h} = \mathbf{\Omega}_{ea}\mathbf{\Omega}_{ee}^{-1} = \mathbf{0}$ and, hence, the conditional asset volatility will equal the unconditional volatility: $\mathbf{\Omega}_{a|e} = \mathbf{\Omega}_{aa} - \mathbf{h}'\mathbf{\Omega}_{ee}\mathbf{h} = \mathbf{\Omega}_{aa}$, where $\mathbf{\Omega}_{a|e}$ denotes the covariance of asset returns conditional on currency returns.

We can summarise these findings into a quick taxonomy of currency hedging based on the behaviour of local returns and currency returns. If currencies carry a risk premium, there will always be a speculative aspect to currency exposure. However, if we assume a zero risk premium to currencies, we have to review currency exposure in terms of its ability to reduce asset risk. Zero correlation between local returns and currency returns will make currencies a noisy asset that adds risk without providing compensation in the form of returns or diversification. Negative correlation between local returns and currency returns makes currencies a hedge asset that reduces total portfolio risk. Hedging out currency risk completely would increase total portfolio risk. Positive correlation between local returns and currency returns would achieve the opposite. In that case over-hedging (where the short position in currencies is larger than the long position in assets carrying currency risk) is optimal.

B1.3 Two-step optimisation

So far we have looked at the simultaneous optimisation of currency and asset positions. Alternatively, we could optimise asset positions in a first step and in the second step choose optimal currency positions conditional on the already established asset positions. The result of this approach, called "partial optimisation", is given below:

$$
\mathbf{w}_{\text{par}}^* = \begin{bmatrix} \mathbf{w}_{a,\text{par}}^* \\ \mathbf{w}_{e,\text{par}}^* \end{bmatrix} = \begin{bmatrix} \lambda \, \mathbf{\Omega}_{aa}^{-1} \mathbf{\mu}_a \\ \lambda \, \mathbf{\Omega}_{ee}^{-1} \mathbf{\mu}_e - h \mathbf{w}_{a,\text{par}}^* \end{bmatrix} \tag{B12}
$$

Terms representing conditional covariance drop out (as by definition it is not taken into account) and there is no feedback of currency positions on asset positions as this has previously been ignored.

Clearly, partial optimisation is sub-optimal (leads to a lower utility) as it ignores the covariances between assets and currencies.

B1.4 One-step (separate) optimisation

The final option for constructing portfolios in the presence of currencies is separate optimisation, also known as "currency overlay":

$$
\mathbf{w}_{\text{sep}}^* = \begin{bmatrix} \mathbf{w}_{a,\text{sep}}^* \\ \mathbf{w}_{e,\text{sep}}^* \end{bmatrix} = \begin{bmatrix} \lambda \, \mathbf{\Omega}_{aa}^{-1} \mathbf{\mu}_a \\ \lambda \, \mathbf{\Omega}_{ee}^{-1} \mathbf{\mu}_e \end{bmatrix} \tag{B13}
$$

"Separate" refers to the fact that asset and currency decisions are taken by different departments in an investment firm which do not take into account each other's positions in a client portfolio. Separate optimisation is dominated by partial optimisation. This can be seen by calculating the difference in utility, U, that both weightings would create:

$$
U\left(\mathbf{w}_{\text{par}}^*\right) - U\left(\mathbf{w}_{\text{sep}}^*\right) = \left(\mathbf{w}_{\text{par}}^* - \mathbf{w}_{\text{sep}}^*\right)\mathbf{\mu} - \frac{1}{2\lambda}\left(\mathbf{w}_{\text{par}}^{*\prime}\mathbf{\Omega}\mathbf{w}_{\text{par}}^* - \mathbf{w}_{\text{sep}}^{*\prime}\mathbf{\Omega}\mathbf{w}_{\text{sep}}^*\right)
$$

$$
= \frac{\lambda}{2}\left(\mathbf{\mu}_a'\,\mathbf{\Omega}_{aa}^{-1}\,\mathbf{\Omega}_{ae}\,\mathbf{\Omega}_{ee}^{-1}\,\mathbf{\Omega}_{ea}\,\mathbf{\Omega}_{aa}^{-1}\,\mathbf{\mu}_a\right) \tag{B14}
$$

As long as $\mathbf{\Omega}_{aa}^{-1}\mathbf{\Omega}_{ae}\mathbf{\Omega}_{ee}^{-1}\mathbf{\Omega}_{ea}\mathbf{\Omega}_{aa}^{-1}$ is positive-definite this will always be the case. Partial and separate optimisation yield the same result if investors find zero hedging optimal.

B1.5 Inclusion of constraints

To conclude this appendix, some constraints will be added to the above solution. As stated in Section 1.1, the optimal solution to the constrained optimisation problem is

$$
\mathbf{w}_{\text{sim}}^* = \begin{bmatrix} \mathbf{w}_{a,\text{sim}}^* \\ \mathbf{w}_{e,\text{sim}}^* \end{bmatrix} = \mathbf{\Omega}^{-1}\mathbf{A}'\left(\mathbf{A}\mathbf{\Omega}^{-1}\mathbf{A}'\right)^{-1}\mathbf{b} + \lambda\,\mathbf{\Omega}^{-1}\left(\mathbf{I} - \mathbf{A}'\left(\mathbf{A}\mathbf{\Omega}^{-1}\mathbf{A}'\right)\mathbf{A}\mathbf{\Omega}^{-1}\right)\mathbf{\mu}
$$

$$
\tag{B15}
$$

If we define

$$\mathbf{A}'\left(\mathbf{A}\,\Omega^{-1}\mathbf{A}'\right)^{-1}\mathbf{b} = \begin{bmatrix} \mathbf{B}_1 \\ \mathbf{B}_2 \end{bmatrix}$$

$$\mathbf{I} - \mathbf{A}'\left(\mathbf{A}\,\Omega^{-1}\mathbf{A}'\right)^{-1}\mathbf{A}\Omega^{-1} = \begin{bmatrix} \mathbf{A}_{11} & \mathbf{A}_{12} \\ \mathbf{A}_{21} & \mathbf{A}_{22} \end{bmatrix} \qquad (B16)$$

we can expand the optimal solution to

$$\begin{bmatrix} \mathbf{w}^*_{a,\,sim} \\ \mathbf{w}^*_{e,\,sim} \end{bmatrix} = \begin{bmatrix} \Omega^{-1}_{a|e}\mathbf{B}_1 - \Omega^{-1}_{a|e}\mathbf{h}'\mathbf{B}_2 \\ \Omega^{-1}_{ee}\mathbf{B}_2 - \mathbf{h}\left(\Omega^{-1}_{a|e}\mathbf{B}_1 - \Omega^{-1}_{a|e}\mathbf{h}'\mathbf{B}_2\right) \end{bmatrix}$$

$$+ \lambda\begin{bmatrix} \Omega^{-1}_{a|e}\left(\mathbf{A}_{11}\boldsymbol{\mu}_a + \mathbf{A}_{12}\boldsymbol{\mu}_e - \mathbf{h}'\mathbf{A}_{21}\boldsymbol{\mu}_a - \mathbf{h}'\mathbf{A}_{22}\boldsymbol{\mu}_e\right) \\ \Omega^{-1}_{ee}\mathbf{A}_{21}\boldsymbol{\mu}_a + \Omega^{-1}_{ee}\mathbf{A}_{22}\boldsymbol{\mu}_e - \mathbf{h}\Omega^{-1}_{a|e}\left(\mathbf{A}_{11}\boldsymbol{\mu}_a + \mathbf{A}_{12}\boldsymbol{\mu}_e - \mathbf{h}'\mathbf{A}_{21}\boldsymbol{\mu}_a - \mathbf{h}'\mathbf{A}_{22}\boldsymbol{\mu}_e\right) \end{bmatrix}$$

$$(B17)$$

Although Equation (B17) looks daunting, it offers a closed-form solution for the optimal hedging problem. It could be used to visually inspect the loss in efficiency when partial rather than simultaneous optimisation is used. However, constraints will in general limit the loss of efficiency – the full correlation structure is limited by the set of constraints and therefore cannot be taken advantage of fully.

APPENDIX C: FACTOR RISK CONTRIBUTIONS
So far we have assumed that we cannot decompose the uncertainty in asset returns into common factors. However, stocks are at least partly driven by characteristics (industry, country, size, etc) which they share with many other stocks. Suppose that we can write the risk premium of a given stock as a combination of these factor returns weighted by their respective factor exposures:[78]

$$\mathbf{r} = \mathbf{X}\mathbf{f} + \mathbf{u}$$

where $\mathbf{r}$ is a $k \times 1$ vector of risk premia (asset return minus cash), $\mathbf{X}$ is a $k \times p$ matrix of factor exposures (sometimes called "loadings", particularly if they are derived from a principal component analysis), $\mathbf{f}$ is a $p \times 1$ matrix of factor returns and $\mathbf{u}$ is a $k \times 1$ vector of asset-specific returns that are both uncorrelated with factor returns and uncorrelated across assets as they are specific to a particular company.[79] The covariance matrix of excess returns can then be expressed as[80]

$$E(\mathbf{r}\mathbf{r}') = E(\mathbf{X}\mathbf{f} + \mathbf{u})(\mathbf{X}\mathbf{f} + \mathbf{u})'$$

$$= E(\mathbf{X f u'}) + E(\mathbf{X f f' X'}) + E(\mathbf{u u'}) + E(\mathbf{u X' f})$$

$$\mathbf{\Omega} = \mathbf{X \Omega}_{ff}\mathbf{X'} + \mathbf{\Omega}_{uu}$$

where $\mathbf{\Omega}_{ff}$ denotes the $p \times p$ covariance matrix of factor returns and $\mathbf{\Omega}_{uu}$ is a $k \times k$ covariance matrix (diagonal matrix) of asset-specific returns. We can now decompose portfolio risk into a common and a specific part:[81]

$$\sigma_p^2 = \mathbf{w' X \Omega}_{ff}\mathbf{X' w} + \mathbf{w' X \Omega}_{uu}\mathbf{w}$$

Using the same logic as before, we get for the marginal factor contribution to risk (MFCTR):

$$\mathbf{MFCTR} = \frac{d\,\sigma_p}{d(\mathbf{X' w})} = \frac{\mathbf{\Omega}_{ff}\mathbf{X' w}}{\sigma_p}$$

where **MFCTR** is an $f \times 1$ vector. The calculations introduced in this appendix will be applied in Chapter 6.

1 The reader is assumed to be familiar with the basics of mean–variance optimisation. A concise review can be found in Elton and Gruber (1995). This chapter will focus on selected issues not commonly found in textbooks.

2 Discussions of the theory of utility can be found in Gollier (2001). Quadratic utility is of the form $u(w) = w - \frac{b}{2}w^2$, where $u(w)$ expresses utility, a measure of happiness, as a function of uncertain wealth, w. In this example greater utility is not strictly an increase in wealth as, depending on the value of b, utility will decline for large enough w. Thus, investors will not always prefer more to less. Moreover, richer investors hold a smaller fraction in risky assets, which is not always plausible (increasing relative risk-aversion).

3 Returns are multivariate normal if they are jointly normal. Normality for a single return series is not enough for multivariate normality. Normality itself is a convenient feature as it allows returns to be easily aggregated across time and across holdings.

   Conceptually, returns cannot be normally distributed as they are naturally truncated at -100% (maximum loss). We will, however, ignore this "technicality", keeping very much in line with most of the literature on portfolio selection. Focusing instead on log returns (which are normally distributed) would add the complication that log returns are not additive (the weighted sum of log returns is not the portfolio log return). More importantly, log returns offer very little additional insight into portfolio construction issues.

4 One common method is to use the average (local) risk premium as input. The average return characterises the expected return, while the median return does not. Working with the risk premium (risky security return minus the risk-free rate) has the advantage that it is more stable than pure returns as it takes out at least part of the interest rate component in returns. However, it is necessary to define what is meant by risk-free rate. If we focus on nominal capital growth, the risk-free rate coincides with the zero rate for the corresponding time horizon (it is risk-free because it is known at the beginning of the time horizon). If instead we focus on real capital growth, the risk-free security becomes inflation-linked bonds, which guarantee a real rate. A further advantage of the local risk premium approach is that it can easily be converted into different home currencies by adding on the

domestic cash rate (domestic cash rate plus local risk premium equals foreign return hedged into home currency).

5 This book follows the convention that vectors and matrices are represented by bold symbols. Estimation errors are dealt with in later chapters (Chapters 3 and 4 in particular).

6 Portfolio diversification lies at the heart of portfolio theory. Adding another asset to a portfolio (keeping total investments constant) will reduce portfolio risk. Suppose that an individual stock return can be written as market return plus stock-specific return $(R_i = R_m + \alpha_i)$ and that k equally weighted stocks are combined into one common portfolio. The risk (variance) of this portfolio can be calculated as

$$\mathrm{var}\left(\sum_{i=1}^{k} w_i R_i \right) = \left(\sum_{i=1}^{k} \frac{1}{k} R_i \right) = \left(\sum_{i=1}^{k} \frac{1}{k} \left(R_m + \alpha_i \right) \right) = \mathrm{var}\left(R_m \right) + \frac{\mathrm{var}\left(\alpha \right)}{k}$$

Adding more assets will result in a portfolio that carries only market risk, with stock-specific risk diversified away. This is also called "micro-diversification". However, groups of stocks are exposed to common macroeconomic factors, and little research has been done on *macro*-diversification, ie, understanding the returns of different asset classes in different economic environments. Questions such as whether hedge funds or commodities are the better hedge against down markets are rarely addressed but would give insight into macro-diversification.

7 The "≈" symbol has been used rather than "=" to emphasise that Equation (1.4) might hold approximately for a wide range of utility functions. Section 1.2 reviews the approximating properties of Equation (1.3).

8 This section will deal with linear equality constraints rather than inequality constraints as little is gained by extending the analysis to constraints that are mathematically more demanding but offer no additional investment insight as commercial solutions are now readily available.

9 Note that $\mathrm{d}(\mathbf{x}'\boldsymbol{\Omega}\mathbf{x})/\mathrm{d}\mathbf{x} = (\boldsymbol{\Omega} + \boldsymbol{\Omega}')\mathbf{x}$, which equals $2\boldsymbol{\Omega}\mathbf{x}$ if $\boldsymbol{\Omega} = \boldsymbol{\Omega}'$, ie, if $\boldsymbol{\Omega}$ is symmetric. See Green (2000, p. 52) for more on this.

10 An adding-up constraint would be written as $\begin{bmatrix} 1 & \cdots & 1 \end{bmatrix} \mathbf{w} = \sum w_i = 1$.

11 However, constraints are sometimes justified as safeguards against bad inputs. We will review this issue in Chapter 3.

12 The reader is referred to the literature on mean–variance spanning tests, which considers whether a new asset added to the investment universe provides an investment opportunity or whether it is spanned (priced) by already existing assets. See Cochrane (2001).

13 See Glen and Jorion (1993).

14 See Ziemba and Mulvey (1998) for a detailed presentation of many asset–liability management issues.

15 Private investors, for example, need to think about liabilities as a real consumption stream after retirement.

16 Writing surplus returns as change in surplus relative to assets rather than relative to surplus has the advantage that surplus returns are always defined (even for zero surplus) and do not become too large (otherwise a surplus rising from 1% to 2% would lead to a 100% surplus return).

17 However, we do not assume f to be fixed (known at start-of-period) as real asset–liability management would also change liabilities (sale, reinsurance, etc).

18 One of the difficulties in asset–liability management arises from the non-existence of a liability-mimicking asset that, if bought, would hedge out all the liability risks completely. This is often caused by inflation-indexed liabilities or final wage-related schemes, which create unhedgeable equity-linked liabilities. Pension funds will always have to accept some liability noise.

19 Each entry in $\boldsymbol{\Omega}_{\mathrm{surplus}}$ can be expressed as $\mathrm{cov}(R_i - f R_l, R_j - f R_l)$.

20 Alternatively, we can define the vector of covariances between assets and our liability as $\Gamma = \begin{bmatrix} \sigma_{1l} \cdots \sigma_{kl} \end{bmatrix}'$. As funding ratio, liability return and liability risk are fixed (known at the start of the investment period), we are left to maximise $\mathbf{w}'\boldsymbol{\mu} - \frac{1}{2}\lambda(\mathbf{w}'\boldsymbol{\Omega}\mathbf{w} - 2f\mathbf{w}'\Gamma)$ subject to constraints. Sharpe and Tint (1990) call the term $2f\mathbf{w}'\Gamma$ "liability hedging credit" as assets that have positive correlation with liabilities add positively to an investor's utility. If the value of assets becomes very high relative to liabilities, the optimisation problem looks increasingly like an asset-only optimisation as f becomes small and there is little effect from the liability-hedging credit.

21 In a simple two-asset case (with the adding-up constraint that both assets have to sum to one), the solution with the smallest surplus volatility is

$$w_1 = \frac{\sigma_{22} - \sigma_{12} + f\left(\sigma_{1l} - \sigma_{2l}\right)}{\sigma_{11} + \sigma_{22} - 2\sigma_{12}}$$

If $(\sigma_{1l} = \sigma_{2l})$, we arrive at the same solution as without liabilities. A special case of this is $\sigma_{1l} = \sigma_{2l} = \mathbf{0}$, which applies to cash-like liabilities.

22 See Chapter 6 on benchmark-relative optimisation.

23 The entry of 0.04 indicates that asset one is characterised by 20% volatility (square root of 4% variance). This means that two-thirds of all return observations lie between the mean return plus or minus two standard deviations, ie, ±20%.

24 The constrained frontier touches the unconstrained frontier where all portfolio weights sum to one.

25 Strictly, investors with quadratic utility would not prefer more wealth to less wealth as utility falls after the satiation point. Quadratic utility also induces increasing absolute risk-aversion (richer individuals hold smaller amounts in risky assets than less rich individuals).

26 See Huang and Litzenberger (1988, p. 60).

27 See Levy and Markowitz (1979).

28 See Favre and Galeano (2001) vs Fung and Hsieh (1997).

29 This is only true if returns are normally distributed. In the case of non-normal returns, the maximum-growth portfolio might not lie on the efficient frontier as positive skewness adds to long-term growth whereas kurtosis detracts from it.

30 This is also called "Kelly betting". See Kelly (1956).

31 See Mossin (1968). Kritzman (2000) also provides an excellent review.

32 Time-varying investment opportunities and their impact on the riskiness of strategic asset allocation decisions are discussed in Campbell and Viceira (2001).

33 See Barberis (2000) and Xia (1999).

34 For an accessible introduction readers are referred to Brandimarte (2001).

35 The selection of asset classes suitable for optimisation is both quantitative and judgmental.

36 See Appendix B of this chapter.

37 A recommended introduction to the practical implementation of cluster analysis is Kaufman and Rousseeuw (1990).

38 This method is also called "agglomerative", whereas methods that begin by uniting all assets in one cluster are termed "divisive".

39 This simple distance function satisfies all required properties for a distance function: the distance to itself is zero; the distance between A and B is the same as that between B and A (symmetry); and the straight-line distance between A and C is always shorter than when a detour is made via B.

40 Historical data sets are available from Hedge Fund Research's website at http://www.hfr.com.

41 Insightful's S-plus contains routines for alternative clustering methods.

42 As a consequence, corporate high yield tends to dominate all other fixed-income classes,

leaving little room for emerging market debt (typically about 17% volatility per annum for JP Morgan EMBI) at almost all risk levels.

43 See Blundell and Ward (1987).

44 Note that this procedure leaves the average return virtually unchanged (for a large enough number of observations, T) –

$$\bar{r}_t^* = \frac{1}{1 - a_1} \bar{r} - \frac{a_1}{1 - a_1} \bar{r} = \bar{r}$$

– but increases the variance estimate. Applying the variance operator to Equation (1.26), we arrive at

$$\sigma^2(r^*) = \frac{1 + a_1^2}{\left(1 - a_1\right)^2} \sigma^2 \mathrm{var}\,(r)$$

UK property volatility rises to about 8% (instead of the naive 3% estimate) and high-yield volatility climbs to 9% (from 6%). Both figures appear much more reasonable than the widely used naive estimates.

45 These sub-indices are not representative of the whole hedge fund universe as the aim here is merely to illustrate the methodology.

46 See Scholes and Williams (1977).

47 Litterman (1996) coined the terms "hot spots" (areas where most of the portfolio risks are concentrated) and "best hedges" (risk-producing positions).

48 Grinold and Kahn (2000) is a complete and highly recommended source on the decomposition of portfolio risk.

49 Maximum diversification is sometimes thought to be achieved with the "equal risk portfolio".

50 Readers are encouraged to repeat all calculations for themselves. The book contains the information required for almost all examples in this and the following chapters.

51 See Bayer (1998).

52 See Jorion (2001).

53 See McCarthy (2000, p. 103).

54 See Chow and Kritzman (2001, p. 58).

55 See De Bever, Kozun and Zwan (2000, p. 283).

56 See Jorion (2001).

57 VAR has come under attack from Artzner et al (1999), who found that as one deviates from the normality assumption on returns, VAR is not necessarily sub-additive, ie, the VAR of a portfolio might be higher than the combined VARs of the single positions.

58 The covariance matrix is, in most applications, estimated either as a multifactor risk model or as a sample covariance matrix (which is ill-conditioned when the number of assets becomes large relative to the number of observations and of limited use in optimisation as it contains random noise as well as significant relationships, but it nevertheless provides a maximum likelihood forecast of risk). The greatest advantages of using the covariance matrix are the reduction of dimensions (low number of factors relative to number of assets), the stability of co-movements (as noise is separated from systematic relations) and the intuitive understanding it affords of the key drivers of portfolio risk (at least for economic multifactor models). Factors are derived either with the use of economic theory (macroeconomic or fundamental factors) or purely on statistical grounds. While statistical models (principal components, etc) are best for portfolio optimisation with regard to passive management, economically based factor models can also serve to identify (and neutralise or sharpen) groups of bets that are linked by common economic factors. The way risk is measured and decomposed has to coincide with the way a risk allocation is decided on; hence, risk management and return forecasting models should not look too different.

59 See Johnston (1984, p. 150).

60 The eigenvalues can also be used to calculate the common variance that is explained by so-called "principal components" (uncorrelated artificial variables that are constructed to maximise explanatory power). The ith component explains $e_i/\Sigma e_i$ of the variance in the three variables (note: eigenvalues are ordered starting with the biggest). In this case the first component explains about 87% of the variance, which directs us towards a strong common trend. (All matrix-oriented programming languages provide routines for calculating eigenvalues. Readers can also use PopTools by Greg Hood.)

61 For a symmetric 3×3 matrix all correlation coefficients must satisfy $\rho_{12}^2 + \rho_{13}^2 + \rho_{23}^2 - 2\rho_{12}\rho_{13}\rho_{23} \leq 1$ to describe a valid relationship.

62 Note that this is a rather technical correction with no relation to the data. In general we would like to use the information available in past returns. See Ledoit (1997) for a Bayesian approach.

63 See Stevens (1998).

64 This statement has been written from a total risk view. If investors look at benchmark-relative risks (or, equivalently, to long/short portfolios), an increase in correlation means that the hedge becomes better.

65 This concept is taken from Chow et al. (1999).

66 This distinguishes the analysis presented in this chapter from approaches that focus on measuring downside correlation by defining the down market with respect to a core asset.

67 One caveat of the described methodology, though, is that Table 1.5 might change if new assets are included. This results directly from the fact that outliers are defined by looking at all assets simultaneously. Thus, what has previously been a normal observation without the new asset could become unusual if the included asset shows an unusual movement from this data point.

68 It can be shown that, for an investor with utility $u(1 + R) = (1 - \gamma)^{-1}(1 + R)^{1-\gamma}$, the optimal solution is given by $w_{equity} = 1/\gamma \times \mu/\sigma^2$. However, if we introduce the probability of dying in year t as δt, this changes to $w_{equity} = 1/\gamma \times [(\mu - \delta t)/\sigma^2]$. One direct consequence of this is that women hold more equities than men as a woman is less likely to die at age t than a man.

69 This model follows Scherer and Ebertz (1998).

70 See Campbell and Viceira (2002), Chapters 6 and 7.

71 Chapters 3 and 4 deal with estimation error in greater detail.

72 Estimation error is given by $\sigma/\sqrt{T} = 0.2/\sqrt{T}$, and the confidence interval is calculated as

$$\left[+\frac{\sigma}{\sqrt{T}} z_a \quad -z_\alpha \frac{\sigma}{\sqrt{T}} \right]$$

where z_α denotes the critical value of a standard normal distribution. In this case $z_\alpha = 1.96$. The sampling error on the annual mean estimate depends only on the length of the data period (in years) and not on the data frequency itself.

73 Campbell, Lo and MacKinlay (1997, p. 364) show that

$$\text{var}(\hat{\sigma}^2) = \left(\frac{T}{\Delta t} - 1 \right)^{-1} 2\sigma^2$$

74 This section follows the work by Jorion (1994).

75 For example, element 1,2 in Ω_{aa} is calculated as

$$\text{cov}(a_1, a_2) = \text{cov}\left(\Delta p_1/p_1 + \Delta s_1/s_1 - c_h, \; \Delta p_2/p_2 + \Delta s_2/s_2 - c_h \right)$$

76 Unitary hedging: currency risk that comes automatically with asset risk is hedged on a one-to-one basis – for example, a 10% position in US assets is hedged with an offsetting −10% position in the US dollar.

77 We suppress cash rates as they are known in advance and do not change the risk numbers.

78 Factor models work well on individual stocks, but they hardly add anything to indices as indices are already very diversified portfolios.

79 Essentially this means that $E(\mathbf{X}\mathbf{f}\mathbf{u}') = \mathbf{0}$.

80 Note that $(\mathbf{A} + \mathbf{B})' = (\mathbf{B}' + \mathbf{A}')$ and $(\mathbf{A}\mathbf{B})' = (\mathbf{B}'\mathbf{A}')$.

81 The same can be done for individual betas:

$$\beta = \frac{\Omega\mathbf{w}}{\mathbf{w}'\Omega\mathbf{w}} = \frac{\mathbf{X}\Omega_{ff}\mathbf{X}'\mathbf{w}}{\mathbf{w}'\Omega\mathbf{w}} + \frac{\mathbf{w}'\Omega_{uu}\mathbf{w}}{\mathbf{w}'\Omega\mathbf{w}}$$

BIBLIOGRAPHY

Artzner, P., F. Delbaen, J. Eber and D. Heath, 1999, "Coherent Measures of Risk", *Mathematical Finance* 9, pp. 203–28.

Barberis, N., 2000, "Investing for the Long Run when Returns are Predictable", *Journal of Finance* 45, pp. 225–64.

Bayer, K., 1998,"Vom traditionellen Management zur Portfolio Factory: Anforderungen und Ziele", in: C. Kutscher and G. Schwarz, *Aktives Portfolio Management* (Zürich: Verlag Neue Züricher Zeitung).

Blundell, G., and C. Ward, 1987, "Property Portfolio Allocation: A Multifactor Model", *Land Development Studies* 4, pp. 145–56.

Brandimarte, P., 2001, *Numerical Methods in Finance* (New York: John Wiley & Sons).

Campbell, J., and L. Viceira, 2002, *Strategic Asset Allocation – Portfolio Choice for Long Term Investors* (Oxford University Press).

Campbell, J., A. Lo and C. MacKinlay, 1997, *The Econometrics of Financial Markets* (Princeton University Press).

Chow, G., and M. Kritzman, 2001, "Risk Budgets", *Journal of Portfolio Management* 27, pp. 56–60.

Chow, G., E. Jacquier, M. Kritzman and K. Lowry, 1999, "Optimal Portfolios in Good Times and Bad", *Financial Analysts Journal* 55, pp. 65–73.

Cochrane, J., 2001, *Asset Pricing* (Princeton University Press).

De Bever, L., W. Kozun and B. Zwan, 2000, "Risk Budgeting in a Pension Fund", in: L. Rahl, *Risk Budgeting* (London: Risk Books).

Elton, E., and M. Gruber, 1995, *Modern Portfolio Theory and Investment Analysis*, Fifth Edition (New York: John Wiley & Sons).

Favre, L., and J. Galeano, 2001, "Portfolio Allocation with Hedge Funds, Case Study of a Swiss Institutional Investor", Working Paper, UBS Warburg.

Fung, W., and D. Hsieh, 1997, "Is Mean Variance Analysis Applicable to Hedge Funds?", Working Paper, Duke University, North Carolina.

Glen, J., and P. Jorion, 1993, "Currency Hedging for International Portfolios", *Journal of Finance* 48, pp. 1865–86.

Gollier, C., 2001, *The Economics of Time and Uncertainty* (Cambridge, MA: MIT Press).

Green, W., 2000, *Econometric Analysis*, Fourth Edition (New York: Prentice-Hall).

Grinold, R., and R. Kahn, 2000, *Active Portfolio Management*, Second Edition (New York: McGraw-Hill).

Huang, C., and R. Litzenberger, 1988, *Foundations of Financial Economics* (New York: North Holland).

Johnston, J., 1984, *Econometric Methods*, Third Edition (New York: McGraw-Hill).

Jorion, P., 1994, "Mean Variance Analysis of Currency Overlays", *Financial Analysts Journal* 50, pp. 48–56.

Jorion, P., 2001, *Value at Risk*, Second Edition (New York: McGraw-Hill).

Kaufman, L., and P. Rousseeuw, 1990, *Finding Groups in Data: An Introduction to Cluster Analysis* (New York: John Wiley & Sons).

Kelly, J., 1956, "A New Interpretation of Information Rate", *Bell System Technical Journal* 35, pp. 917–26.

Kritzman, M., 2000, *Puzzles of Finance* (New York: John Wiley & Sons).

Ledoit, O., 1997, "Improved Estimation of the Covariance Matrix of Stock Returns with an *better ......* Application to Portfolio Selection", Working Paper, University of California, Los Angeles.

Levy, H., and H. Markowitz, 1979, "Approximating Expected Utility by a Function of the Mean and Variance", *American Economic Review* 69, pp. 308–17.

Litterman, B., 1996, "Hot Spots and Hedges", *Journal of Portfolio Management*, Special Issue, pp. 52–75.

McCarthy, M., 2000, "Risk Budgeting for Pension Funds and Investment Managers Using VAR", in: L. Rahl., *Risk Budgeting* (London: Risk Books).

Mossin, J., 1968, "Optimal Multiperiod Portfolio Policies", *Journal of Business* 41, pp. 215–29.

Scherer, B., and T. Ebertz, 1998, "A Simple Model for Lifetime Asset Allocation", *Journal of Private Portfolio Management* 1, pp. 27–30.

Scholes, M., and J. Williams, 1977, "Estimating Betas From Nonsynchronous Data", *Journal of Financial Economics* 14, pp. 327–48.

Sharpe, W., and L. Tint, 1990, "Liabilities – A New Approach", *Journal of Portfolio Management* 16, pp. 5–11.

Stevens, G., 1998, "On the Inverse of the Covariance Matrix in Portfolio Analysis", *Journal of Finance* 53, pp. 1821–7.

Xia, Y., 1999, "Learning about Predictability: The Effect of Parameter Uncertainty on Dynamic Optimal Consumption and Asset Allocation", Working Paper, University of California, Los Angeles.

Ziemba, W., and J. Mulvey, 1998, *Worldwide Asset and Liability Modelling* (Cambridge University Press).

Incorporating Deviations from Normality: Lower Partial Moments

This chapter deals with non-normality, a prominent shortcoming of traditional portfolio analysis. We first review key issues that arise one is faced with non-normality in data series. The main focus of the chapter, however, is the application of lower partial moments as one way of dealing with asymmetric return distributions. A second, more general method will be presented in Chapter 5.

2.1 NON-NORMALITY IN RETURN DATA

2.1.1 Single-period returns: visualising and testing for non-normality

This and the next two sections will deal with non-normality (which was identified in Chapter 1 as a potential shortcoming of the traditional Markowitz framework) and its impact on portfolio choice. We will not attempt to arrive at some definitive "cookbook recipe" for constructing a portfolio but, rather, to establish the key issues to keep in mind when doing so. These are:

❑ Are returns normal?
❑ Are deviations from normality statistically significant?
❑ Are these deviations stable, ie, forecastable?
❑ Will non-normality vanish over time?
❑ Can we model a simple non-normal alternative?

Most of these questions are covered in this section, though the last two are answered in Sections 2.1.2 and 2.1.3, respectively.

2.1.1.1 Returns are not normal

The first question is easy enough to answer: as is recognised in asset management, returns are not normally distributed.[1] This is important because the assumption of normality makes calculations involving risk much simpler than they are with non-normal alternatives, allowing one to easily aggregate asset risks both over time and across assets.[2] Most financial models rely heavily on the normality assumption.[3]

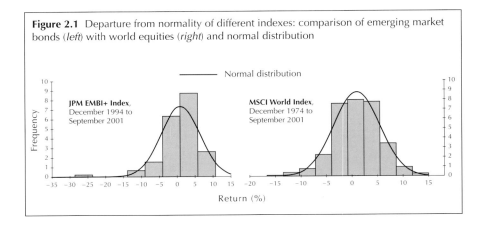

Figure 2.1 Departure from normality of different indexes: comparison of emerging market bonds (*left*) with world equities (*right*) and normal distribution

However, the degree of non-normality differs between financial time series. This can be seen by comparing histograms (empirical distributions) of returns for world equities and emerging market bonds with a normal distribution. This is done using the MSCI World Index and the JP Morgan EMBI+ Index in Figure 2.1.

Returns on equities in the MSCI World Index, which represents many stocks diversified across regions and sectors, are closer to normality than returns on emerging market bonds, where the JP Morgan EMBI+ Index contains a small number of bonds with a regional concentration in Latin America. This is hardly surprising, as – provided that they show little correlation – the more assets an index contains, the smaller the deviation from non-normality will be. However, if correlation increases at certain times (as seen recently in emerging markets), extreme returns in single holdings will not be diversified away and the empirical distribution will show significant negative "skewness".[4] Ignoring non-normality in developed markets presents less of a problem than it does in emerging markets.[5] Hence, it is necessary to judge each type of market on its merits as to whether it is worth the effort to model non-normality explicitly.

2.1.1.2 Statistical significance of deviations
If we obtain an empirical data sample like a financial time series we would not, of course, expect a relatively small number of random drawings from it to be distributed exactly normally. However, we need some way other than visual inspection of measuring non-normality so that we have an objective basis for judging whether deviations from normality are statistically significant.

Deviations from normality are often summarised in two measures known as "skewness" and "kurtosis". *Skewness* measures the asymmetry of a distribution; a distribution is negatively skewed if it has a long tail to the left and positively skewed if its long tail is to the right. Skewness can be calculated (and tested for significance) by using

$$\text{skew} = \frac{1}{T} \sum_{i=1}^{T} \frac{(r_i - \mu)^3}{\hat{\sigma}^3} \sim N\left(0, \sqrt{6/T}\right) \tag{2.1}$$

where T is the number of observations, r_i is the return in period i, μ is the mean, σ is the standard deviation, and N stands for normal distribution. A symmetric distribution (like the normal bell curve) has zero skewness as all realisations are equally scattered to the left and right of the mean.

Kurtosis measures the "peakedness" of a distribution – that is, the size of the peak relative to the tails. The distributions of illiquid asset classes or those with periodic jumps are flatter than the normal distribution as they are characterised by a high probability of small movements and large jumps (both positive and negative), along with a low probability of intermediate movements. These characteristics give their distributions "fat" tails – ie, values tend to spread into the extremes of the distribution. Excessive kurtosis (relative to the kurtosis of three for a normal distribution) can be calculated, and tested for significance, using

$$\text{kurtosis} = \frac{1}{T} \sum_{i=1}^{T} \frac{(r_i - \mu)^4}{\hat{\sigma}^4} - 3 \sim N\left(0, \sqrt{24/T}\right) \tag{2.2}$$

We can use both measures *and* simultaneously test for normality using the Jarque–Bera (JB) test:[6]

$$JB = T\left(\frac{\text{skewness}^2}{6} + \frac{\text{kurtosis}^2}{24}\right) \sim \chi^2 \, (2) \tag{2.3}$$

which has a chi-square distribution with two degrees of freedom.[7] Applying the JB test to real data gives the results in Table 2.1. With the exception of US government bonds, almost all series show statistically significant deviations from normality at the 5% level, indicated by a p-value below 0.05. The results also show that even an index with relatively few and highly correlated assets, such as the MSCI EMF, can be almost normally distributed, contrary to the rule of thumb mentioned earlier.

2.1.1.3 Stability of deviations – "persistency"
Statistically significant non-normality alone is generally not enough to justify the effort to model non-normality. To make them exploitable deviations from normality have to be stable, or persistent, across time periods. Otherwise, the error maximisation property in the portfolio optimisation process takes effect and portfolios that are deliberately constructed to show positive in-sample skewness will fail out-of-sample.

Table 2.1 Testing for normality – application of Jarque–Bera test to selected indexes (monthly data)

	JPM US Gov.	MSCI EMF	SB WGBI	JPM EMBI+	MSCI World
Mean (%)	0.69	−0.57	0.73	0.92	0.98
Maximum (%)	4.35	16.71	4.02	10.71	14.99
Minimum (%)	−2.69	−29.22	−2.01	−28.74	−16.63
Volatility (%)	1.31	8.55	1.05	5.45	4.55
Skewness	0.05	−0.64	0.12	−1.97	−0.22
Kurtosis	3.11	3.96	3.86	11.22	3.91
JB test	30.17	6.12	6.65	21.62	13.62
p-value	0.92	0.05	0.04	0.00	0.00
No. observations	189	57	201	93	321

Data for all series end September 2001 – longest series available.
JPM US Gov., JPM US Government Bonds; MSCI EMF, Morgan Stanley Capital International Emerging Markets Free Index; SB WGBI, Salomon Brothers World Government Bond Index; JPM EMBI+, JP Morgan Emerging Markets Bond Index Plus; MSCI World, MSCI Emerging Markets Free.

Unfortunately, authors are divided on the persistency issue.[8] Rather than reviewing the literature, we offer a test for persistency of skewness that can easily be applied to determine whether it is worth modelling non-normality for particular assets:[9]

1. Choose an asset universe – emerging markets, for example.
2. Split the data set into two non-overlapping time periods of equal length.
3. Calculate skewness, kurtosis or asymmetric semivariance (given by the semivariance minus half the variance) for each time period.[10]
4. Run a regression of the form

$$\text{skew} - \text{measure}_{t+1} = a + b \cdot \text{skew} - \text{measure}_t + \varepsilon_t \qquad (2.4)$$

Persistency is indicated by a significant slope parameter and a high R^2.

This test will be illustrated with data for emerging debt markets – specifically, data from JP Morgan EMBI+ sub-indices for the countries included in Figure 2.2.

The data run from August 1994 to November 2001 and are split into time series of equal length. We run the regression given by Equation (2.4) and use the excess semivariance as a measure of skewness. The resulting fit is also included in Figure 2.2. The *t*-value on the slope coefficient (0.63) is statistically significant (2.53), while the regression explains 44% of the variance in excess skewness. The result indicates that there is persistency in the excess skewness and justifies – indeed calls for – the modelling of non-normality in these emerging market debt returns.

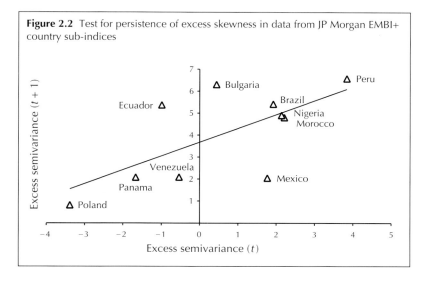

Figure 2.2 Test for persistence of excess skewness in data from JP Morgan EMBI+ country sub-indices

2.1.2 Normality and multi-period returns

When defending the assumption that multi-period returns are distributed normally we have a powerful ally: the central limit theorem (CLT). This states that the *sum* of independent and identically distributed variables converges to a normal distribution as long as the variables have finite variances.[11] Convergence takes place after approximately 30 random numbers have been added up. Correspondingly, the *product* of random variables gives *lognormally* distributed variables.[12] Hence, multi-period returns are better described using a lognormal distribution as they are effectively products of single-period returns.

2.1.2.1 Convergence to normality – simulation example

We can simulate the consequences of the CLT with one of the most non-normally distributed returns encountered in portfolio construction exercises: portfolio insurance.[13] Suppose that we engage in a monthly protective put strategy by buying one at-the-money put option per asset. We will assume that the underlying asset returns 0.83% per month with a volatility of 5%. The put option price is about 2% (assuming a 3.5% annual risk-free rate). Monthly returns for this strategy can be calculated as

$$R_{month,i} = \frac{\max[100 - S_i, 0] + S_i}{100 + \text{Put}} = \frac{\max[100, S_i]}{100 + \text{Put}} \quad (2.5)$$

where the asset price is normalised to 100 at the beginning of each month. The histogram of 10,000 monthly draws and a fitted normal distribution are shown in Figure 2.3.

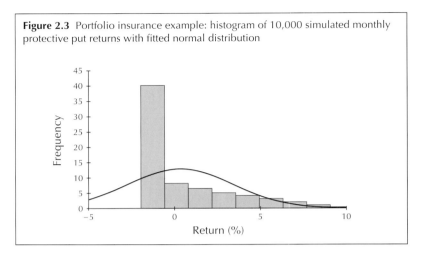

Figure 2.3 Portfolio insurance example: histogram of 10,000 simulated monthly protective put returns with fitted normal distribution

Portfolio insurance transforms small probabilities of large losses into large probabilities of small losses. Volatility now becomes a seriously misleading concept as it massively overestimates the probability of losses. In fact, it becomes more a measure of upside potential than of downside risk. Negative one-sigma events cannot occur as the put protection compensates for losses in the underlying asset. The positive skewness in the distribution makes the average return an easily misinterpreted number. This is sometimes deliberately used in marketing pitches as, for skewed distributions, mean and median returns can be very different: distributions with a positive skew have a mean return that is much higher than the median return. The average return is no longer the outcome where about half the returns are lower and half are higher. In fact, in this example, returns will fall below the average in about 65% of all cases (with a negative median). Thus, measuring the costs of portfolio insurance by the difference in mean returns is potentially misleading.

Suppose now that we continue this strategy over 30 months – ie, using 30 monthly resets of monthly protective puts. The annualised return in this case is given by

$$R_{30\,\text{month}} = \frac{30}{12} \sqrt[30]{\prod_{i=1}^{30} \left(1 + R_{\text{month},i}\right)}$$

The results derived from 10,000 simulations of rolling over 30 monthly protective puts can be seen in Figure 2.4. After 30 periods our very non-normal protective put returns have converged, as expected, to a lognormal distribution (the solid curve). This is why mainstream asset allocators feel little need to model non-normality in long-term asset allocation studies.[14]

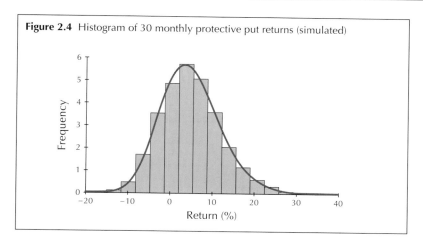

Figure 2.4 Histogram of 30 monthly protective put returns (simulated)

2.1.2.2 Convergence to normality – some problems with real data

So far, this chapter has considered a textbook case. The Monte Carlo simulations in the previous section were drawn from a normal distribution of asset returns with finite variance, and protective put returns were generated using Equation (2.5) under the assumption (construction) that asset returns are drawn independently.[15] Doing so leads to the familiar convergence to normality, as seen in the CLT. With real data, however, the assumptions that allow us to invoke the CLT might not be realistic.[16]

First, although single-period returns may be uncorrelated, they are not independent, as the CLT requires. For example, volatility tends to cluster, in that high- and low-volatility regimes tend to persist for a while; squared returns (a proxy for volatility) are significantly correlated; and, in general, Garch models – time-series models that capture dependency in second moments – fit the data reasonably well.[17]

A second, more technical, argument is that return distributions do not necessarily exhibit finite variance. In fact, if single-period returns show infinite variance (distributions with a tail index, α, ≤ 2), the same logic that underlies the CLT also provokes convergence to a class of fat-tailed distributions. Their sum will then converge to a so-called "α-stable distribution" (which includes the normal distribution as a special case if $\alpha = 2$). The parameter α plays an important role in extreme value theory. Estimation and inference of α is relatively straightforward.[18] It has been shown that, if we order returns $r_1 \leq r_2 \leq \cdots r_{T_{tail}} \leq \cdots r_T$, we can estimate the tail index from

$$\hat{\alpha}^{-1} = \frac{1}{T_{tail}} \sum_{i=T_{tail}}^{1} \log\left(\frac{r_i}{r_{T_{tail}+1}}\right) \qquad (2.6)$$

where T_{tail} is the number of observations in the tail and $T_{tail} + 1$ is the observation where the tail is assumed to start. Unfortunately, there is no hard and fast rule on how to determine T_{tail}. Practitioners plot the tail index against the choice of T_{tail} – in what is known as a "hill" plot – and choose the tail index where the curve becomes more or less horizontal (the tail index is robust against changes in the number of tail observations).[19] To test the null hypothesis, H_0, that $\alpha < 2$ against $H_1: \alpha \geq 2$ (the value of two divides distributions with fat tails but finite variance from distributions with infinite variance), we can use[20]

$$\sqrt{T_{tail}} \; (\hat{\alpha} - \alpha) \sim N(0, \alpha^2) \tag{2.7}$$

It should be noted that, to be reliable, this test procedure needs extreme values to be present in the data set (as is generally typical of extreme value theory); hence we need enough data to be reasonably sure that extreme events have been sampled in the empirical distribution.[21]

2.1.3 Modelling non-normality with a mixture of normal distributions

Models that can be understood intuitively and fit the data well have the greatest chance of receiving attention from practitioners. As market participants tend to think in terms of regimes – eg, periods of different volatility – it is natural to model a distribution as a combination of two (or more; see Hamilton, 1994) normal distributions, with each distribution representing a different regime. Shifts from one regime to another take place randomly with a given probability. Moreover, mixtures of normal distributions can model skewness as well as kurtosis and generally fit the data much better than a non-normal alternative.[22]

The probability density function for a mixture of two normal distributions is a probability-weighted sum of normal density functions:[23]

$$f_{MoN}(r) = p f_{high}(r) + (1-p) f_{low}(r)$$

$$f_{high}(r) = \frac{1}{2\pi\sigma_{high}^2} \exp\left(-\frac{1}{2} \frac{(r - \mu_{high})^2}{\sigma_{high}^2}\right)$$

$$f_{low}(r) = \frac{1}{2\pi\sigma_{low}^2} \exp\left(-\frac{1}{2} \frac{(r - \mu_{low})^2}{\sigma_{low}^2}\right) \tag{2.8}$$

where $f_{MoN}(r)$ is the combined density of the high-volatility, $f_{high}(r)$, and low-volatility, $f_{low}(r)$, regimes, while p denotes the probability of experiencing a draw from the high-volatility regime. The log-likelihood function, $\log(L)$, can be written in the usual way:

$$\log(L) = \log\left(\prod_{i=1}^{T} f_{MoN}(r_i)\right) = \sum_{i=1}^{T} \log\left(f_{MoN}(r_i)\right)$$

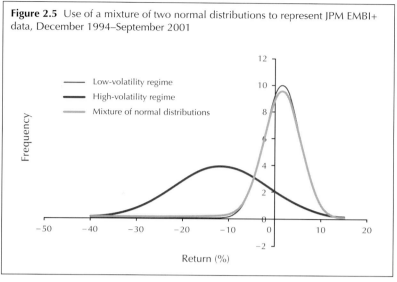

Figure 2.5 Use of a mixture of two normal distributions to represent JPM EMBI+ data, December 1994–September 2001

$$= \sum_{i=1}^{T} \log \left(p \, \frac{1}{2\pi\sigma_{\text{high}}^2} \exp\left(-\frac{1}{2} \frac{\left(r - \mu_{\text{high}}\right)^2}{\sigma_{\text{high}}^2} \right) \right.$$

$$\left. + (1-p) \frac{1}{2\pi\sigma_{\text{low}}^2} \exp\left(-\frac{1}{2} \frac{\left(r - \mu_{\text{low}}\right)^2}{\sigma_{\text{low}}^2} \right) \right) \qquad (2.9)$$

We can now apply maximum-likelihood estimation by maximising Equation (2.9) with respect to μ_{high}, σ_{high}^2, μ_{low}, σ_{low}^2 and p. If applied to the EMBI+ data used in Section 2.1, we get the frequency distribution represented by the grey curve in Figure 2.5.

Essentially, the EMBI+ data can be split into a high-volatility (10.22%) and a low-volatility (3.99%) regime. High volatility arises from market jumps, which are, on average, negative (−11.6%). High-volatility regimes have a modest probability (5.3%) and, hence, a limited influence on the combined distribution (which is found by probability-weighting both regimes and adding them up for every return level).

Figure 2.5 shows that <u>if there are two regimes and one has a much greater probability of occurrence than the other, fitting a mixture of two normal distributions does not *necessarily* result in a bimodal distribution.</u> However, a mixture is preferable as it allows for distributions that are skewed to the left, thus capturing the long left tail in the data much better than the normal alternative.[24]

2.2 LOWER PARTIAL MOMENTS

2.2.1 Illustration of approach using empirical distribution and single return series

So far this chapter has established that, depending on the nature of the data and the time horizon, the assumption of normality might not be close enough to reality. Now we want to describe how non-normality can be incorporated in portfolio construction applications.

We start with the general observation that uncertain returns, $\tilde{R}$, can be decomposed into a threshold return, γ, plus an upside measure, expressed by $\max[\tilde{R} - \gamma, 0]$, which is either positive or zero, minus a downside measure, denoted by $\max[\gamma - \tilde{R}, 0]$, which is also either positive or zero (all measures are relative to the threshold). In combination we get

$$\tilde{R} = \underbrace{\gamma}_{\text{threshold}} + \underbrace{\max[\tilde{R} - \gamma, 0]}_{\text{upside}} - \underbrace{\max[\gamma - \tilde{R}, 0]}_{\text{downside}} \qquad (2.10)$$

Suppose that our threshold return is -5%. A return of -15% can then be expressed as

$$-5\% + \underbrace{\max[-15\% - (-5\%), 0]}_{0\%} - \underbrace{\max[-5\% - (-15\%), 0]}_{10\%} = -15\%$$

Measures that try to capture the downside of a return distribution are called lower partial moments, while measures that focus on the upside of a distribution are called upper partial moments. The value of risk measures that capture non-normality increases the more return distributions deviate from normality. Moreover, as investors seem to be primarily concerned about downside deviations, some authors call for more behaviourally motivated risk measures that recognise the gap between theoretical risk measures and those used by practitioners.[25]

Lower partial moments are characterised by a threshold – if returns fall beneath this threshold, a "risky" scenario is indicated – and large negative deviations from the threshold are penalised. Starting from Equation (2.10), the lower partial moment of the mth degree (which defines the penalty) and threshold, γ, in its *ex-post* form can be written as[26]

$$\text{lpm}(\gamma, m) = E\max\left[(\tilde{R} - \gamma)^m, 0\right] = \frac{1}{T}\sum_{i=1}^{T}(\tilde{R}_i - \gamma)^m d_i$$

$$d_i = \begin{cases} 0, & R_i > \gamma \\ 1, & R_i \leq \gamma \end{cases} \qquad (2.11)$$

where the function d_i (indicator function) counts the cases in which the *ex-post* return is at the threshold value. The parameter m describes how the penalty function is shaped.

What can we use to determine our choice of threshold return and the

Table 2.2 Choice of threshold return

Threshold return (γ)	Objective
Zero return	Nominal capital protection
Inflation	Real capital protection
Risk-free rate	Target minimum-opportunity costs
Actuarial rate	Actuarial funding protection
Moving target (benchmark)	Target opportunity costs

curvature of the penalty function in Equation (2.11)? Popular threshold values are based on actuarial target returns (in the case of pension funds), loss-aversion (ie, a target return of zero), or purchasing power protection (where the threshold return equals average period inflation). These and other economically plausible possibilities are summarised in Table 2.2.

Effectively, the indicator function decides which observations will enter the calculations in Equation (2.11). If the threshold is set very much to the left of a distribution, relatively few observations will determine the calculation of the respective lower partial moment as extreme events are rare by definition.

The second parameter we control is m. When m is equal to zero, we get the shortfall probability – often used in institutional asset management – denoted by lpm(γ, 0). Anything to the power of zero equals one, and hence Equation (2.11) will add up any value of one for which the indicator function is itself one. Dividing by the total number of observations, we get the probability of underperformance. A key problem with the lpm(γ, m) risk measure is that all underperformance is perceived to be equally undesirable; thus a threshold underperformance by five basis points would have the same impact on our risk measure as an underperformance by 2,500 basis points. Most practitioners feel uncomfortable with lpm(γ, 0) as this might actually lead to risk-seeking behaviour if the return requirement is so high that only the most lucky draw from the most risky asset could help. Setting m equal to one, we get lpm(γ, 1),[27] which gives us the average underperformance.[27] As lpm(γ, 1) implies risk-neutrality for all return realisations below the threshold (only the average counts, not the dispersion), it also determines the boundary between risk-averting and risk-seeking behaviour. Although there is no theoretical limit to increase in m, for portfolio construction exercises we will restrict ourselves to lpm(γ, 2), which can be interpreted as the shortfall variance.[28] This measures the dispersion of underperformance and comes closest in interpretation to the usual variance measure.[29] The higher m is, the more weight is given to underperformance for a given distribution. The more skewed a distribution, the higher the value for a given lower partial moment. This can be illustrated as follows.

59

Table 2.3 Application of lpm risk measure to two hypothetical assets

	Asset 1		Asset 2	
Return (%)	−0.82	21.61	10.39	32.82
Probability (%)	25	75	75	25
Moments of distribution				
Mean, μ	16		16	
Variance, σ	9.71		9.71	
Skew	−1.15		0.04	
Risk measure (lpm (γ, m))				
lpm: 16, 0	25%		75%	
lpm: 16, 1	−4.21		−4.21	
lpm: 16, 2	70.75		23.58	
lpm: 16, 3	−1190		−132.2	

First two rows give downside and upside performance for the two assets.

Suppose we have two assets with the probability distributions given in Table 2.3 and that we choose a threshold return equal to the distribution mean, μ. Although both assets show the same mean and variance, asset two provides much less downside risk than asset one as its distribution is less skewed. This is clearly shown by the risk measure results in the table, the lower partial moments for $m \geq 2$ attributing less risk to asset two. However, the calculations also show that the ranking of the two assets depends on the choice of m; for example, asset one looks favourable if we consider shortfall risk but inferior when we look at shortfall variance. The choice is therefore one investors should consider carefully.

2.2.1.1 Calculation of Equation (2.11) – an example
A simple example will help to understand the mechanics of calculating Equation (2.11) when real data are involved. Suppose we obtain the return realisations given in Table 2.4 when we use a threshold return of −5%. Equation (2.11) is then employed to calculate the lower partial moments given at the bottom of the table. Effectively, only three observations (those shaded in the table) are used to calculate the downside risk measures as these are the only observations for which returns fall below −5%.

In contrast, a variance-based approach would use the full sample information. Although the problem of estimation error will not be addressed in detail until the next chapter (some comments with respect to the lpm method described so far can be found in Section 2.2.3.1), suspicion should already have been aroused by the superficiality of the method of estimating lower partial moments presented so far. For example, the same shortfall probability result would have been obtained for any threshold return between 0% and −13%.

Table 2.4 Example of lower partial moment calculation using Equation (2.11)

γ = −5% (handwritten)

R_i	d_i	$(R_i - \gamma)^0$	$(R_i - \gamma)^1$	$(R_i - \gamma)^2$
19.50	0	1	24.50	600.46
−33.43	1	1	−28.43	808.07
−33.43	1	1	−28.43	808.07
−13.29	1	1	−8.29	68.80
−13.29	1	1	−8.29	68.80
12.66	0	1	17.66	311.96
10.18	0	1	15.18	230.33
24.75	0	1	29.75	885.34
26.30	0	1	31.30	979.63
34.43	0	1	39.43	1554.60
7.73	0	1	12.73	162.01
12.61	0	1	17.61	310.02
−13.52	1	1	−8.52	72.54
−13.52	1	1	−8.52	72.54
4.89	0	1	9.89	97.77
21.62	0	1	26.62	708.56
11.79	0	1	16.79	281.92
0.38	0	1	5.38	28.99
43.34	0	1	48.34	2336.82
24.45	0	1	29.45	867.45
Calculated lpm risk measure for m = 0, 1 and 2		**lpm (γ, 0)** 0.15	**lpm (γ, 1)** −2.26	**lpm (γ, 2)** 47.47

(handwritten annotations: "why is this row repeated?", "why are all negative returns repeated?")

2.2.2 Lower partial moments and multiple return series

So far, this section has estimated lower partial moments for a single return series, but how can we express the co-movements of assets in a lower partial moments framework? Will we be able to aggregate these risk measures in a portfolio with the same ease as within classical portfolio theory? Starting from our definition of lower partial moments in Equation (2.11) and concentrating on downside variance,[30] we can extend the equation in a very natural way:[31]

$$\text{lpm}_{ij}(\gamma, 2) = \frac{1}{T}\sum_{i=1}^{T}(R_i - \gamma)(R_j - \gamma)\,d_i \qquad (2.12)$$

Effectively, this means that Equation (2.12) will only use those occurrences where $d_i = 1$ – ie, where asset i underperforms and does not achieve its threshold return. In the same way, we can define the co-lower partial moment of return on asset j, R_j, with asset i, R_i, thus:

$$\text{lpm}_{ij}(\gamma, 2) = \frac{1}{T}\sum_{i=1}^{T}(R_i - \gamma)(R_j - \gamma)\,d_j \qquad (2.13)$$

Table 2.5 Co-lower partial moments calculated for two uncorrelated return series

Series 1		Series 2		Equation (2.12)	Equation (2.13)
R_i	d_i	R_j	d_j	$(R_i - \gamma)(R_j - \gamma)d_i$	$(R_i - \gamma)(R_j - \gamma)d_j$
19.5	0	−27.8	1	0.0	−558.1
16.52	0	−27.9	1	0.0	−493.7
−33.43	1	−19.2	1	403.6	403.6
23.95	0	−35.4	1	0.0	−879.9
−13.29	1	−3.9	0	−9.2	0.0
12.66	0	21.0	0	0.0	0.0
10.18	0	30.1	0	0.0	0.0
24.75	0	28.9	0	0.0	0.0
26.30	0	43.8	0	0.0	0.0
34.43	0	−12.6	1	0.0	−297.7
7.73	0	11.2	0	0.0	0.0
12.61	0	33.7	0	0.0	0.0
3.10	0	−14.3	1	0.0	−75.1
−13.52	1	37.6	0	−363.4	0.0
4.89	0	35.9	0	0.0	0.0
21.62	0	11.0	0	0.0	0.0
11.79	0	−2.8	0	0.0	0.0
0.38	0	−8.1	1	0.0	−16.4
43.34	0	5.2	0	0.0	0.0
24.45	0	−23.9	1	0.0	−557.6

In general (apart from lucky coincidences), we find that $d_i \neq d_j$, which means that we cannot come up with a symmetric co-lower partial moment matrix using the definition in Equations (2.12) and (2.13). An example of this can be seen in Table 2.5, where the numbers have been generated from two uncorrelated normal distributions with an average return of 10% and a volatility of 20% each.

We calculate the lower partial moments for assets i and j (and vice versa) according to Equations (2.12) and (2.13) and get

$$\text{lpm}_{ij}(\gamma, 2) = \frac{1}{T} \sum_{i=1}^{T} (R_i - \gamma)(R_j - \gamma)\, d_i = \frac{1}{20}(403.6 - 9.2 - 363.4) = 1.6$$

$$\text{lpm}_{ij}(\gamma, 2) = \frac{1}{T} \sum_{i=1}^{T} (R_i - \gamma)(R_j - \gamma)\, d_j$$

$$= \frac{1}{20}(-558.1 - \ldots - 292.2 - 297.7 - 75.1 - 16.4 - 557.6) = -123.7$$

The estimates are highly asymmetric (they differ substantially) and prone to the same estimation error problem that we have already seen with lower partial moments for a single asset. This asymmetry makes the application of standard (critical line) portfolio optimisers impossible.

However, with the advent of more general optimisers we can optimise (ie, minimise) lower partial moments in a simple Excel spreadsheet using the following short procedure:

Step 1 Fill k columns, where k is the number of assets, and T rows, where T is number of return observations or time periods, with the returns for the respective assets. Returns could either be historical data or obtained from fitted and bootstrapped distributions. Make the number of observations large so there are as few gaps in the distribution as possible. (See the recommended method in Section 2.2.3.2 for how to estimate lower partial moments correctly.)

Step 2 Calculate portfolio returns for each time period (row) for a given weight vector and calculate the lower partial moment of choice on the series of portfolio returns using the steps shown in Table 2.4.

Step 3 Use an optimiser to minimise lower partial moments, subject to a return constraint (and other constraints of choice).[32]

Step 4 Repeat Step 3 for different target returns to trace out an efficient frontier.

Fortunately, most properties we know from traditional mean–variance optimisation carry over to the lower partial moments framework. It has been shown that a continuous frontier exists, but also that the usual two-fund separation properties hold (the frontier becomes a straight line and we can separate preferences from relative asset weights) as soon as we include cash in the universe.[33]

However, this still leaves the problem that lower partial moments are not symmetric. To circumvent this, a symmetric lower partial moment measure has been described[34] that allows one to construct a symmetric lower partial moment matrix.[35] This procedure takes the individual lower partial moments and "glues" them together using ordinary correlations:

$$\text{lpm}_{ij}^{\text{symmetric}}(\gamma, 2) = \sqrt{\text{lpm}_i(\gamma, 2)} \, \sqrt{\text{lpm}_j(\gamma, 2)} \, \rho_{ij} \qquad (2.14)$$

This allows us to calculate the lower partial moment of the portfolio as the usual quadratic form

$$\text{lpm}_p(\gamma, 2) = \sum_{i=1}^{k} \sum_{j=1}^{k} w_i \, w_j \, \text{lpm}_{ij}^{\text{symmetric}}(\gamma, 2) \qquad (2.15)$$

Because this procedure reduces estimation error, it is more robust and will therefore improve out-of-sample performance.[36]

2.2.3 How to estimate lower partial moments correctly

Lower partial moments can be estimated the right or the wrong way. Unfortunately, a lot of criticism of lower partial moments as a concept has been caused by practitioners misguidedly using the incorrect estimation method, ie, utilising empirical return distributions.[37] However, we should not confuse practical matters of implementation (the problem of estimation) with conceptual issues. Hence, this section does not deal with conceptual concerns (for these, see Section 2.3) but instead focuses on implementation.[38]

2.2.3.1 The wrong way, or how to maximise estimation error
The flawed method of estimating lower partial moments, using the empirical distribution to calculate Equation (2.11), has been considered in some detail in Sections 2.2.1 and 2.2.2. As lower partial moments are based on the left tail of a distribution – the downside of asset returns – and as extreme realisations are by definition rarely observed, we suspect that estimation error might be a problem when lower partial moments are used. We also suspect that estimation error increases the more extreme the threshold we choose. A larger estimation error than given by variance-based risk measures would be a serious handicap to implementation as portfolio optimisation algorithms tend to leverage estimation error by taking on extreme positions. To appreciate the potential for estimation error in lower partial moment estimates we will look at a simple sampling experiment.

Suppose we have an asset with a monthly mean of 1% and a monthly volatility of 5.77%. We want to simulate the dispersion of our estimates of shortfall probability, $\mathrm{lpm}(\gamma, 0)$, and standard deviation (ie, volatility). To reflect the dispersion of both correctly in a standard histogram (showing estimates of the same magnitude), we choose the threshold value, γ, so that the true probability of shortfall equals the true volatility. Choosing a threshold value of -8.09%, we get (see Appendix A for numerical interpretation of expressions like (2.16)):

$$\mathrm{lpm}(-8.09\%, 0) = \int_{-\infty}^{-8.09\%} (R-\gamma)^0 f(R) \, \mathrm{d}R = 5.77\% \qquad (2.16)$$

We now draw 60 monthly observations, estimate shortfall probability and standard deviation and repeat this procedure 1,000 times. The histogram of estimates is plotted in Figure 2.6 and shows the much wider dispersion of the shortfall probability estimates. This confirms the belief that estimation error is a potentially serious problem for the implementation of lower partial moments methods.

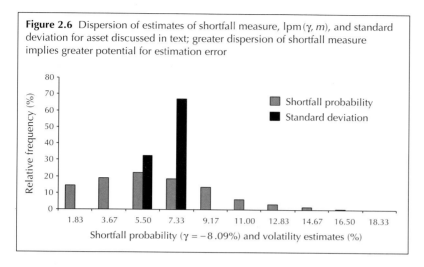

Figure 2.6 Dispersion of estimates of shortfall measure, lpm (γ, m), and standard deviation for asset discussed in text; greater dispersion of shortfall measure implies greater potential for estimation error

2.2.3.2 Best practice

We have seen that using the (discrete) empirical distribution gives flawed results. Using instead the volatility estimates and calculating the shortfall probability using Equation (2.16) would obviously have led to much less diverse results. We recommend a similar route for estimating lower partial moments. Essentially, this is a multi-step procedure that can be automated:[39]

Step 1 Specify the candidate distributions to be fitted, making sure that they are consistent with the possible range of return realisations.

Step 2 Estimate all candidate distributions and find the distribution that best fits the data empirically, ie, determine the distribution function $\hat{f}(R)$ using appropriate methods.

Step 3 Integrate the best-fit distribution found in Step 2 to calculate the desired lower partial moment (see Appendix A for suitable integration techniques):

$$\mathrm{lpm}(\gamma, m) = \int_{-\infty}^{\gamma} (R - \gamma)^m \hat{f}(R)\, dR \qquad (2.17)$$

Two points with regard to Step 1. First, clearly it would be imprudent to consider fitting a normal distribution to a guaranteed fund product (like a protective put) as negative three-sigma events will not be feasible – put protection will in most cases not allow negative returns of this size. Second, although maximum-likelihood methods are widely used, we will focus on the merits of fit-based estimation methods as they are significantly easier to grasp.[40] Moreover, they can be implemented in a straightforward way using accessible spreadsheet technology. These methods maximise the similarity between the empirical cumulative probability of the data and the theoretical cumulative probability of the fitted distribution.

One merit of fit-based methods is that they use the distribution function of the data directly. This is done in the next three steps:

Step 4 Rank all observations in a return series in ascending order, starting with the smallest realisation. Extract the empirical cumulative distribution by calculating $F(R_i) = i/T$, where i is the rank of the ith observation and T is the total number of observations.

Step 5 Given a set of starting values for the distributional parameters in our candidate distribution, calculate the distance between the empirical and the theoretical (fitted) cumulative distribution function. The most common procedure is to calculate the absolute distance $|F(R_i) - \hat{F}(R_i)|$, but other penalty functions are also applicable. Calculate the total variation.

Step 6 Repeat Step 5 until the total variation is minimised or, alternatively, until the Kolmogorov–Smirnov statistic, D, given by[41]

$$D = \max_i(D_i) = \max_i\left(\left|F(R_i) - \hat{F}(R_i)\right|\right) \qquad (2.18)$$

is minimised to find the best-fitting combination of parameters.

Note, however, that Equation (2.18) is determined by the largest distance, so it might rank a distribution that does not fit in general above a distribution that fits very well apart from a single data point – which essentially is the logic of any min–max criterion (choosing the minimum difference over a range of maximums). Additionally, since the vertical difference between $F(R_i)$ and $\hat{F}(R_i)$ itself has a distribution:

$$\hat{\sigma}^2(D_i) = \frac{\hat{F}(R_i)\left[1 - \hat{F}(R_i)\right]}{T}$$

and since it becomes more volatile as we come closer to the centre of the distribution, the Kolmogorov–Smirnov statistic will pay considerably less attention to fitting the tails, which is potentially hazardous for lower partial moment estimation.

Step 6* An alternative to the Kolmogorov–Smirnov statistic is the Anderson–Darling statistic, A, calculated as:[42]

$$A^2 = \int_{-\infty}^{+\infty} \frac{\left[F(R_i) - \hat{F}(R_i)\right]^2}{\hat{\sigma}^2} \hat{f}(R)\, dR \qquad (2.19)$$

This puts less emphasis on the highly variable values (scaling them

Figure 2.7 Fit of logistic distribution to S&P500 Index data using the Anderson–Darling statistic (Step 6* in text)

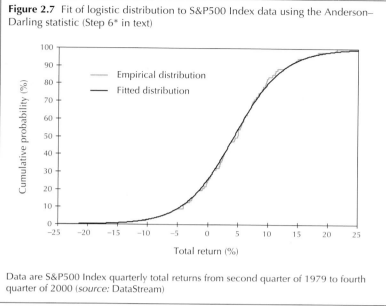

Data are S&P500 Index quarterly total returns from second quarter of 1979 to fourth quarter of 2000 (*source:* DataStream)

down by their respective variance) and more emphasis on the more likely values (weighting distances by their relative importance).

The results of an example calculation for S&P500 Index data are shown in Figure 2.7. The fitted logistic distribution, which has an Anderson–Darling statistic value of 0.14, can be written as

$$\hat{f}(R) = \frac{z}{\beta(1+z)^2}, \qquad z = \exp\left(-\frac{R-\alpha}{\beta}\right),$$

$$\alpha = 0.043028, \quad \beta = 0.040792$$

$$\hat{F}(R) = \frac{1}{1+z}$$

Step 7 The last step is numerical integration of the fitted distribution function. As we already know $\hat{F}(R_i)$, the evaluation of a target semivariance (target rate of 0%) becomes much easier; numerical integration essentially means multiplying the probability of falling into a bucket by the average value of that bucket (see Appendix A). Hence the lower partial moment integral can be approximated by

$$\int_{-\infty}^{0} \hat{f}(R) R^2 \, dR = \sum_i \left[\hat{F}(R_{i+1}) - \hat{F}(R_i)\right] \left[\frac{R_{i+1} + R_i}{2}\right] = 3.17\%$$

As the difficulty of the approach recommended here is to find the best-fitting distribution (a set of candidate distributions has to be estimated and the best-fitting distribution has to be selected using statistical criteria) and because these distributions change (causing a stability problem), it has also been proposed that a more continuous – ie, less arbitrary – distribution should be created by repeatedly sampling from the empirical distribution (known as bootstrapping). Typically, one would use monthly data and sample 12 realisations to create a single annual return. Repeating this procedure 1,000 times would give a smooth distribution of annual returns. However, doing this would also destroy the non-normality in the data as the independent draws generated by the bootstrapping procedure would generate a (log) normal distribution – an instance of the central limit theorem at work again. Hence this procedure is not recommended.

2.3 A COMPARISON OF LOWER PARTIAL MOMENTS-BASED AND VARIANCE-BASED METHODS IN PORTFOLIO CHOICE

So far, this chapter has critically reviewed the assumption of normality of asset returns, introduced downside risk measures and described the estimation problems that arise when these measures are used. In this section we want to comment on the use of downside risk measures in portfolio optimisation compared to Markowitz optimisation.

There is fierce debate between supporters and critics of classical or mean–variance-based portfolio theory.[43] One battleground is utility theory: is a preference for downside risk compatible with rational decision-making (ie, expected utility maximisation), and are such preferences plausible?[44] How well do mean–variance-based solutions approximate expected utility?[45] Another area of contention is actual portfolio allocations: how different are portfolios constructed using the two approaches? From a practical point of view, the last question is much the most interesting as it is very difficult to contradict a client who claims to have non-mean–variance preferences. Hence, we will concentrate on how variance-based portfolios compare with portfolios constructed using lower partial moments.

Introducing lower partial moments into portfolio optimisation merely requires a change of risk measure. Instead of minimising variance, we minimise $\text{lpm}(\gamma, m)$ with respect to the vector of portfolio weights, subject to a return constraint, a budget constraint and whichever other constraints require

$$\min_{\mathbf{w}} \text{lpm}(\gamma, m)$$

$$\mathbf{w}'\mathbf{R} = \overline{R}$$

$$\mathbf{w}'\mathbf{I} = 1$$

$$\dots \tag{2.20}$$

Figure 2.8 Effect of skewness in asset returns on portfolio allocations obtained using lower partial moments (Equation (2.20))

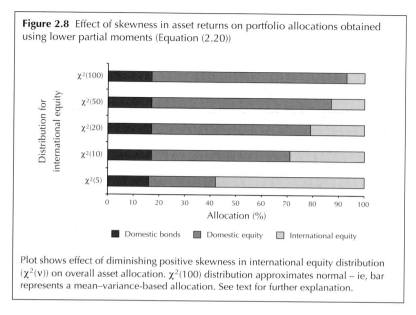

Plot shows effect of diminishing positive skewness in international equity distribution ($\chi^2(v)$) on overall asset allocation. $\chi^2(100)$ distribution approximates normal – ie, bar represents a mean–variance-based allocation. See text for further explanation.

Changing the required return, we can trace out an efficient frontier – ie, plot the portfolios that result from Equation (2.20).

Suppose that we want to investigate how skewness in asset returns affects the optimal portfolio allocations obtained from Equation (2.20) and how these allocations compare with mean–variance-based portfolios. A three-asset example will demonstrate the issues. We will assume, for illustration only, that domestic bonds (5% volatility) and domestic equity (15% volatility) are normally distributed, whereas international equity (20% volatility) has a skewed distribution with various degrees of skewness. Specifically, international equity is assumed to be distributed as $\chi^2(v)$, where v denotes the different degrees of freedom.

Samples of correlated returns (10,000 observations each) are created using the fact that $\chi^2(v)$ has mean v and standard deviation $\sqrt{2v}$.[46] This allows us to model international equity returns with the desired mean and volatility. Although $\chi^2(v)$ is positively skewed (a desirable trait for lower partial moments), it will approach the normal distribution as $v \to \infty$.[47] This means that we can observe how a continuous shift from skewed distributions to a normal distribution affects portfolio composition. Correlations between variables are maintained by using the rank order correlation method.[48] For each feasible weight vector we calculate the risk characteristics using the series of 10,000 portfolio return observations.

Figure 2.8 shows the result of this experiment. We set a 7% annual return while minimising downside volatility with respect to a zero-loss return target, ie, lpm$(0, 2)$. For very positively skewed international equity returns (small v), this asset class dominates the allocation. This is different from mean–variance-based solutions – approximated in Figure 2.8 by the bar for $\chi^2(100)$ – which fail to detect the desired feature of positive skewness and so prefer the asset with lower volatility (domestic equity), which is actually riskier. As international equity returns approach normality both solutions coincide. This is not surprising as, in a normally distributed world, a portfolio with low downside risk is, in fact, merely a portfolio with low volatility. If, for example, investors were concerned with the probability of loss rather than the volatility of returns, the set of efficient solutions would not change; as long as returns are normally distributed we will find that, for any given return, the portfolio with the lowest probability of loss is also the one with minimum volatility. Hence, the set of efficient portfolios stays the same (all are mean–variance-efficient portfolios), although, depending on their loss-aversion, investors might choose different portfolios.

Contrarily, if returns are significantly non-normal, solutions provided under the normality assumption will depart dangerously from the level of downside protection that could have been achieved if non-normality had been properly addressed. Non-normal returns will result in lower partial moment-minimised portfolios that dominate (plot above) mean–variance portfolios in mean lower partial moment space while being dominated in mean–variance space as a different objective is optimised.[49] The degree of non-normality and the investor's conviction about its stability will determine the choice of methodology.

To end this section, some brief comments should be made about how the choice of target return affects the difference between variance-based and shortfall variance-based (lpm-based) allocations. As the maximum-return portfolio is composed from the maximum-return assets, risk measures play almost no role in its construction. This changes as we move to the minimum-risk portfolio, where assets are chosen purely on the basis of their riskiness. Hence the difference between lpm-based and variance-based portfolio construction will, other things being equal, increase as we move towards lower return requirements. A similar logic applies to the threshold return: the more it deviates to the left from the mean return, the more the allocations differ. We can summarise by saying that that differences between the two methods increase with skewness, decrease with return requirements and decrease with threshold return.[50] To the extent that skewness can be predicted (see Section 2.1), lower partial moment-based allocations are a powerful alternative to traditional portfolio construction.

2.4 SUMMARY

Lower partial moments offer a convenient way to model non-normality in returns data but still use an optimisation framework that is very much related to traditional Markowitz optimisation (and identical if symmetric co-moments are assumed). However, estimation error is a serious problem in implementation – much more so than with variance-based measures. The problem can be partially overcome using the procedures reviewed in this chapter and suggested in the associated literature. Whether the modelling effort leads to solutions that are statistically different in-sample from traditional solutions depends critically on the degree of skewness. Whether these solutions add out-of-sample value depends on the persistence of deviations from non-normality. Dogmatic views of any persuasion are of little help.

APPENDIX A: INTEGRATION TECHNIQUES FOR CALCULATING LOWER PARTIAL MOMENTS

There are three ways to calculate lower partial moments by integration after best-fitting a distribution to the historical data. The first and easiest way is to use a software package, like Matlab, Maple or Mathematica, that is capable of undertaking symbolic math calculations.

However, often we do not have a package like this at hand, we cannot integrate it into our other routines, or there is no simply no closed-form solution. In this case we have to *numerically integrate* the expression for the lower partial moment.

A1 Numerical integration

Suppose we need to calculate the shortfall probability for a normal distribution representing an asset with 3% average return and 6% volatility. For arbitrary continuous distributions we find that

$$\mathrm{lpm}(0,0) = \int_{-\infty}^{0} f(R)\,\mathrm{d}R \qquad (A1)$$

In the present case, assuming normality, we already know that

$$f(R) = \frac{\dfrac{1}{\sigma\sqrt{2\pi}}\,\mathrm{e}^{-(R-\mu)^2}}{2\sigma^2}$$

which allows us to set up a spreadsheet as in Table A1.

We will use the trapezium rule to illustrate the concept of numerical integration.[51] The whole area under the bell-shaped curve is divided into vertical strips of equal width. This is done in the first column of Table A1, where we have chosen a width of 2% between two realisations of R_i. The smaller the width, the more precise our approximations will become. Note that our grid points (R_i) cover about three standard deviations from the mean in both directions ($-15\% = 3\% - 3 \times 6\% \leq R_R \leq 3\% + 3 \times 6\% = 21\%$).

For each grid point we calculate the density $f(R_i)$, as in the second column of Table A1. Now the area under the bell curve between any two grid points can be approximated by a rectangle; for example, the area between -6% and -8% is approximated by a rectangle with a width of 2% and an average height of $(2.2 + 1.2)/2 = 1.7$. This value goes in the third column in the row for $R_i = -6\%$.

The fourth column contains the probabilities of a return falling between any two values. Continuing our example, the probability of a return falling between -6% and -8% is approximately

$$\underbrace{\underbrace{\frac{\left| f(-6\%) - f(-8\%) \right|}{2}}_{\text{height}} \underbrace{2\%}_{\text{width}}} = 3\%$$

This calculation is repeated for all buckets along column three. Summing up the relevant entries, we get the shortfall probability according to

Table A1 Example of numerical integration

R_i (%)	$f(R_i)$	$\dfrac{\left\| f(R_i) - f(R_{i-1}) \right\|}{2}$	$\dfrac{\left\| f(R_i) - f(R_{i-1}) \right\|}{2} \Delta R$	$\dfrac{\left\| f(R_i) - f(R_{i-1}) \right\|}{2} \Delta R (R_i + R_{i-1})/2$ (%)
-16	0.0			
-14	0.1	0.08	0.00	-0.025
-12	0.3	0.21	0.00	-0.054
-10	0.6	0.46	0.01	-0.102
-8	1.2	0.94	0.02	-0.169
-6	2.2	1.70	0.03	-0.238
-4	3.4	2.76	0.06	-0.276
-2	4.7	4.03	0.08	-0.242
0	5.9	5.28	0.11	-0.106
2	6.6	6.21	0.12	0.124
4	6.6	6.56	0.13	0.393
6	5.9	6.21	0.12	0.621
8	4.7	5.28	0.11	0.740
10	3.4	4.03	0.08	0.726
12	2.2	2.76	0.06	0.608
14	1.2	1.70	0.03	0.442
16	0.6	0.94	0.02	0.281
18	0.3	0.46	0.01	0.158
20	0.1	0.21	0.00	0.078

$$\text{lpm}(0,0) = \int_{-\infty}^{0} f(R)\,\mathrm{d}R \approx \frac{\left|f(-14\%) - f(-16\%)\right|}{2}\,2\% + \ldots$$

$$+ \frac{\left|f(0) - f(-2\%)\right|}{2}\,2\% = 30\%$$

Obviously, the entries in column four have to sum up to one – ie, the area under the curve is one.

We can extend our analysis by calculating the average conditional loss:[52]

$$\text{average conditional loss} = \frac{\int_{-\infty}^{0} f(R)\,R\,\mathrm{d}R}{\int_{-\infty}^{0} f(R)\,\mathrm{d}R} \tag{A2}$$

Practitioners sometimes do this when moving from domestic to global stocks to give clients a feel for risk. The average conditional loss adds up all probability-weighted losses. However, as we want to calculate the average conditional loss (ie, the average loss after a loss took place), we have to standardise (divide) by the probability of making a loss (already known to be 30%). The fifth column in Table A1 numerically integrates $\int_{-\infty}^{0} f(R)R\,\mathrm{d}R = -1.21\%$. Hence the average conditional loss becomes

$$\text{average conditional loss} = \frac{-1.21\%}{30\%} = -4.04\%$$

A2 Monte Carlo integration

The second method considered here is Monte Carlo integration. Essentially this is a "brute force" method – not elegant, but it does work if computing time is inexpensive.

The process is as follows. Take a limited number of random draws from the estimated distribution. Calculate the desired lower partial moment, or any other statistic – like that in Equation (A2). Increase the data set by sampling further from the estimated distribution and plot the calculated risk figure. As the window of sampled data increases the estimate will start to stabilise. How fast the empirical values converge to the true fixed value depends on which statistic is calculated. The further out into the tail we are looking, the longer convergence takes.

The result of this process (mirroring the assumptions in Section 2.2.3) can be seen in Figure A1. Depending on what criteria are set for convergence, it will take about 250 draws of 20 observations each, ie, 5,000 data points, until the estimate converges (stabilises). The first 20 data points

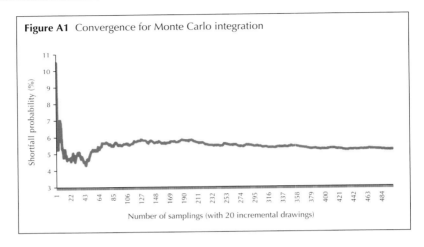

Figure A1 Convergence for Monte Carlo integration

result in a shortfall probability of 10.5%. After another 50 drawings, each with 20 observations, this value drops to about 5%, but many more drawings are required for further convergence.

1   See Mandelbrot (1963) or Fama (1965) for early references and Duffie and Pan (1997) for a more recent review.
2   See Jorion (2001, p. 104).
3   See Bamberg and Dorfleitner (2001) for a review.
4   See Bekaert *et al.* (1998) for a review of distributional characteristics for emerging market debt.
5   However, it should be noted that high-frequency returns in developed markets (hourly or daily returns) also exhibit considerable non-normality (much higher than monthly returns), so this may be fallacious for those with short time horizons.
6   See Bera and Jarque (1987).
7   An alternative test for the significance of higher moments is to take the deviations from the mean return, raise them to the power of three or four (also accounting for normal kurtosis) and regress them against a constant. The *t*-value on the constant measures significance.
8   While studies by Singleton and Wingender (1986) or Peiro (1994 and 1999) show no persistence in skewness, others, such as Nawrocki (1991), have been more optimistic.
9   This test is taken from Kahn and Stefek (1996).
10 For a symmetric distribution this term should be zero.
11 This is the so-called Lindberg–Levy form. The Lindberg–Feller version is even stronger as it states that the sum of random variables is normally distributed even if they all come from different distributions. See Green (2000, p. 116)
12 If the sum of one-period logarithmic returns, $\Sigma \ln(1 + R_i)$, is normal (CLT), the multi-period return $e^{\Sigma \ln(1+R_i)}$ is lognormal (a random variable is lognormal if its log is normal).
13 See Bookstaber and Langsam (1988) as a classic reference.
14 See Siegel (2000).
15 The proposed simulation procedure ignores any intertemporal dependence that might exist in the data.
16 As convergence by definition takes time, most investors do not have the luxury to wait until convergence occurs; even long-term investors have short-term reporting horizons that make the application of the CLT less applicable.

17 Garch is the abbreviated form of "generalised autoregressive conditional heteroscedasticity". An up-to-date review of Garch modelling can be found in Alexander (2001, Chapter 4).

18 See Mills (1999, p. 186).

19 See the S-plus code from McNeil (2001), which produces hill plots as well as more sophisticated estimators for tail indices.

20 See Hall (1982).

21 An unexpected feature of fat-tailed distributions is that large multi-period losses grow with $T^{1/\alpha}$ rather than with $T^{1/2}$ for the normal distribution. For large enough time horizons the fat-tailed distributions ($\alpha > 2$) will show lower probabilities of large multi-period losses. See Embrechts (2000) and, in particular, Danielson and DeVries (2000, p. 91).

22 See Kim and Finger (2000) for a very recent application to investigate the breakdown of correlation between markets.

23 This section draws on Hamilton (1994, p. 684).

24 We could also test the significance of the mixture of normals relative to the unconditional normal distribution, as suggested in Kim and Finger (2000), using a likelihood ratio test. The test statistic is given as

$$-2c\ln\left(\frac{L_{\text{constrained}}}{L_{\text{unconstrained}}}\right) \sim \chi^2(4), \qquad c = \frac{N-3}{N}$$

where N is the number of observations and $L_{\text{constrained}}$ denotes the value of the constrained likelihood function (where the parameters are equal between regimes). The value of the test statistic is 12.16, against a critical value of 9.48 (for the 5% confidence level). Hence the mixture-of-distributions model is statistically different from its simple alternative.

25 See Stutzer (2000).

26 As *ex ante* and *ex post* should not be different in large samples, we use an equals sign in Equation (2.11), even though this is technically incorrect, as E is the *ex-ante* expectations operator.

27 Note that this is different from the conditional underperformance, which is the average underperformance if underperformance occurs.

28 If we set $\gamma = \bar{\mu}$ (where the threshold equals the distribution mean), we arrive at a measure called "semivariance" because it calculates the variance of return realisations below the mean return:

$$\text{lpm}(\bar{\mu},2) = \frac{1}{T}\sum_{i=1}^{T}(R_i - \bar{\mu})^2 d_i, \qquad d_i = \begin{cases} 0, & R_i > \bar{\mu} \\ 1, & R_i \le \bar{\mu} \end{cases}$$

However, for every $d_i = 1$, we know that $1 - d_i = 0$. It is now easy to show that

$$\text{lpm}(\bar{\mu},2) + \text{upm}(\bar{\mu},2) = \frac{1}{T}\sum_{i=1}^{T}(R_i - \bar{\mu})^2 d_i + \frac{1}{T}\sum_{i=1}^{T}(R_i - \bar{\mu})^2 (1-d_i)$$

$$= \frac{1}{T}\sum_{i=1}^{T}(R_i - \bar{\mu})^2 = \sigma^2$$

In the case of symmetric distributions this term simplifies even further and we get

$$2\,\text{lpm}(\bar{\mu},2) = \sigma^2$$

which can be used as a simple normality check. If the variance is roughly twice the semivariance, it is close to symmetry (symmetry does not imply normality, though, as distributions might be symmetric but still exhibit fat tails (see Section 2.1).

29 Higher-order lower partial moments can be interpreted as shortfall skewness, kurtosis, etc.

30 A more general formulation for lower partial co-movements would write lower partial co-moments as

$$\text{lpm}_{ij}(\gamma, m) = \frac{1}{T} \sum_{i=1}^{T} (R_i - \gamma)^{m-1}(R_j - \gamma)\, d_i$$

31 See Harlow (1991). It is worth mentioning that Markowitz (1959) was the first to introduce downside risk measures into the portfolio management arena. However, as he used a slightly different concept than the current mainstream definition in Equation (2.11), it is not followed in this context.

32 Examples of such optimisers include Palisade Evolver and Frontline Solver. Note that this does not necessarily lead to the optimal solution (as described in Chapter 5) and is effectively close to scenario optimisation.

33 See Hogan (1974) for a review of semivariance and Bawa (1978) for a generalisation of all lower partial moments.

34 Nawrocki (1991) deserves credit for introducing symmetric lower partial co-movements.

35 The cause of asymmetry in Table 2.4 was estimation error. It is true that symmetry is a technically convenient property, but it is not one that we would expect economically.

36 See Nawrocki (1991, p. 470), who modelled the out-of-sample performance of alternative risk measures.

37 See Sortino and Forsey (1996) versus Kaplan and Siegel (1994).

38 Rom and Fergurson (1993 and 1994) can be seen as a typical example of a heated conceptual debate. A more balanced view can be found in Kahn and Stefek (1996).

39 Rather than fitting the whole distribution, it is possible to use the Fisher and Cornish approximation (see Hull, 2000, p. 366) to calculate the percentiles of a distribution merely by calculating skewness and kurtosis. We know from basic statistics that the α-percentile of a normal distribution is given as $\mu - z_\alpha \sigma$, where z_α represents the α-percentile of a standard normal distribution. The Fisher and Cornish approximation will "adjust" z_α to reflect non-normality. In the case of skewness only we get $\mu - z_\alpha^* \sigma$, with $z_\alpha^* = z_\alpha + \frac{1}{6}(z_\alpha^2 - 1)$ skew. If the skew is negative (longer left tail), z_α^* will be even more negative (the result of adding a negative number to an already negative number).

40 See Vose (2001) for an excellent review of these techniques.

41 Further references can be found in Vose (2000), who also gives a concise description of distribution fitting.

42 See Anderson and Darling (1952).

43 See the debate between Rom and Fergurson (1993 and 1994) and Kaplan and Siegel (1994) in the *Journal of Investing*, where business interests meet dogmatics.

44 See Fishburn (1997) and Bawa (1978), who show that dominance of mean- and lower partial moment-based decision rules is a necessary condition for expected utility maximisation (despite not showing sufficiency).

45 See Levy and Markowitz (1979) or Fung and Hsieh (1997).

46 We also assume that correlation between domestic bonds and domestic equity is 0.2 and that between domestic bonds and international equity it is 0.1, while equities are correlated with 0.7. Bond returns are expected to be 4.5%, while equity markets are supposed to deliver 7.5% annual returns. The caveat here is the assumption of the presence of positive skewness, which comes without penalty in expected returns as investors would bid up the prices of these assets, lowering the expected returns. Issues like this are dealt with in the literature on asset pricing using higher moments. See Arditti and Levy (1976) and Krauss and Litzenberger (1976), or Lai (1991) and Chunhachinda *et al.* (1997) for more recent studies.

47 However, the distribution will not become perfectly symmetric as the normal distribution peaks at its mean while $\chi^2(v)$ peaks at $v - 2$.

48 Simplified, this means to correlate ranks of the individual distributions rather than continuous realisations. See Iman and Conover (1982).

49 Mean lower partial moment space refers to a two-dimensional graph where the x-axis charts the calculated lower partial moments and the y-axis represents portfolio mean.

50 This also means that these differences will tend to decrease with the number of assets, as portfolio skewness should be diversified away, and that they are probably less relevant to active risks (tracking error) as the possibility of long and short positions should diversify skewness away even faster.

51 See Ostajewski (1990) for an introduction to numerical integration. A spreadsheet-based treatment of this can be found in Mesina (2001).

52 See Jorion (2001, p. 97)

BIBLIOGRAPHY

Alexander, C., 2001, *Market Models* (Chichester: John Wiley & Sons).

Anderson, T., and D. Darling, 1952, "Asymptotic Theory of Certain Goodness of Fit Criteria Based on Stochastic Processes", *Annals of Mathematical Statistics* 23, pp. 193–212.

Arditti, F., and H. Levy, 1976, "Portfolio Efficiency Analysis in Three Moments: The Multi-period Case", *Journal of Finance* 30, pp. 797–809.

Bamberg, G., and G. Dorfleitner, 2001, "Fat Tails and Traditional Capital Market Theory", Working Paper, University of Augsburg.

Bawa, V., 1978, "Safety First, Stochastic Dominance and Optimal Portfolio Choice", *Journal of Financial and Quantitative Analysis* 13, pp. 255–71.

Bekaert, G., C. Erb, C. Harvey and T. Viskanta, 1998, "Distributional Characteristics of Emerging Markets Returns and Asset Allocation", *Journal of Portfolio Management* 24, pp. 102–15.

Bera, A., and C. Jarque, 1987, "A Test for Normality of Observations and Regression Residuals", *International Statistical Review* 55, pp. 163–72.

Bookstaber, R., and J. A. Langsam, 1988, "Portfolio Insurance Trading Rules", *Journal of Futures Markets* 8(1), pp. 15–32.

Chunhachinda, P., S. Dandapani, S. Harnid and A. Prakash, 1997, "Portfolio Selection and Skewness: Evidence from International Stock Markets", *Journal of Banking and Finance* 21, pp. 143–67.

Danielson, J., and C. DeVries, 2000, "Value at Risk and Extreme Returns", in P. Embrechts, *Extremes and Integrated Risk Management* (London: Risk Books), pp. 85–106.

Duffie, D., and J. Pan, 1997, "An Overview over Value at Risk", *Journal of Derivatives* 4(3), pp. 7–49.

Embrechts, P., 2000, *Extremes and Integrated Risk Management* (London: Risk Books).

Fama, E., 1965, "The Behaviour of Stock Market Prices", *Journal of Business* 38, pp. 34–105.

Fishburn, P., 1997, "Mean Risk Analysis with Risk Associated with Below-Target Returns", *American Economic Review* 67(2), pp. 116–26.

Fung, W., and D. Hsieh, 1997, "Is Mean Variance Analysis Applicable to Hedge Funds?", Working Paper, Duke University.

Green, W., 2000, *Econometric Analysis*, Fourth Edition (New York: Prentice-Hall).

Hall, P., 1982, "On Some Simple Estimates of an Exponent of Regular Variation", *Journal of the Royal Statistical Society* 44, pp. 37–42.

Hamilton, J., 1994, *Time Series Analysis* (Princeton University Press).

Harlow, W., 1991, "Asset Allocation in a Downside Risk Framework", *Financial Analysts Journal* 47, pp. 28–40.

Hogan, W., 1974, "Toward the Development of an Equilibrium Based Capital Market Model Based on Semivariance", *Journal of Financial and Quantitative Analysis* 9, pp. 1–11.

Hull, C., 2000, *Options, Futures and Other Derivatives,* Fourth Edition (New Jersey: Prentice-Hall).

Iman, R., and W. Conover, 1982, "A Distribution Free Approach to Inducing Rank Order Correlation Among Input Variables", *Communications in Statistics* 11, pp. 311–34.

Jorion, P., 2001, *Value at Risk,* Second Edition (New York: McGraw-Hill).

Kahn, R., and D. Stefek, 1996, "Heat, Light and Downside Risk", Barra Research Paper.

Kaplan, P., and L. Siegel, 1994, "Portfolio Theory is Alive and Well", *Journal of Investing* 3, pp. 18–23.

Kim, J., and C. Finger, 2000, "A Stress Test to Incorporate Correlation Breakdown", Riskmetrics Paper.

Krauss, A., and R. Litzenberger, 1976, "Skewness Preference and the Valuation of Risky Assets", *Journal of Finance* 31, pp. 1085–100.

Lai, T., 1991, "Portfolio Selection With Skewness, A Multiple Objective Approach", *Review of Quantitative Finance and Accounting* 1, pp. 293–305.

Levy, H., and H. Markowitz, 1979, "Approximating Expected Utility by a Function of Mean and Variance", *American Economic Review* 69, pp. 308–17.

Mandelbrot, B., 1963, "The Variation of Certain Speculative Prices", *Journal of Business* 36, pp. 394–419.

Markowitz, H., 1959, *Portfolio Selection: Efficient Diversification of Investments* (New Haven: Yale University Press).

McNeil, A., 2001, "EVIS (SPLUS Code for Extreme Value Theory)", www.math.ethz.ch/ ~mcneil.

Mesina, M., 2001, *Numerische Mathematik mit Excel* (Poing: Franzis Verlag).

Mills, T., 1999, *The Econometric Modelling of Financial Time Series,* Second Edition (Cambridge University Press).

Nawrocki, D., 1991, "Optimal Algorithms and Lower Partial Moment: Ex Post Results", *Journal of Applied Economics* 23, pp. 465–70.

Ostajewski, A., 1990, *Advanced Mathematical Models* (Cambridge University Press).

Peiro, A., 1994, "The Distribution of Stock Returns: International Evidence", *Journal of Applied Financial Economics* 4, pp. 431–9.

Peiro, A., 1999, "Skewness in Financial Returns", *Journal of Banking and Finance* 23, pp. 847–62.

Rom, B., and K. Fergurson, 1993, "Post Modern Portfolio Theory Comes of Age", *Journal of Investing* 2, pp. 11–17.

Rom, B., and K. Fergurson, 1994, "Portfolio Theory is Alive and Well: A Response", *Journal of Investing* 2, pp. 24–44.

Siegel, J., 2000, *Stocks for the Long Run* (New York: McGraw-Hill).

Singleton, J., and J. Wingender, 1986, "Skewness Persistence in Common Stock Returns" , *Journal of Financial and Quantitative Analysis* 21, pp. 335–41.

Sortino, F., and H. Forsey, 1996, "On the Use and Misuse of Downside Risk", *Journal of Portfolio Management* 22, pp. 35–42.

Stutzer, M., 2000, "A Portfolio Performance Index and its Implications", *Financial Analysts Journal* 56, pp. 30–8.

Vose, D., 2001, *Risk Analysis* (Chichester: John Wiley & Sons).

Portfolio Resampling and Estimation Error

This chapter introduces estimation error as an additional problem for traditional Markowitz-based portfolio construction. In contrast to Chapter 4,
which also deals with estimation error but with a more decision-theoretic
foundation, this chapter presents two heuristic methods that seem to be
widespread among practitioners. In Sections 3.1 and 3.2 we use Monte
Carlo methods to visualise the effect of estimation error on portfolio
construction. We will distinguish between estimation error (when the
distribution parameters are stable but we do not have enough data) and
non-stationarity (the distribution parameters are unstable). The next four
sections focus on the main topic of this chapter: resampled efficiency as
a meaningful concept for portfolio construction.[1] The chapter concludes
with an interpretation of investment constraints in the light of portfolio
resampling.

3.1 VISUALISING ESTIMATION ERROR: PORTFOLIO RESAMPLING

The estimated parameters used in asset allocation problems – typically,
point estimates of means, variances and correlations – are calculated
using just one possible realisation of a return history. Even if we assume
stationarity (constant mean, non-time-dependent covariances), we can
only expect point estimates of risk and return inputs to equal the true distribution parameters if our sample is very large. The difference between
estimated and true distribution parameters when samples are not sufficiently large is estimation error. The effect of estimation error on optimal
portfolios can be captured by a Monte Carlo procedure called portfolio
resampling.[2]

Portfolio resampling works like this. Suppose we estimated both the
variance–covariance matrix, $\hat{\Omega}_0$, and the return vector, $\hat{\mu}_0$, using T observations, where Ω is a $k \times k$ covariance matrix of excess returns (asset return
minus cash), and μ is a $k \times 1$ vector of average excess returns. Our point
estimates are random variables as they are calculated from random returns.

Now, what we need to do is to model the randomness of the inputs.
Portfolio resampling does this by drawing repeatedly from the return

distribution given by our point estimates. We create an equivalent statistical sample with T observations (the same as the original data). For this new, artificially created data set we can estimate new inputs $\hat{\Omega}_1$ and $\hat{\mu}_1$. By repeating this procedure n times we get n new sets of optimisation inputs: $\hat{\Omega}_1, \hat{\mu}_1$ to $\hat{\Omega}_n, \hat{\mu}_n$. For each of these inputs we can now calculate a new efficient frontier spanning from the minimum-variance portfolio to the maximum-return portfolio. We calculate m portfolios along the frontier and save the corresponding allocation vectors $\mathbf{w}_{11}, \ldots, \mathbf{w}_{1m}$ to $\mathbf{w}_{n1}, \ldots, \mathbf{w}_{nm}$. Evaluating all m frontier portfolios for each of the n runs, with the original optimisation inputs $\hat{\Omega}_0, \hat{\mu}_0$, will force all portfolios to plot below the original efficient frontier. This is because any weight vector optimal for $\hat{\Omega}_i$ and $\hat{\mu}_i$ ($i = 1, \ldots, n$) cannot be optimal for $\hat{\Omega}_0, \hat{\mu}_0$. Therefore, all portfolio weights result in portfolios plotting below the efficient frontier as the weights have been derived from data that contain estimation error. Hence, the result of the resampling procedure is that estimation error in the inputs is transformed into uncertainty about the optimal allocation vector.

3.1.1 Resampling: an example

The mechanics of portfolio resampling are best illustrated by an example.[3] Suppose an analyst downloaded 18 years of data and calculated historical means and covariances, arriving at the inputs given in Table 3.1.[4]

Running a standard mean–variance optimisation (ie, minimising portfolio risk subject to a return constraint, whereby the returns vary from the return of the minimum-variance portfolio to the return of the maximum-return portfolio) would, for the data set above, result in the asset allocations along the efficient frontier shown in Figure 3.1.[5] Here we have chosen to calculate $m = 25$ portfolios, dividing the difference between the minimum and maximum return into 25 steps.

As investors familiar with traditional portfolio optimisation would have predicted, the resulting allocations look very concentrated as some assets never even enter the solution. Also, small changes in risk-aversion may

Table 3.1 Input data for portfolio resampling example

Asset	Variance–covariance matrix $(\hat{\Omega}_0)$								Return vector $(\hat{\mu}_0)$
	Canada	France	Germany	Japan	UK	US	US bonds	E bonds	
Canada	30.25								0.39
France	15.85	49.42							0.88
Germany	10.26	27.11	38.69						0.53
Japan	9.68	20.79	15.33	49.56					0.88
UK	19.17	22.82	17.94	16.92	36.12				0.79
US	16.79	13.30	9.10	6.66	14.47	18.49			0.71
US bonds	2.87	3.11	3.38	1.98	3.02	3.11	4.04		0.25
Euro bonds	2.83	2.85	2.72	1.76	2.72	2.82	2.88	2.43	0.27

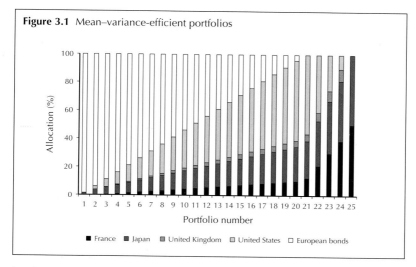

Figure 3.1 Mean–variance-efficient portfolios

lead to widely different portfolios. Allocation vectors (portfolio numbers) 20 and 23 are quite different in weightings. Given the uncertainty about the degree of investors' risk-aversion, this is an unattractive feature of traditional portfolio optimisation.

Suppose instead that the resampling procedure described above is applied. Each new weight vector (calculated from resampled inputs) can be interpreted as a set of statistically equal weights. However, as only the original set of weights, w_0, is optimal for the original set of inputs, $\hat{\Omega}_0$, $\hat{\mu}_0$, all other portfolios must plot below the efficient frontier; their weight estimates are the direct result of sampling error. Figure 3.2 shows the efficient frontier (envelope) and the resampled portfolios derived using the resampling technique we have described. The dispersion arises owing to the great variation in statistically equal weight vectors.

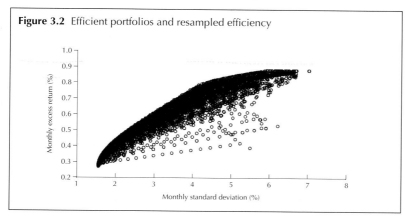

Figure 3.2 Efficient portfolios and resampled efficiency

Increasing the number of draws, T, forces the data points closer to the original frontier as the dispersion of inputs becomes smaller. This is equivalent to reducing sampling error. However, it is not clear from this resampling exercise where the "better" frontier lies. Section 3.3 will deal with this problem directly.

3.2 ERRORS IN MEANS AND COVARIANCES

It has long been established that portfolio optimisation suffers from error maximisation.[6] As we have seen, inputs into the efficient frontier algorithm are measured with error, and the optimiser tends to pick those assets with very attractive features (high return and low risk and/or correlation) and tends to short or deselect those with the worst features. These are exactly the cases where estimation error is likely to be highest, hence maximising the impact of estimation error on portfolio weights. If, for example, assets have high correlations, they appear similar to the quadratic programming algorithm. An algorithm that takes point estimates as inputs and treats them as if they were known with certainty (which they are not) will react to tiny differences in returns that are well within measurement error.[7] The problem gets worse as the number of assets rises because this increases the chance of outliers.

Portfolio resampling allows us to clearly distinguish the impact of the uncertainty due to estimation errors in means from that due to estimation errors in variance.[8] To measure the estimation errors in means only, we resample from the variance–covariance matrix, $\hat{\Omega}_0$, and return vector, $\hat{\mu}_0$, as before, – the difference in the case of estimation errors in means only being that we optimise using resampled means $\hat{\mu}_i$, $i = 1, \ldots, n$, and the

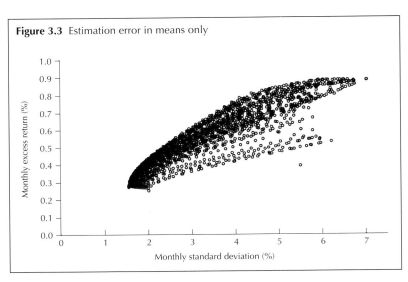

Figure 3.3 Estimation error in means only

original variance–covariance matrix $\hat{\Omega}_0$. The result for the data in Section 3.1 is plotted in Figure 3.3, which shows the still impressive dispersion of the risk–return points compared with Figure 3.2.

Alternatively, we can reoptimise using resampled covariance matrices but treating means as known. The result of this can be seen in Figure 3.4, where the data in Figure 3.3 are included for comparison. The dispersion of risk–return points is considerably reduced when estimation error is confined to variances.

So far, we have assumed that the only source of estimation error is sampling error, ie, that it is caused by insufficient data. If this were so, the problem would only be temporary – one that would not concern researchers in 200 years' time, for example, when data would be plentiful. However, there is a second source of estimation error, known as "non-stationarity". A time series is said to be non-stationary if its variance changes over time, its autocovariance is time- and also lag-dependent, or its mean changes over time.[9] When there is non-stationarity the researcher might be well advised to use shorter data sets. Extending the length of a data series might reduce the contribution of sampling error to estimation error, but at the same time it could increase that of non-stationarity.[10]

Sometimes estimation error can be observed directly from the data by estimating rolling volatilities and examining their variation. However, this approach can produce misleading results, as Figure 3.5 shows. Sampling error alone can create wide fluctuations in resampled volatilities, even for stationary data. The grey symbols in the figure are the rolling volatilities estimated from random draws from a normal distribution with the same mean and covariance as the historic data.

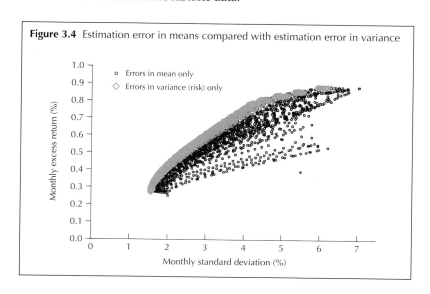

Figure 3.4 Estimation error in means compared with estimation error in variance

Figure 3.5 Rolling volatility of historical returns compared with rolling volatility of random draws from normal distribution with the same mean and variance

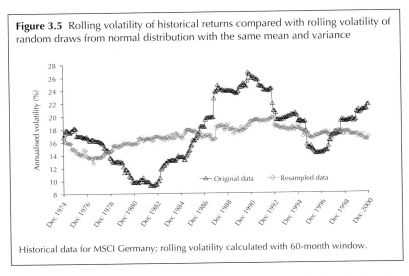

Historical data for MSCI Germany; rolling volatility calculated with 60-month window.

What we need, therefore, is a test statistic to judge whether fluctuations in rolling volatility are significant enough to reject stationarity. As we do not know the distribution of rolling volatilities under the null hypothesis, H_0, of stationarity, we have to construct a test statistic. A convenient way of doing this is Monte Carlo simulation.

Step 1 Calculate rolling volatilities for historical data using $\sigma_t^2(l) = 1/l \sum_{i=t}^{t+l} (r_i - \bar{r})^2$, where l is the window length. Record the maximum and minimum volatilities as a measure of dispersion.

Step 2 Estimate the mean and volatility of the historical series.

Step 3 Using the distribution parameters obtained in Step 2, draw from a normal distribution to create a time series of simulated returns with the same length as the historical data.[11] Record the maximum and minimum volatilities.

Step 4 Repeat Step 3 1,000 times. Watch the convergence of the estimates to determine the number of samplings. Then sort the results, or plot the distribution. Read the critical values for the desired confidence level from the distribution.

When this is done, we are left with the simple exercise of comparing the historical minimum and maximum volatilities (about 8% and 28% – see Figure 3.5) with their Monte Carlo-derived distributions. Figure 3.6 shows the histograms for both statistics. In this case the Monte Carlo experiment supports our intuition that the historical estimates are too extreme to have been produced by sampling error – none of the 1,000 simulations produced higher maximum (or minimum) volatilities. Hence we can conclude that it is unlikely that the data have been drawn from a stationary distribution.[12]

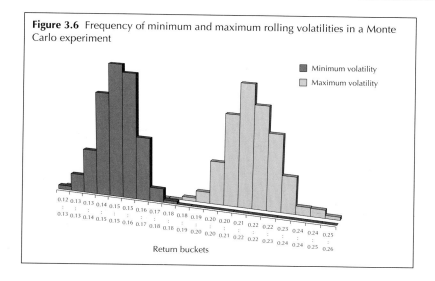

Figure 3.6 Frequency of minimum and maximum rolling volatilities in a Monte Carlo experiment

3.3 RESAMPLED EFFICIENCY

We have seen in Section 3.2 that the quadratic optimisation algorithm employed is too powerful for the quality of the input. This is not necessarily a problem of the mechanism itself but, rather, calls for a refinement of the input. Recently, a new concept called "resampled efficiency" has been introduced into the asset management world to deal with estimation error.[13] The objective of this and the next few sections is to describe this new technology, compare it with established procedures and point to some peculiarities of the approach.

The basis of the approach is to establish a "resampled frontier". *resampled frontier* Portfolios along this frontier are defined as an "average of the rank-associated mean–variance-efficient portfolios"[14] (for further explanation see Appendix B). Averaging maintains an important portfolio characteristic – that the weights sum to one – which is probably the main practical justification for the averaging procedure. However, the method is heuristic: it has no economic justification based on the optimising behaviour of rational agents.

The resampled weight for a portfolio of rank m (portfolio number m along the frontier) is given by

$$\overline{\mathbf{w}}_m^{\text{resampled}} = \frac{1}{n} \sum_{i=1}^{n} \mathbf{w}_{im} \tag{3.1}$$

where $\mathbf{w}_{im}$ denotes the $k \times 1$ vector of the mth portfolio along the frontier for the ith resampling. The procedure can be summarised as follows:

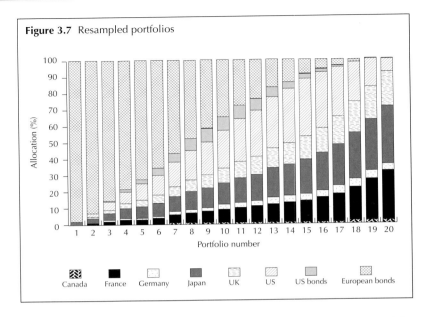

Figure 3.7 Resampled portfolios

Step 1 Estimate the variance–covariance matrix and the mean vector of the historical inputs. (Alternatively, the inputs can be prespecified.)

Step 2 Resample, using the inputs created in Step 1, taking T draws from the input distribution; the number of draws, T, reflects the degree of uncertainty in the inputs. Calculate a new variance–covariance matrix from the sampled series. Estimation error will result in different matrices from those in Step 1.

Step 3 Calculate an efficient frontier for the inputs derived in Step 2. Record the optimal portfolio weights for m equally distributed return points along the frontier.

Step 4 Repeat Steps 2 and 3 many times.[15] Calculate average portfolio weights for each return point. Evaluate a frontier of averaged portfolios with the variance–covariance matrix from Step 1 to plot the resampled frontier.

Instead of adding up portfolios that share the same rank, one could alternatively add up portfolios that show the same risk–return trade-off. This can easily be done by maximising $U = \mu - \frac{1}{2\lambda_m}\sigma^2$ for varying λ_m and then averaging the λ_m-associated portfolios, as demonstrated in Appendix B. Utility-sorted portfolios are theoretically preferable as they indicate risk–return trade-offs that an investor with a given risk-aversion would actually choose if in a position to repeatedly make choices under different risk–return environments.

Resampled portfolios show a higher diversification, with more assets

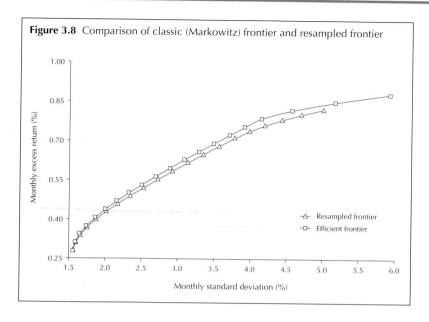

Figure 3.8 Comparison of classic (Markowitz) frontier and resampled frontier

entering the solution, than classically constructed portfolios (compare Figure 3.7 with Figure 3.1). They also exhibit less sudden shifts in allocations, giving a smooth transition as return requirements change. In the eyes of many practitioners these are desirable properties.

Owing to the apparent over-diversification relative to return forecasts, the resampled frontier will show different weight allocations and will plot below the classically derived efficient frontier, as shown in Figure 3.8, and it does not reach the same maximum return as the classic frontier. Whereas the maximum-return solution in the classic frontier contains only the maximum-return asset(s), the averaging process prohibits this kind of solution for the resampled frontier. Both frontiers are relatively similar in risk–return space (as seen in Figure 3.8) but quite different in weight space, a feature that can be seen by comparing Figures 3.1 and 3.7.

risk-return-space is different from weight-space

One of the problems of using the average criterion can be appreciated by more closely inspecting the distribution of resampled weights for a particular rank-associated portfolio. Portfolio 12 in Figure 3.7 has an average allocation into US equities of about 23%. However, if we look at the distribution of resampled US equity weights for this portfolio in Figure 3.9, we find that in most of the runs (more than 500 out of 1,000), the actual weight given was between 0% and 5% and the 20%–25% columns are trivial. The average of 23% seems to be heavily influenced by the few lucky (ie, favourable) draws leading to significant allocations. This point is discussed further in Section 3.6.

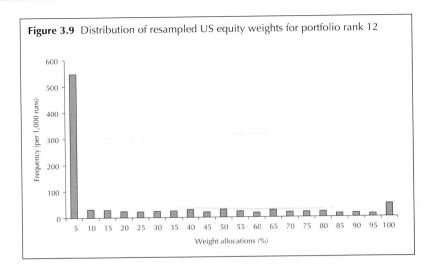

Figure 3.9 Distribution of resampled US equity weights for portfolio rank 12

3.4 DISTANCE MEASURES

Effectively, the resampling procedure provides the distribution of portfolio weights, giving us what we need to test whether two portfolios are statistically different. The difference can be measured as distance in a k-dimensional vector space, where k is the number of assets. The Euclidean measure for the distance of a vector of portfolio weights of portfolio i ($\mathbf{w}_i$) to portfolio p ($\mathbf{w}_p$) is given by

$$\left(\mathbf{w}_p - \mathbf{w}_i\right)'\left(\mathbf{w}_p - \mathbf{w}_i\right) \tag{3.2}$$

Statistical distance, however, is computed as

$$\left(\mathbf{w}_p - \mathbf{w}_i\right)'\hat{\boldsymbol{\Sigma}}^{-1}\left(\mathbf{w}_p - \mathbf{w}_i\right) \tag{3.3}$$

where $\boldsymbol{\Sigma}$ is the variance–covariance matrix of portfolio weights. The test statistic represented by this expression is distributed as χ^2 with degrees of freedom equal to the number of assets, k.[16]

An example will illustrate this. Suppose we have two assets each with 10% mean and 20% volatility, that the correlation between both assets is zero and that the risk-aversion coefficient, λ, is 0.2. The optimal solution without estimation error is given by

$$\mathbf{w}^* = \begin{bmatrix} w_1^* \\ w_2^* \end{bmatrix} = \lambda\boldsymbol{\Omega}^{-1}\boldsymbol{\mu} = 0.2 \cdot \begin{bmatrix} \dfrac{1}{0.2^2} & 0 \\ 0 & \dfrac{1}{0.2^2} \end{bmatrix}\begin{bmatrix} 0.1 \\ 0.1 \end{bmatrix} = \begin{bmatrix} 0.5 \\ 0.5 \end{bmatrix}$$

We will calculate optimal portfolios without adding-up constraints. By definition, holdings in these portfolios do not have to add up to one.

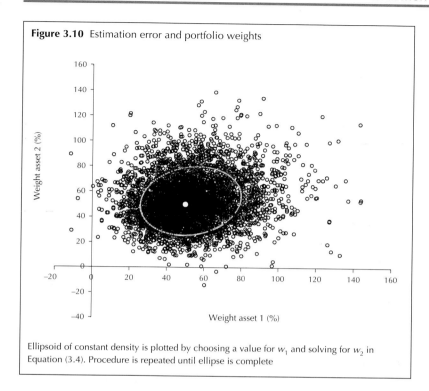

Figure 3.10 Estimation error and portfolio weights

Ellipsoid of constant density is plotted by choosing a value for w_1 and solving for w_2 in Equation (3.4). Procedure is repeated until ellipse is complete

In which case resampling would make no sense as all resampled weights would plot on a straight line (from 100% weight 1 to 100% weight 2). Indeed, one might be tempted to conclude that they are not portfolios as the assets do not add up, but one could think of cash as a third (filling) asset as cash would leave marginal risks as well as total risks unchanged.

Although, as we have just calculated, the optimal solution is a 50% allocation into each asset, the estimated weights are scattered around this solution. Comparing the vector difference to the critical value of χ^2 yields a measure of how statistically different a portfolio is.[17] The ellipsoid in Figure 3.10 is a line of constant density consistent with Equation (3.3) for the vector distance between the optimal portfolio without estimation error and its resamplings. In our two-asset example, lines of constant density can be obtained from

$$p\left(w_1 - w_1^*, w_2 - w_2^*\right) = \frac{1}{2\pi \det(\mathbf{\Sigma})^{\frac{1}{2}}} e^{-\frac{1}{2}\begin{bmatrix} w_1 - w_1^* \\ w_2 - w_2^* \end{bmatrix}' \mathbf{\Sigma}^{-1} \begin{bmatrix} w_1 - w_1^* \\ w_2 - w_2^* \end{bmatrix}}$$

(3.4)

$$\mathbf{\Sigma}^{-1} = \begin{bmatrix} 27.93 & 0.005 \\ 0.005 & 27.76 \end{bmatrix}$$

However, introducing long-only constraints (effectively truncating weights at zero and one) invalidates the normality assumption for the distribution of portfolio weights. Michaud (1998) uses a different distance measure, widely applied in asset management, which recognises that two portfolios with the same risk and return might actually exhibit different allocations. He defines the distance between two portfolios as

$$\left(\mathbf{w}_p - \mathbf{w}_i\right)' \hat{\mathbf{\Omega}}_0 \left(\mathbf{w}_p - \mathbf{w}_i\right) \tag{3.5}$$

which is equivalent to the squared tracking error (volatility of return difference between portfolios i and p). Michaud's procedure runs as follows:

Step 1 Define a portfolio against which differences can be tested. For example, this could be the current asset allocation. Calculate Equation (3.5) for all resampled portfolios, ie, resample under new forecasts.

Step 2 Sort portfolios in descending order by tracking error, TE.

Step 3 Define TE_α as the critical tracking error for the $\alpha\%$ level (ie, if 1,000 portfolios are resampled and the critical level is 5%, look at the tracking error of a portfolio which is 50th from the top). Hence, all portfolios for which

$$\left(\mathbf{w}_p - \mathbf{w}_i\right)' \hat{\mathbf{\Omega}}_0 \left(\mathbf{w}_p - \mathbf{w}_i\right) \geq TE_\alpha^2 \tag{3.6}$$

are labelled statistically different. We can now ascertain whether a newly reoptimised portfolio (assuming no estimation error) is statistically different from the current asset allocation.

Step 4 Finally, calculate the minimum and maximum allocations for each asset within the confidence region.

The uncertainty about the optimal weights can be visualised for a three-asset example, but this becomes quite difficult for higher dimensions. It should be noted that similarity is defined with respect to the optimal weight vector rather than in terms of risk and return, so two portfolios could be very similar in terms of risk and return but very different in their allocations. This is a known feature as it is widely recognised that risk–return points below the frontier are not necessarily unique.

Although Michaud's test procedure is intuitive, it should be noted that the dispersion in weights is large, so it will be difficult to reject the hypothesis that both portfolios are statistically equal even if they are not. The power of the test suggested here is therefore low.

3.5 PORTFOLIO RESAMPLING AND LINEAR REGRESSION

If there were no long-only constraint, we could effectively find optimal portfolios using a simple regression approach as portfolio optimisation would then become a linear problem. Suppose we downloaded k (number of assets) time series of excess returns from a databank – ie, total return, R, minus cash rate, c, with T observations each. We can combine these excess returns in a matrix, $\mathbf{X}$, with each column containing one return series. Regressing these excess returns against a constant[18]

$$\mathbf{1}_{T \times 1} = \mathbf{X}_{T \times k} \mathbf{w}_{k \times 1} + \mathbf{u}_{T \times 1} \tag{3.7}$$

yields

$$\hat{\mathbf{w}} = (\mathbf{X}' \mathbf{X})^{-1} \mathbf{X}' \mathbf{1} \tag{3.8}$$

where $\mathbf{1}$ denotes a $T \times 1$ vector of ones and $\mathbf{u}$ is the $T \times 1$ vector of regression residuals. This can be interpreted as coming closest to a portfolio with zero risk (the vector of ones shows no volatility) and unit return. This would present an arbitrage opportunity. Rescaling the optimal weight vector will yield the "characteristic portfolio" (one that is optimal with respect to the characteristic $\hat{\boldsymbol{\mu}}$):

$$\hat{\mathbf{w}}_{\text{characteristic}}^* = \frac{\hat{\boldsymbol{\Omega}}_0^{-1} \hat{\boldsymbol{\mu}}_0}{\boldsymbol{\mu}_0' \hat{\boldsymbol{\Omega}}_0^{-1} \hat{\boldsymbol{\mu}}_0} \tag{3.9}$$

Alternatively, a constrained regression, with a linear constraint on portfolio weights, can be run to create portfolios that meet particular return requirements. This framework can then be used to test restrictions on individual regression coefficients (estimated portfolio weights), as well as restrictions on groups of assets, and test whether they are significantly different from zero.[19]

Such a regression framework also puts a central problem of portfolio construction into a different, well-known perspective. Highly correlated asset returns mean highly correlated regressors, with the obvious consequences arising from multicollinearity: high standard deviations on portfolio weights (regression coefficients) and identification problems (difficulty of distinguishing between two similar assets). Simply downtesting and excluding insignificant assets will result in an outcome that is highly dependent on the order of exclusion, with no guidance on where to start.[20] This is a familiar problem both to the asset allocator and to the econometrician.

Portfolio resampling can be interpreted as a simulation approach to obtaining the distribution of weight estimates by Monte Carlo methods, as in Equation (3.7). The centre of the distribution is calculated in the same way as in portfolio resampling – ie, by averaging the coefficient

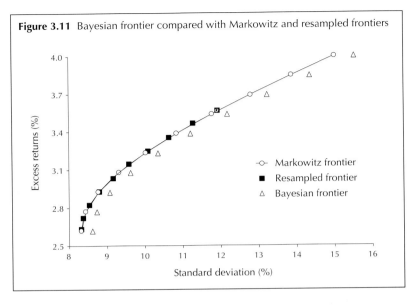

Figure 3.11 Bayesian frontier compared with Markowitz and resampled frontiers

estimates for a particular asset. Instead of taking the structural form of the model as given and simulating the error term, resampling simulates a whole new set of data, which is equivalent to assuming that the regressors are stochastic.[21] This can be illustrated by writing Equation (3.7) in the usual textbook form –

$$y = \beta_1 x_1 + \cdots + \beta_k x_k + u, \quad \beta_i = w_i, \quad x_i = R_i - c, \quad y = 1 \qquad (3.10)$$

– which can be estimated using any standard regression software. Drawing new return data from the variance–covariance matrix and re-estimating Equation (3.10) n times, we can calculate the average weight for asset $j = 1, \ldots, k$ by averaging over the regression coefficients ($\hat{\beta}_i = \hat{w}_i$).

$$\overline{w}_j = \frac{1}{n} \sum_{i=1}^{n} \hat{w}_{ij}, \qquad j = 1, \ldots, k \qquad (3.11)$$

While this is not necessary for portfolios without long-only constraints (as the distribution of the regressors is known), portfolio resampling is more general than the regression approach as it can also be applied to portfolios with long-only constraints, where the weight distribution is not known. Essentially, this means bootstrapping the unknown distribution of a test statistic. If an asset is, for example, included in 70 of 1,000 runs for a given rank or utility score, it will get a p-value of 7%. This approach can also be extended through Bayesian analysis using standard textbook results. Priors are set on the distribution of portfolio weights instead of asset returns.

3.6 PITFALLS OF PORTFOLIO RESAMPLING

It is common sense that estimation error will result in an increase in portfolio risk. This has been captured in the Bayesian literature on portfolio construction (see Chapter 4). Taking the simplest case of a two-asset portfolio, any combination of two assets would be efficient. All resampled portfolios will still plot on the efficient frontier and no portfolio will plot below, although the frontier might be shorter as sometimes the order of assets reverses so that the averaged maximum-return portfolio will not contain 100% of the higher-return asset.

Let us examine the two-asset case in more detail. Suppose that we have two uncorrelated assets with estimated volatilities of 10% and 15%, that we use 60 monthly observations to estimate the frontier and that average returns over cash are 4% and 2% per annum. Figure 3.11 plots the results for a traditional, a resampled and a Bayesian frontier.[22] The increase in risk is only captured using the Bayesian frontier, where, for the same expected return (expected returns will not change with the introduction of estimation error under uninformative priors), each portfolio is shown to expose the investor to more risk because Bayesian methods leverage up the variance–covariance matrix but leave the return vector unchanged. In direct contrast, in the resampled frontier estimation error shows up only as a shortening of the frontier, not as an increase in risk for every return level. Instead, uncertainty about the mean shows up as a reduction on the maximum expected mean return. This is not plausible.

Now let us consider two assets with the same expected return but one has significantly higher volatility. One could think of this as an international fixed-income allocation on a hedged and an unhedged basis. Most practitioners (and the mean–variance optimiser) would exclude the higher-volatility asset from the solution unless it had some desirable correlations. How would resampled efficiency deal with these assets? Repeatedly drawing from the original distribution will result in draws for the volatile asset with highly negative, as well as highly positive, returns. Quadratic programming will invest heavily in this asset in the latter case and short the asset in the former case. However, as shorting is not allowed for portfolios with long-only constraints, this will result in positive allocation for high positive average return draws and zero allocations for high negative average return draws. This is different from an unconstrained optimisation, where large long positions would be offset (on average) by large negative positions. Consequently, an increase in volatility will lead to an increase in the average allocation. Hence, a worsening Sharpe ratio would be accompanied by an increase in weight. Again, this is not a plausible result; it arises directly from the averaging rule in combination with a long-only constraint, which creates an optionality for the allocation of the corresponding asset. Assets are either in or out but never negative. This intuitive line of reasoning can be made explicit through an example based on the data set given in Table 3.1.

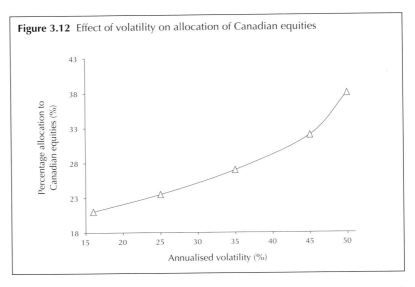

Figure 3.12 Effect of volatility on allocation of Canadian equities

We will use only the equity data for Canada, France and Germany and the fixed-income data for European bonds. Also, we will reduce the sample size to 60 monthly observations, as this is a more realistic time-frame for most practical applications. We will vary only the volatility of the asset with the lowest return, Canadian equities, and look at their allocation in the maximum-return portfolio (although Canadian equities have the lowest return, their allocation tends to peak at the maximum-return portfolio). As volatility rises – and Sharpe ratio falls – allocations at the high-return end rise. In fact, deterioration in the risk–return relationship for Canadian equities is accompanied by an increased weight, as shown in Figure 3.12. This is not a result of higher volatility leading to higher estimation error – as this phenomenon does not arise in long/short portfolios – but is a direct result of averaging over long-only portfolios as the long-only constraint creates "optionality".

Another problem of resampled efficiency is that it violates basic requirements for efficient portfolios. The first such requirement is that the efficient frontier does not contain upward-bending parts.[23] Any upward-bending part would imply that one could construct portfolios superior to the frontier by linearly combining two frontier portfolios. How could such a situation arise when the concept of resampled efficiency is used? As we have already mentioned, the difference between the resampled and the classic efficient frontier is due to overdiversification.

As the return requirements rise, the maximum-return portfolio tends to a state in which it contains a single asset. There might well be instances where overdiversification diminished as we moved towards the maximum-return solution as these solutions do tend to be concentrated in the high-return asset. This is exactly the case with the resampled frontier

Figure 3.13 Upward-bending resampled frontier

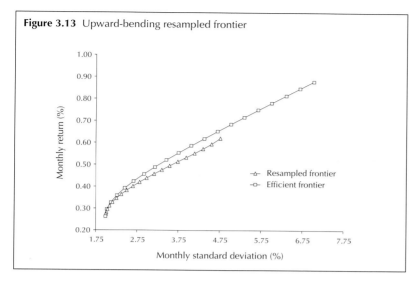

shown in Figure 3.13. It is certainly true that the true test of resampled efficiency is out-of-sample performance in a Monte Carlo study. However,
upward-bending parts in an efficient frontier are difficult to justify.

A second basic violation of modern portfolio theory is that resampling
(with long-only constraints) changes the structure of the maximum Sharpe
ratio portfolio. This is neither intuitive nor theoretically correct as estimation error will increase the holding of cash for every level of risk-aversion
(as all risky assets are perceived to be riskier) but will not change the structure of the maximum Sharpe ratio portfolio. The reason for this is that
risk-averse investors will increase their cash holdings as cash is not only
free of volatility risk but is also free of estimation risk. Resampling, on the
other hand, is very likely to change the relative weights within the maximum Sharpe ratio portfolio as it tends to overallocate to the more volatile
assets. Moreover, whereas the tangency portfolio (maximum Sharpe ratio)
contains no cash even in the presence of estimation error, it will always
include cash in the case of resampling as cash will always be sampled in
(at least for some runs).

The most important criticism of resampled efficiency arises from its
statistical foundation, as all resamplings are derived from the same vector
and covariance matrix, $\hat{\Omega}_0, \hat{\mu}_0$. Because the true distribution is unknown,
all resampled portfolios suffer from the deviation of the parameters
$\hat{\Omega}_0, \hat{\mu}_0$ from $\Omega_{true}, \mu_{true}$, in very much the same way. Averaging will not
help much in this case as the averaged weights are the result of an input
vector, which is itself very uncertain. Hence it is fair to say that all portfolios inherit the same estimation error. The special importance attached
to $\hat{\Omega}_0, \hat{\mu}_0$, finally limits the analysis.

3.7 CONSTRAINED PORTFOLIO OPTIMISATION

We will now leave the concept of resampled efficiency and turn to the most common procedure for avoiding "unreasonable" solutions: constrained portfolio optimisation. Constraining the set of possible solutions will, if binding, lead to a shift of the efficient frontier downwards and to the right. Although constraints are often motivated by legal constraints,[24] or preferences,[25] in this section we will assume that they are used by the investor to safeguard against "unreasonable" solutions caused by estimation error in inputs. Effectively, constraints are used to enforce some kind of diversification. Although it has already been shown that the accompanying reduction of risk is not enough to compensate for the lowered return, this section will focus on how constraints change the distribution of explicit forecasts.[26] We do this with the simulation framework used in this chapter.

Suppose that, in addition to the historical means, we have a vector of forecasts

$$\boldsymbol{\mu}_f = (2\%\ \ 1\%\ \ 1\%\ \ 1\%\ \ 1\%\ \ 1\%\ \ 0\%\ \ 0\%)$$

We shall also assume that the investor would prefer to avoid concentrated portfolios and so will constrain the optimal solution as given below:

$$
\underbrace{\begin{pmatrix} 1 \\ 0 \\ 0 \\ 0 \\ 0 \\ 0 \\ 0 \\ 0.1 \\ 0.1 \end{pmatrix}}_{\mathbf{w}^{\text{lower}}}
\leq
\underbrace{\begin{pmatrix} 1 & 1 & 1 & 1 & 1 & 1 & 1 & 1 \\ 1 & 0 & 0 & 0 & 0 & 0 & 0 & 0 \\ 0 & 1 & 0 & 0 & 0 & 0 & 0 & 0 \\ 0 & 0 & 1 & 0 & 0 & 0 & 0 & 0 \\ 0 & 0 & 0 & 1 & 0 & 0 & 0 & 0 \\ 0 & 0 & 0 & 0 & 1 & 0 & 0 & 0 \\ 0 & 0 & 0 & 0 & 0 & 1 & 0 & 0 \\ 0 & 0 & 0 & 0 & 0 & 0 & 1 & 0 \\ 0 & 0 & 0 & 0 & 0 & 0 & 0 & 1 \end{pmatrix}}_{\mathbf{A}}
\underbrace{\begin{pmatrix} w_1 \\ w_2 \\ w_3 \\ w_4 \\ w_5 \\ w_6 \\ w_7 \\ w_8 \end{pmatrix}}_{\mathbf{w}}
\leq
\underbrace{\begin{pmatrix} 1 \\ 0.3 \\ 0.3 \\ 0.3 \\ 0.3 \\ 0.3 \\ 0.3 \\ 0.3 \\ 0.3 \end{pmatrix}}_{\mathbf{w}^{\text{upper}}}
$$

No asset is allowed to enter as a short position (ie, we impose a long-only constraint). No asset weight may be higher than 30% and all asset weights have to add up to 100%. Assuming λ, the risk-aversion coefficient, to be 0.038, the solution to the problem[27]

$$\mathbf{w}'\boldsymbol{\mu}_f - \frac{\lambda}{2}\mathbf{w}'\boldsymbol{\Omega}_0\mathbf{w}$$

$$\mathbf{w}^{\text{lower}} \leq \mathbf{A}\mathbf{w} \leq \mathbf{w}^{\text{upper}} \tag{3.12}$$

is given by the constrained optimal allocation vector

$$\mathbf{w}^* = (30\%\ \ 0\%\ \ 12\%\ \ 11\%\ \ 0\%\ \ 27\%\ \ 10\%\ \ 10\%)'$$

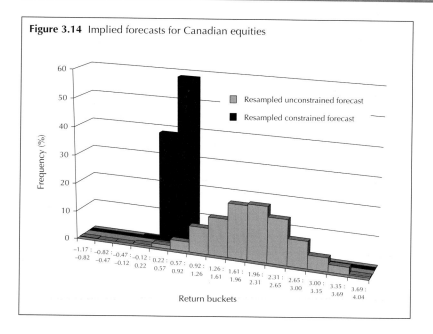

Figure 3.14 Implied forecasts for Canadian equities

To appreciate the effect of investment constraints on optimal portfolio choice, it is informative to compare the implied returns of constrained and unconstrained portfolios. This can be done by backing out (solving for those returns that make current weights optimal) the implied returns of the new portfolio allocation to see how the constraints change our original return forecasts.[28] However, we would like to do this for a variety of optimisations, allowing us to directly compare the distribution of input return forecasts (reflecting estimation error) and the distribution of implied return forecasts from the constrained portfolios (reflecting a combination of constraints and estimation error) using the resampled portfolios. These implied returns are those that would make an investor arrive at the constrained portfolio without having constraints in the first place.

To do this we resample the optimisation in Equation (3.12) 1,000 times, calculating for each run

$$\mu_i^{\text{implied}} = \frac{\hat{\Omega}_i \mathbf{w}_i^*}{\hat{\sigma}_i^{*2}} \mu_i^* = \lambda \hat{\Omega}_i \mathbf{w}_i$$

The result of this procedure for asset 1 (Canadian equities) is plotted in Figure 3.14. The unconstrained implied forecasts show a much greater variation than the constrained implied forecasts. We also find that the implied returns from the constrained optimisation exhibit a significantly lower average. This is a direct effect of the binding upper constraint, which brings down the marginal contribution to risk and, hence, the implied returns. Constraining portfolio weights can be interpreted as equivalent to a high-conviction (low estimation risk) forecast. This is not necessarily intuitive as constraints have been introduced because investors do not believe in high-conviction forecasts in the first place.

3.8 CONCLUSION

Portfolio resampling offers an intuitive basis for developing tests for the statistical difference between two portfolios, as represented by their weight vectors. Therefore it is generally the methodology of choice for this purpose.

It is not clear, however, why averaging over resampled portfolio weights should offer a solution for dealing with estimation error in optimal portfolio construction. In the case of long/short portfolios, averaged resampled portfolios offer no improvement over traditional Markowitz solutions; in fact, both solutions – ie, frontiers – may coincide. When long-only constraints are applied, resampled efficiency leads to more diversified portfolios; as diversified portfolios are well known to beat Markowitz portfolios out-of-sample, Michaud's (1998) finding that resampled efficiency beats simple Markowitz portfolios out-of-sample is hardly surprising.[29]

It not clear either to what extent this out-of-sample superiority can be generalised as portfolio resampling has some unwanted features, as has been shown in this chapter. Deteriorating Sharpe ratios, caused by higher volatility, lead to an increased allocation for more volatile assets in the high-return portfolios because favourable return realisations lead to large allocations, while unfavourable drawings lead to zero allocations at most (due to the phenomenon of "optionality"). Another disadvantage is that the efficient frontiers may have turning points, changing from a concave section to a convex section. It is also interesting to note that at least three assets are needed for the methodology to show the increased risk arising from estimation error.

Although the ultimate test of any portfolio construction methodology is out-of-sample performance, Markowitz methods are not the appropriate benchmark for assessing resampled efficiency; one would like to know how the latter compares with Bayesian alternatives, which do not exhibit the problems mentioned above and have a strong foundation in decision theory. Although it is not clear why resampled efficiency should be optimal, it remains an interesting heuristic for dealing with an important problem.

Constraining the set of efficient solutions is well accepted among most practitioners because it is very much in the tradition of choosing weights rather than generating return forecasts and it also expresses a deep mistrust of quantitative solutions. However, the more constrained portfolios become, the less power is given to the variance–covariance matrix and the investor ends up with an assumed, rather than a derived, solution. Resampling has shown that constraints transform a large return forecast with considerable estimation error into a smaller forecast with much less estimation error. As just stated, this is not an obvious result as the use of constraints reflects the fact that investors do not believe in high-conviction forecasts in the first place.

So far we have seen that estimates for the optimal weight vector which rely on only one source of information – historical data, or forecasts with the same uncertainty attached – are much too noisy for the optimisation algorithm. Incorporating additional information, in the form of priors, is the only way to overcome this problem. The next chapter will therefore turn to Bayesian statistics as a way of constructing more meaningful information.

APPENDIX A: LINEAR REGRESSION AND CHARACTERISTIC PORTFOLIOS

Starting from Equation (3.8) and multiplying by T/T we get

$$\hat{w} = \left(X'X \frac{T}{T} \right)^{-1} X'1$$

$$= \left(X'X \frac{1}{T} \right)^{-1} \frac{1}{T} X'1$$

$$= \left(X'X \frac{1}{T} \right)^{-1} \hat{\mu}_0$$

where

$$\hat{\mu}_0 = \frac{1}{T} X'1 = \frac{1}{T} \left[\sum x_1 \cdots \sum x_k \right]'$$

Rewriting the equation for the variance–covariance matrix gives

$$\hat{\Omega}_0 = \frac{\left(X - 1\hat{\mu}_0' \right)' \left(X - 1\hat{\mu}_0' \right)}{T}$$

$$= \frac{\left(X'X - T\hat{\mu}_0 \hat{\mu}_0' - T\hat{\mu}_0 \hat{\mu}_0' - \hat{\mu}_0 1'1 \hat{\mu}_0' \right)}{T}$$

$$= \frac{X'X}{T} - \hat{\mu}_0 \hat{\mu}_0'$$

$$\frac{X'X}{T} = \hat{\Omega}_0 + \hat{\mu}_0 \hat{\mu}_0'$$

Using the result in Green (2000, p. 32, 2.66), we now write

$$\hat{w} = \left(X'X\frac{1}{T} \right)^{-1} \hat{\mu}_0$$

$$= \left(\hat{\Omega}_0 + \hat{\mu}_0\hat{\mu}_0' \right)^{-1} \mu_0$$

$$= \left(\hat{\Omega}_0^{-1} - \frac{\hat{\Omega}_0^{-1}\hat{\mu}_0\hat{\mu}_0'\hat{\Omega}_0^{-1}}{1 + \hat{\mu}_0'\hat{\Omega}_0^{-1}\hat{\mu}_0} \right) \hat{\mu}_0$$

$$= \frac{\hat{\Omega}_0^{-1}\hat{\mu}_0}{1 + \hat{\mu}_0'\hat{\Omega}_0^{-1}\hat{\mu}_0}$$

Scaling this weight vector accordingly leads to the results in the text.

APPENDIX B: RANK-ASSOCIATED VERSUS LAMBDA-ASSOCIATED PORTFOLIOS

Resampled efficiency is defined as averaging over the rank-associated portfolios, as described in Section 3.3. Effectively, this means averaging over portfolios that have been given the same name (ie, rank $1, 2, \ldots, m$). Portfolios carrying rank 1 are the respective minimum-variance portfolios, while portfolios carrying rank m are the maximum-return portfolios. All other portfolios are ranked in between according to their expected returns. The distance between the minimum-variance and maximum-return portfolios is divided into equal parts.

Instead of adding up portfolios that share the same rank, one could add up portfolios that show the same risk–return trade-off. This can easily be done by maximising $U = \mu - \frac{1}{2\lambda_m}\sigma^2$ for varying λ_m and then averaging the λ_m-associated portfolios. To show how close the results given by both methods are, we will resample a hypothetical three-asset case.

Assume that returns are drawn from a multivariate normal distribution with parameters

$$\mu_0 = \begin{bmatrix} 5 \\ 10 \\ 15 \end{bmatrix}, \quad \Omega_0 = \begin{bmatrix} 25 & 0 & 0 \\ 0 & 100 & 0 \\ 0 & 0 & 225 \end{bmatrix}$$

We solve a simple unconstrained optimisation like $w_i^* = \lambda\Omega_i^{-1}\mu_i$, where i represents the ith simulation and λ has been set to 2.72. This yields the distribution of lambda-associated portfolios. Rank-associated portfolios

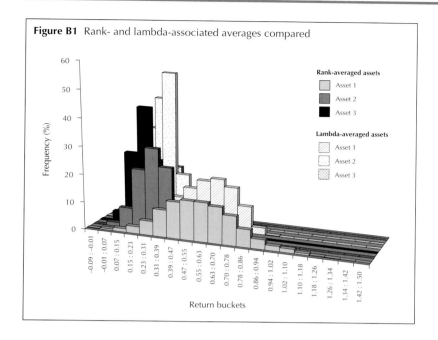

Figure B1 Rank- and lambda-associated averages compared

are found by first finding out where the return of the original $(\hat{\mathbf{\Omega}}_0, \hat{\mathbf{\mu}}_0)$ lambda-associated portfolio ranks on the range between the minimum-variance and maximum-return portfolios and then calculating optimal weights for each run. The distribution of resampled weights is given in Figure B1. Although mean allocations are virtually identical, it is interesting to note that lambda-associated portfolios show a slightly smaller variation in weights. The small experiment conducted in Figure B1 confirms what Michaud (1998) has already pointed out: both averaging mechanisms yield very similar results.

1   The patent for the procedure, issued in December 1999 under the title "Portfolio Optimization by Means of Resampled Efficient Frontiers", is held by its inventors, Richard and Robert Michaud. The procedure is worldwide patent pending and New Frontier Advisors, LLC, Boston, MA, has been granted exclusive worldwide licensing rights.
2   Jorion (1992) describes portfolio resampling as one method of addressing sampling error. Sampling error is the only form of estimation risk if the true underlying parameters are stable but there are insufficient data to estimate them precisely.
3   See Scherer (2002).
4   All examples are illustrated using the original data from Michaud (1998, pp. 17, 19). For these data $T = 216$ and $k = 8$. An entry of 30.25 stands for a standard deviation of $\sqrt{30.25} = 5.5$. Converted into annual volatility, this becomes $\sqrt{12} \times 5.5 = 19.05$. The corresponding new estimate is 0.39 per month, which is equivalent to a risk premium of 4.68 per year.
5   Markowitz (1991) and Sharpe (1970) are classic references.
6   See Michaud (1989) or Nawrocki (1996).

7   This problem has been extensively reported and empirically studied. Examples are Best and Grauer (1991), Chopra and Ziemba (1993) or Jobson and Korkie (1983).

8   It is well known that variance estimation can be improved by reducing the data interval, eg, from monthly to daily (assuming no correlation in first or second moments). The same is not true for estimates of means as the precision rises only for the average daily return and not for the annual average. A detailed exposition of this can be found in Neftci (2000).

9   See Mills (1999, Chapter 3).

10 Broadie (1993) is the only source (to the author's knowledge) to address non-stationarity in return series as a problem for portfolio construction.

11 Alternatively, we could bootstrap (assigning equal probability to each return) from historical data. However, both methods yield similar results as long as the data are reasonably normal.

12 The method described could also be used to test whether the difference between maximum and minimum volatilities (range) is significantly different from what one would expect if the data were stationary.

13 Michaud (1998) describes his methodology well in his book *Efficient Asset Management*.

14 Michaud (1998, p. 50).

15 As the number of samplings grows, statistical tests can be applied with greater confidence. However, this comes at the expense of computing time. For many applications 500 samplings will suffice.

16 The idea of this test statistic is that it is obviously not enough to look at weight differences only; small weight differences for highly correlated assets might be of greater significance than large weight differences for assets with negative correlation.

17 Critical values of χ^2 can be found in any statistical software package, including EXCEL.

18 This can be done using any econometrics package by running a regression of ones against all asset returns, excluding an intercept, hence forcing the regression through the origin in excess-return space (maximising the Sharpe ratio). See also Equation (19) in Jobson and Korkie (1983).

19 See Britten-Jones (1999).

20 Specifically, a procedure in which one omits the most insignificant asset, re-estimates and again omits the most insignificant asset. This is repeated until no insignificant asset is left.

21 See Maddala (2001, p. 600) on bootstrapping data rather than residuals.

22 See Chapter 4 on Bayesian methods with regard to portfolio construction problems.

23 For a review of efficient set mathematics, see Huang and Litzenberger (1988).

24 Constraints come in many forms. We can distinguish between long-only constraints (minimum holding of 0% and maximum holding of 100%), add-up constraints (portfolio weights must sum to 100%), individual constraints (upper and lower bounds on single asset), group constraints (groups of assets have to stay within boundaries), total risk constraints (portfolio beta has to stay within boundaries, volatilities must not exceed given level), risk contribution constraints (risk budgets) and return constraints (return contribution from group of assets). Implicitly we have limited the list to linear constraints.

25 For example, a constraint with a given level of ordinary income (coupon and dividend payments) has to be maintained.

26 See Grauer and Shen (2000).

27 The risk-aversion parameter is derived from the risk–return trade-off implicit for an investor holding the benchmark portfolio and an unconditional return expectation for the benchmark of 3.5%.

28 This has been suggested by Grinold and Easton (1998), who also show how to explicitly calculate which constraint contributes how much of the difference between original and implied constrained forecasts.

29 See Jorion (1992) or Chopra, Hensel and Turner (1993).

BIBLIOGRAPHY

Best, M., and R. Grauer, 1991, "On the Sensitivity of Mean Variance Efficient Portfolios to Changes in Asset Means: Some Analytical and Computational Results", *Review of Financial Studies* 4, pp. 314–42.

Britten-Jones, M., 1999, "The Sampling Error in Estimates of Mean Variance Efficient Portfolios", *Journal of Finance* 54, pp. 655–71.

Broadie, M., 1993, "Computing Efficient Frontiers using Estimated Parameters", *Annals of Operations Research* 45, pp. 21–58.

Chopra, V., C. Hensel and A. Turner, 1993, "Massaging Mean Variance Inputs: Returns from Alternative Global Investment Strategies, in the 1980's", *Management Science* 39, pp. 845–55.

Chopra, V., and W. Ziemba, 1993, "The Effects of Errors in Means, Variances and Covariances on Optimal Portfolio Choice", *Journal of Portfolio Management*, Winter, pp. 6–11.

Grauer, R., and F. Shen, 2000, "Do Constraints Improve Portfolio Performance?", *Journal of Banking and Finance* 24, pp. 1253–74.

Green, W., 2000, *Econometric Analysis*, Fourth Edition (New Jersey: Prentice-Hall).

Grinold, R., and K. Easton, 1998, "Attribution of Performance and Holdings", in W. Ziemba and J. Mulvey, *Worldwide Asset and Liability Management* (Cambridge University Press).

Huang, C.-F., and R. Litzenberger, 1998, *Foundations for Financial Economics* (New York: Prentice-Hall).

Jobson, J., and B. Korkie, 1983, "Statistical Inference in Two Parameter Portfolio Theory with Multiple Regression Software", *Journal of Financial and Quantitative Analysis* 18, pp. 189–97.

Jorion, P., 1992, "Portfolio Optimization in Practice", *Financial Analysts Journal* 48, pp. 68–74.

Maddala, G., 2001, *Econometrics*, Third Edition (New York: John Wiley & Sons).

Markowitz, H., 1991, *Portfolio Selection: Efficient Diversification of Investments*, Second Edition (New York: Blackwell).

Michaud, R., 1989, "The Markowitz Optimization Enigma: Is Optimized Optimal?", *Financial Analysts Journal* 45, pp. 31–42.

Michaud, R., 1998, *Efficient Asset Management: A Practical Guide to Stock Portfolio Optimization and Asset Allocation* (Oxford University Press).

Mills, T., 1999, *The Econometric Modelling of Financial Time Series*, Second Edition (Cambridge University Press).

Nawrocki, D., 1996, "Portfolio Analysis with a Large Universe of Assets", *Applied Economics* 28, pp. 1191–8.

Neftci, S., 2000, *An Introduction to the Mathematics of Financial Derivatives*, Second Edition (San Diego: Academic Press).

Scherer, B., 2002, "Portfolio Resampling: Review and Critique", *Financial Analysts Journal*, Forthcoming.

Sharpe, W., 1970, *Portfolio Theory and Capital Markets* (New York: McGraw-Hill).

4

Bayesian Analysis and Portfolio Choice

4.1 AN INTRODUCTION TO BAYESIAN ANALYSIS
4.1.1 Theoretical foundations

We have seen in the previous chapter that confining ourselves solely to the information available within a sample will not allow us to tackle the effect of parameter uncertainty on optimal portfolio choice. Not only do we need non-sample information (eg, additional data) to overcome this problem, but it would also be irrational of us to ignore other information based on the experience or insights – also called *priors* or *preknowledge* – of investors, statisticians and financial economists. The optimal combination of sample and non-sample information is found in Bayesian statistics. As Nobel laureate Harry Markowitz put it, "the rational investor is a Bayesian".[1]

To appreciate the implications of Bayesian statistics for portfolio choice we first need to understand the main differences between the Bayesian approach to statistics and the traditional, or "frequentist", approach. The traditional approach creates point estimates for distributional parameters. Estimates are either significant and believed to be 100% true, or insignificant and not believed at all, depending on the researcher's requirement with respect to significance.[2] For example, we either set the risk premium of currencies to zero (as we have found, statistically it has been insignificantly different from zero, but not zero itself), or we set it to a particular sample estimate that has been significantly different from zero, albeit by a narrow margin. The frequentist approach often uses maximum-likelihood methods to produce point estimates, where maximising the likelihood function maximises the probability that the data have been generated from a distribution with the estimated parameters. Instead of a point estimate, Bayesian analysis produces a density function (*posterior density*) for the parameters involved, given the observed data. It does so by combining sample information (*likelihood functions*) with prior beliefs. Priors can be interpreted as the odds a researcher would be willing to accept if forced to bet on the true parameters before investigating the data. Hence, the subjective notion of probability (degree of belief) used by Bayesians is opposite to the objective notion of probability employed by frequentists (how many counts would be achieved by repeated sampling).

Suppose we have a history of risk premia (simple returns minus cash) for a single time series of a particular asset, and that this history is summarised in a return vector $\mathbf{r} = (r_1\ r_2\ r_3 \dots r_T)'$, where $r_i = R_i - c_i$. Suppose also that we are interested in estimates of mean and variance summarised in a parameter vector $\mathbf{\theta} = (\mu\sigma^2)'$. Then the probability of obtaining the data (the return series) and the parameters can be written either as $p(\mathbf{r}, \mathbf{\theta}) = p(\mathbf{r}|\mathbf{\theta})p(\mathbf{\theta})$ or, alternatively, as $p(\mathbf{r}, \mathbf{\theta}) = p(\mathbf{\theta}|\mathbf{r})p(\mathbf{r})$.[3] Equating both expressions we get Bayes' theorem:

$$\underbrace{p\left(\mathbf{\theta}|\mathbf{r}\right)}_{\substack{\text{Posterior} \\ \text{density}}} = \frac{\overbrace{p\left(\mathbf{r}|\mathbf{\theta}\right)}^{\substack{\text{Likelihood} \\ \text{function}}}\ \overbrace{p\left(\mathbf{\theta}\right)}^{\text{Prior}}}{p\left(\mathbf{r}\right)} \qquad (4.1)$$

The posterior distribution $p(\mathbf{\theta}|\mathbf{r})$ of the parameters describes our information about $\mathbf{\theta}$ after we have observed the data, given our preknowledge before observing the sample information. Information in the data is captured via the likelihood function $p(\mathbf{r}|\mathbf{\theta})$, which is the estimated probability of observing the data if the true parameter was $\mathbf{\theta}$. Prior information is captured in $p(\mathbf{\theta})$, which gives us the odds that a risk-neutral investor would place on a bet about the value of $\mathbf{\theta}$. Equation (4.1) is often written in a slightly different form:

$$p\left(\mathbf{\theta}|\mathbf{r}\right) \propto p\left(\mathbf{r}|\mathbf{\theta}\right)p\left(\mathbf{\theta}\right) \qquad (4.2)$$

where $\propto$ means proportional to. The reason both statements are equivalent is that $p(\mathbf{r})$ does not depend on $\mathbf{\theta}$ and, with the data already known, it can just be thought of as a normalising factor to guarantee that the area under the posterior density integrates to one.

Equation (4.2) represents the core of Bayesian statistics. It is applied to a formulated prior distribution and the resulting expression is manipulated to find the posterior density. This is a technically complex procedure (albeit slightly less so than it might otherwise be because it is not necessary to employ maximisation techniques as in maximum-likelihood estimation) and certainly beyond the scope and intention of this book, but a simple "how to do it" example is given in the next section.

In most asset allocation problems, however, we are interested in the *predictive distribution* (the distribution of as yet unknown future returns) for the return series as this distribution directly defines an investor's utility.[4] The predictive distribution can be written as

$$p\left(\tilde{\mathbf{r}}|\mathbf{r}\right) = \int p\left(\tilde{\mathbf{r}}|\mathbf{\theta}\right)p\left(\mathbf{\theta}|\mathbf{r}\right)\mathrm{d}\mathbf{\theta} \qquad (4.3)$$

where $\tilde{\mathbf{r}}$ denotes the data not known at this time. The distribution is conditioned only by the observed data, **r**, and not by any fixed realisation of $\boldsymbol{\theta}$. This expression looks daunting, but we can give it a simple simulation interpretation since the integral on the right-hand side can be evaluated using Monte Carlo integration.[5] First we draw n times from the posterior distribution $p(\boldsymbol{\theta}|\mathbf{r})$ to get n parameter vectors ($\boldsymbol{\theta}_1$ to $\boldsymbol{\theta}_n$), and then we draw from the return distribution for each parameter vector – ie, we draw from $p(\tilde{\mathbf{r}}|\boldsymbol{\theta}_1)$ to $p(\tilde{\mathbf{r}}|\boldsymbol{\theta}_n)$ to get $p(\tilde{\mathbf{r}}|\mathbf{r})$, where $\tilde{\mathbf{r}} = (\tilde{r}_1 \, \tilde{r}_2 \, \tilde{r}_3 \, \ldots \, \tilde{r}_n)'$.

4.1.1 Application exercise

A simple example will illustrate the procedure.[6] Suppose that we have a single time series of risk premia that are assumed to come from a standard Brownian motion model of asset prices. The risk premia are normally distributed with an estimated mean, $\hat{\mu}$, of 0.3% per month and an estimated monthly standard deviation, $\hat{\sigma}$, of 6%. These estimates have been arrived at using 60 monthly observations. Suppose further that we have no prior information about the mean and variance of this series apart from what is called an "uninformed" or "uninformative" prior of the form $p(\boldsymbol{\theta}) = \sigma^{-2}$, which expresses our uncertainty about the estimates we have obtained. We want to study the effect of a lengthening time horizon in the presence of estimation error – that is, what effect estimation error has on the predictive distribution if an investor's time horizon increases.

It has been shown by Zellner (1971) that, given our assumptions, the solution to Equation (4.2), ie, the posterior density, is given by

$$p\left(\sigma^2 \,|\, \mathbf{r}\right) \sim \text{Inverse gamma} \left(\frac{T-1}{2}, \frac{1}{2}\left(\mathbf{r} - \frac{\mathbf{r}\mathbf{1}}{T}\right)'\left(\mathbf{r} - \frac{\mathbf{r}\mathbf{1}}{T}\right) \right) \qquad (4.4)$$

$$p\left(\mu \,|\, \mathbf{r}, \sigma^2\right) \sim N\left(\frac{\mathbf{r}\mathbf{1}}{T}, \frac{\sigma^2}{T} \right) \qquad (4.5)$$

We can now evaluate Equation (4.3) using a two-step procedure.

Step 1 First we draw from the posterior distribution of our parameters. To do this we first sample from Equation (4.4) 1,000,000 times. We then input these 1,000,000 values of σ^2 to generate 1,000,000 values for μ. It is evident that the uninformative prior does not change the expected mean as values in Equation (4.5) are drawn from a normal distribution with a mean equal to the sample mean. This is a general feature of non-informative priors – they just add uncertainty about the range of mean returns, not about the average itself.

Step 2 Next we sample from our model of stock returns (a normal distribution conditional on a particular fixed parameter vector) for each pair of inputs σ^2 and μ, ie, we sample from $\tilde{r}_i \sim N(\mu_i, \sigma_i^2)$.

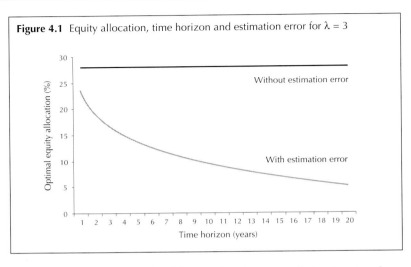

Figure 4.1 Equity allocation, time horizon and estimation error for $\lambda = 3$

This is repeated for different time horizons, T, by drawing from $\tilde{r}_{iT} \sim N(\mu_i T, \sigma_i^2 T)$. For each time horizon we are now able to calculate the mean and volatility of returns. We can then calculate the optimal equity allocation, as a function of time horizon, for a given risk tolerance, λ, using

$$w^*_{\text{Equity}} = \mu \lambda^{-1} \sigma^{-2} = 0.003 \frac{1}{3} \frac{1}{0.06^2} = 27.7\%$$

The results for a risk tolerance of three are plotted in Figure 4.1. As the figure shows, in our simple model setting the presence of estimation error creates obvious negative time horizon effects. These are the result of an uncertainty about the mean return that adds increasingly to the total variation of returns as the horizon lengthens. After as little as one year there is already a substantial drop in the optimal equity allocation. (Appendix B extends this analysis by introducing forecastability.) In contrast, as shown by the upper curve in Figure 4.1, in the absence of estimation error we would get the usual result that there is no link between time horizon and the appropriate equity allocation.[7]

As we have already mentioned, prior distributions describe an investor's view before he sees the data. This ensures the independence used in Equation (4.2). We can distinguish between *uninformative* priors and *informative* priors. Uninformed priors add no additional information to the data – they just express the possible range of parameter estimates. Therefore, adding an uninformative prior to our return data increases the uncertainty about future returns but not the average outcome. Informed priors *do* change the average expected outcome; an informed prior stating that all average returns are equal would lead us to the minimum-variance port-

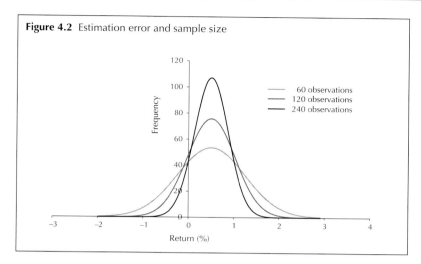

Figure 4.2 Estimation error and sample size

folio, while an informed prior whose average returns were close to the return equilibrium would move us in the direction of the market portfolio.

Bayesian analysis is different from resampling (which was discussed in Chapter 3). Resampling draws repeatedly from the data without adding any new source of information to the historical data. The true distribution is still unknown (as we do not know the true parameters) and, as mentioned in Chapter 3, all resampled portfolios inherit the same estimation error relative to the true distribution.

4.2 THE SIMPLEST CASE

So far, we have identified estimation error as a serious problem, we have visualised the effect of uncertainty in the input on the distribution of optimal weight estimates, and we have ascertained that the addition of non-sample information is the only way to arrive at more realistic allocations. In this section we will illustrate Bayesian methods by looking at the simplest case of a single return series for which we want to estimate the mean return, assuming its variance is known in advance. This assumption is well justified by the small sampling error on variance estimates.

Suppose we have a time series of risk premia $\mathbf{r} = (r_1 \ r_2 \ r_3 \ldots r_T)'$, for which the estimation error on the average return will depend on the number of observations available. We will estimate an average return of 0.5% per month with a monthly volatility of 5.77% (20% per annum). The same estimate carries stronger information if it is obtained using a larger sample – ie, there is less uncertainty about the average return. This relationship is plotted in Figure 4.2, from which it can be seen that, as the number of data points rises, $p(\mathbf{r}|\boldsymbol{\theta})$ becomes more "peaky" and the distribution concentrates more and more over the estimated value.[8] As the sample size approaches infinity the interval degenerates to a single point above the mean value.

How, technically, would we get the posterior distribution? We know from Equation (4.2) that $p(\mu \mid r) \propto p(r \mid \mu)p(\mu)$. Let us assume that our data points in r are independent draws from a normal distribution and that the conjugate prior is the exponential of a quadratic form $p(\mu) = \exp(a\mu^2 + b\mu + c)$ parameterised as[9]

$$p(\mu) \propto \exp\left(-\frac{1}{2\varphi^2}\left(\mu - \mu_{prior}\right)^2\right)$$

Hence we can describe $p(\mu)$ with $\mu \sim N\left(\mu_{prior}, \varphi^2\right)$. The likelihood function of T points drawn from a normal distribution with known variance is given by multiplying the likelihoods for each individual data point.[10] Equation (4.2) then becomes

$$p(\mu \mid r) \propto p(\mu) \prod_{i=1}^{T} p\left(r_i \mid \mu\right)$$

$$\propto \exp\left(-\frac{1}{2\varphi^2}\left(\mu - \mu_{prior}\right)^2\right) \prod_{i=1}^{T} \exp\left(-\frac{1}{2\sigma^2}\left(r_i - \mu\right)^2\right)$$

$$\propto \exp\left\{-\frac{1}{2}\left(\frac{\left(\mu - \mu_{prior}\right)^2}{\varphi^2} + \frac{\sum_{i=1}^{T}\left(r_i - \mu\right)^2}{\sigma^2}\right)\right\} \qquad (4.6)$$

The solution to this expression is given below (a derivation is given in Appendix A). The predictive mean comes from a normal distribution

$$\mu \sim N\left(\mu_{predictive}, \; \varphi_T^2\right)$$

with parameters

$$\mu_{predictive} = \left(\frac{1}{\varphi_T^2}\mu_{prior} + \frac{T}{\sigma^2}\hat{\mu}\right)\left(\frac{1}{\varphi_T^2} + \frac{T}{\sigma^2}\right)^{-1}$$

$$\frac{1}{\varphi_T^2} = \frac{1}{\left(\dfrac{1}{\varphi^2} + \dfrac{T}{\sigma^2}\right)} \qquad (4.7)$$

The predictive mean, $\mu_{predictive}$, is a weighted average of the prior mean, μ_{prior}, and the historical mean, μ. The weights given to both sources of

Figure 4.3 Effect of additional information

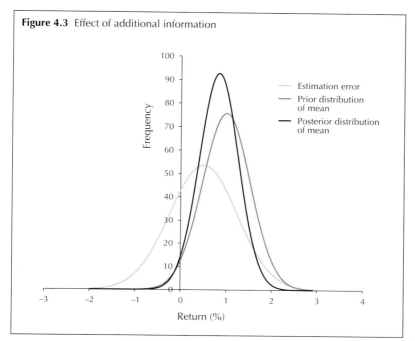

Return (%)

$$Precison = \frac{1}{\sigma^2}$$

information will depend on the precision of the respective information. Precision is defined as one divided by variance. The less volatile the information, the greater its precision. As more data become available the prior information becomes increasingly irrelevant and the predictive mean approaches the historical mean. The general form of Equation (4.7) can be found throughout this chapter.

Figure 4.3 illustrates the effect of adding a second source of information when it is assumed that the prior is twice as precise as the sample estimate. When prior information is added to the data our combined estimate is more precise than either source, as can be seen from a narrower, more peaked, distribution.

We can also give a sample interpretation to Figure 4.3.[11] Suppose we have two independent samples of information and that the sample sizes differ, the second source of information containing twice as many data. If we take the grand mean (the sample mean of the combined data set) and estimate its estimation error, we arrive at the same peaked distribution for the posterior mean as in Figure 4.3.

The findings above can be summarised as follows:

❏ For short time series (new asset classes, initial public offerings (IPOs), new managers, etc), prior information will dominate. The longer the time series, the less important the prior will be.

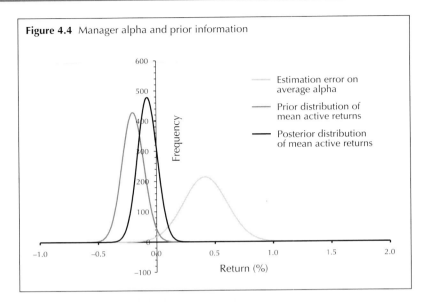

Figure 4.4 Manager alpha and prior information

❏ Volatile asset classes exhibit large estimation errors and are therefore more amenable to the application of prior information.

❏ High uncertainty about the information content of a prior will result in little weight being given to this extra information.

We will finish this section with a practical application example.[12] Suppose we have historical information on an individual manager. We are confident about our risk forecast of a 5% annual tracking error, which is based on 60 monthly observations. The average annual alpha is also 5%. Additionally, we already know, from a host of empirical studies,[13] that as a direct consequence of transaction costs the average alpha in the asset management industry is likely to be negative.[14] Suppose we put a confidence in our prior assumption of −2.4% alpha per annum (equivalent to saying we are as confident as if this had been based on a sample of 240 data points), how would we view the alpha-generating capabilities of this particular manager after we combined historical data and our prior view? Substituting the inputs into Equation (4.7) and plotting the distributions yields the results presented in Figure 4.4.

Figure 4.4 shows that, in our example, prior information leads to a serious reduction in alpha expectations as the information carries little uncertainty. The posterior distribution tries to compromise between prior information and data information by finding a distribution that agrees as much as possible with both information sources. A reduced alpha forecast will obviously affect the decision whether to adopt active or passive management, as will be seen in Chapter 7.

4.3 GENERAL MULTIVARIATE CASE

So far, we have introduced some basic Bayesian principles. Now we will outline a general approach that allows investors to express priors on means and variances and investigate their application to portfolio selection problems.[15] This section deals with *statistical* priors as we assume that informative priors are derived without reference to an economic equilibrium model. Priors derived from economic models are dealt with in the next section.

Suppose we have k assets, for each of which there are T observations. Returns are assumed to follow a multivariate normal distribution with mean vector $\boldsymbol{\mu}$ and covariance matrix $\boldsymbol{\Omega}$. However, their true values are unknown and we only observe their sample equivalents, ie, $\mathbf{r} \sim N(\hat{\boldsymbol{\mu}}, \hat{\boldsymbol{\Omega}})$. First we will allow priors on mean returns, assuming that the mean returns are multivariate normal as formulated below:

$$\boldsymbol{\mu} \sim N\left(\boldsymbol{\mu}_{\text{prior}}, \boldsymbol{\Psi}_{\text{prior}}\right) \tag{4.8}$$

The covariance matrix $\boldsymbol{\Psi}_{\text{prior}}$ reflects our priors on the covariation of average returns, not on the covariation of asset returns. If we think, for example, that two markets should have very similar average returns (say, the Dutch and the German bond markets), we can reflect this through $\boldsymbol{\Psi}_{\text{prior}}$. We will also allow priors on the covariance of returns. The uncertainty about the true covariance matrix is modelled as an inverse Wishart distribution with v degrees of freedom:[17]

$$\boldsymbol{\Omega} \sim W^{-1}\left(v, \boldsymbol{\Omega}_{\text{prior}}\right) \tag{4.9}$$

The parameter v reflects the uncertainty about our prior information on $\boldsymbol{\Omega}$, expressed via $\boldsymbol{\Omega}_{\text{prior}}$. It expresses the number of draws from $\boldsymbol{\Omega}$ that we would use to calculate the covariance matrix $\boldsymbol{\Omega}_{\text{prior}}$ if we gave our priors a sample interpretation. Setting v equal to T means that our prior information is as reliable as the historical estimate $\hat{\boldsymbol{\Omega}}$.

The predictive distribution of asset returns has both a mean vector and a covariance matrix, which can be expressed as[18]

$$\boldsymbol{\mu}_{\text{predictive}} = \left(\boldsymbol{\Psi}_{\text{prior}}^{-1} + \hat{\boldsymbol{\Omega}}^{-1}T\right)^{-1}\left(\boldsymbol{\Psi}_{\text{prior}}^{-1}\boldsymbol{\mu}_{\text{prior}} + \hat{\boldsymbol{\Omega}}^{-1}T\hat{\boldsymbol{\mu}}\right) \tag{4.10}$$

$$\boldsymbol{\Omega}_{\text{predictive}} = \underbrace{\frac{T+1+v}{T+v-k-2}}_{\substack{\text{Leverage to}\\\text{reflect}\\\text{estimation}\\\text{error}}}\left(\underbrace{\frac{v}{v+T}}_{\substack{\text{Prior}\\\text{weight}}}\boldsymbol{\Omega}_{\text{prior}} + \underbrace{\frac{T}{v+T}}_{\substack{\text{Sample}\\\text{weight}}}\hat{\boldsymbol{\Omega}}\right) \tag{4.11}$$

Predictive means and covariances are linear mixtures of prior and historical (sample estimate) information. Both components are weighted according to their precision.[19] In the case of equal precision, where v equals T or Ψ_{prior}^{-1} equals $\hat{\Omega}^{-1}T$, we arrive at equal weightings. The term for the predictive variance also includes $(T + v - k - 2)^{-1}(T + v + 1)$, which adjusts for pure estimation risk. Additional information ($v > 0$) reduces estimation risk, whereas a larger number of assets increases estimation risk. Estimation risk enters the formula as a leverage factor on the covariance matrix. Risk is increasing as there is now uncertainty attached to point estimates, which have previously been treated as being known without uncertainty. Fewer data mean higher covariance leverage. Uncertainty also rises with the number of assets as there is a greater likelihood that one asset will show an unusual estimate.

The framework outlined above allows us to accommodate different sets of priors. If we put ourselves in the position of having no prior opinion about the parameters (a general non-informative case, also called Jeffreys' prior), we set v equal to zero (where we have no information about covariance) and make Ψ_{prior} infinite, ie, there is a large uncertainty about the range of forecasts.[20] Equations (4.10) and (4.11) then become

$$\mu_{predictive} = \hat{\mu}, \quad \Omega_{predictive} = \frac{T+1}{T-k-2}\hat{\Omega} \qquad (4.12)$$

This confirms that if returns are multivariate normal and we assume a diffuse prior, our estimates for the mean vector remain unchanged.[21] This is intuitive as uncertainty about the expected value shows up in the difference between mean and realisation. There is, however, no uncertainty about an expected value. The variation of returns increases by a constant factor so that the new variance–covariance matrix is just leveraged up (see Equation 4.12).[22] Estimation error affects all assets in the same, proportional, way, with the scaling factor depending on sample size – small sample sizes result in greater uncertainty and, hence, larger scalings.[23] However, instead of being multivariate normal, the predictive distribution of asset returns with estimation error follows a multivariate t-distribution. The admissibility of mean–variance analysis now depends critically on the assumption of quadratic utility. If investors show quadratic utility, the scaling of the covariance matrix can be interpreted as a scaling in risk-aversion. In this case, estimation error will result in a higher pseudo-risk-aversion, and this in turn has five consequences:

❑ For each return requirement the optimal portfolio will show higher risk due to the scaling.
❑ The composition of portfolios along the efficient frontiers will stay the same because for any original risk-aversion there exists an equal rescaled risk-aversion.

❑ Investors are likely to find different portfolios as the risk–return trade-off changes, ie, flattens.
❑ If the utility function is not quadratic, the mean–variance representation of the problem holds only approximately; alternative models might be better suited to deal with this.[24]
❑ The inclusion of cash will leave the composition of the maximum Sharpe ratio portfolio unchanged. Investors will react to estimation risk with an increase in cash, which is the only asset free of investment risk and estimation risk. They will not change the composition of the minimum-variance portfolio as estimation risk affects all assets in the same way.

Rational investors will use the predictive distribution (including estimation risk and prior information) to calculate their expected utility. However, as purely non-informative priors do not change the set of efficient portfolios, such priors have been widely ignored. Instead, there has been more interest in informative priors.

How should we implement the view on volatility separately from prior information on correlations? As the covariance matrix uses correlations and volatilities simultaneously, we have to split the covariance matrix into a symmetric correlation matrix and a diagonal volatility matrix:

$$\Omega_{prior} = \underbrace{\begin{pmatrix} \sigma_1 & 0 & \cdots & 0 \\ 0 & \sigma_2 & \cdots & 0 \\ \vdots & \vdots & \ddots & \vdots \\ 0 & 0 & \cdots & \sigma_k \end{pmatrix}}_{\sigma_{prior}} \underbrace{\begin{pmatrix} 1 & \hat{\rho}_{12} & \cdots & \hat{\rho}_{1k} \\ \hat{\rho}_{21} & 1 & \cdots & \hat{\rho}_{2k} \\ \vdots & \vdots & \ddots & \vdots \\ \hat{\rho}_{k1} & \hat{\rho}_{k2} & \cdots & 1 \end{pmatrix}}_{\hat{\rho}} \underbrace{\begin{pmatrix} \sigma_1 & 0 & \cdots & 0 \\ 0 & \sigma_2 & \cdots & 0 \\ \vdots & \vdots & \ddots & \vdots \\ 0 & 0 & \cdots & \sigma_k \end{pmatrix}}_{\sigma_{prior}}$$

This allows us to input priors on volatilities but leave correlations unchanged. As more and more data become available, the prior becomes less important and we approach the sample estimates

$$\left(\mu_{predictive} \xrightarrow[T \to \infty]{} \hat{\mu} ; \ \Omega_{predictive} \xrightarrow[T \to \infty]{} \hat{\Omega} \right)$$

– a basic feature of Bayesian methods. However, this is not the case with the Black–Litterman (B–L) model, which is reviewed in the next section.

4.4 SPECIAL CASE: BLACK–LITTERMAN
4.4.1 General outline
The previous section presented a general framework for combining historical sample information with additional non-sample information. However, the problem remains that if we do not have an informative prior, we cannot arrive at an unambiguous and economically meaningful default allocation.[25] In this case it would be prudent to hold the market

portfolio (combined with cash to adjust for varying risk appetites) rather than an optimal portfolio based on historical averages. How can we anchor our predictive distribution to a portfolio that is well known to investors and already serves as a passive alternative – ie, the market portfolio?

Again, we use two independent sets of information to generate the predictive distribution.[26] Let us begin with the anchor: instead of assuming that returns come from a historical distribution $r \sim N(\hat{\mu}, \hat{\Omega})$, it is assumed that returns come from

$$r \sim N(\boldsymbol{\pi}, \tau\hat{\Omega}) \qquad (4.13)$$

where $\boldsymbol{\pi}$ denotes the equilibrium returns (those returns that would give the market portfolio if used in an optimisation) and τ reflects the level of belief in the equilibrium returns. The smaller τ is, the more weight is given to the equilibrium returns (historical uncertainty is scaled down). Investors' priors provide the second source of information about mean returns. It is assumed that the investor has some knowledge about the distribution of returns that allows him to forecast them according to

$$\boldsymbol{\mu}_{\text{prior}} = \mathbf{r} + \boldsymbol{\varepsilon}, \boldsymbol{\varepsilon} \sim N(\mathbf{0}, \boldsymbol{\Gamma}) \qquad (4.14)$$

where $\boldsymbol{\Gamma}$ is the variance–covariance of forecast errors. Prior views are regarded as unbiased estimators of future returns, whereas forecasting errors are seen as pure noise. The elements of $\boldsymbol{\Gamma}$ can be easily determined if we already use a quantitative forecasting model. In that case, we can scale down the elements on the main diagonal by using the explained variance available from the respective forecasting models:

$$\boldsymbol{\Gamma} = \begin{pmatrix} \sigma_1^2(1-R_1^2) & 0 & 0 \\ 0 & \ddots & 0 \\ 0 & 0 & \sigma_k^2(1-R_k^2) \end{pmatrix} \qquad (4.15)$$

In Equation (4.15) we implicitly assume that we forecast "true" alpha because only asset-specific risk (idiosyncratic risk) will show, by definition, zero correlation across assets. If we were to forecast total returns (or risk premia), we would very likely find forecast errors to be positively correlated. However, keeping in mind that $IC = \sqrt{R^2}$, we can use the information coefficient (IC) – the correlation between a forecast return and the return actually realised – to link forecasting skills to the covariance matrix of forecasting errors. High skills (high IC) shrink the diagonal terms in $\boldsymbol{\Gamma}$ and thus give more weight to high-skill forecasts.

Alternatively, we can use a more judgmental approach, transforming typical qualitative forecasts into a quantitative view. For example, an investor who is 90% sure that the return on the US market will be between 5% and 15% in fact believes the average return to be about 10% with a volatility of about 3.33% (assuming normality); we can say this because we know that 90% of all data lie within three standard deviations ($10\% \pm 1.5 \times 3.33\%$).

Analogous to Equations (4.7) and (4.10), the mean predictive return (refined forecast) can be calculated as a matrix-weighted average of two information sources:[27]

$$\boldsymbol{\mu}_{\text{predictive}} = \left(\boldsymbol{\Gamma}^{-1} + \tau^{-1}\hat{\boldsymbol{\Omega}}^{-1} \right)^{-1} \left(\boldsymbol{\Gamma}^{-1}\boldsymbol{\mu}_{\text{prior}} + \tau^{-1}\hat{\boldsymbol{\Omega}}^{-1}\boldsymbol{\pi} \right) \qquad (4.16)$$

where again $\tau^{-1}\hat{\boldsymbol{\Omega}}^{-1}$ measures the precision (confidence) in the forecasts of equilibrium returns. The parameter τ plays a similar role to T in Equation (4.10), and $\boldsymbol{\Gamma}^{-1}$ measures the precision of our prior views. Although a slightly different interpretation is given to the matrices involved, Equations (4.10) and (4.16) have the same solution.

4.4.2 A three-asset example

A simple three-asset example can be used to provide further insight into the mechanics. Suppose we have three highly correlated markets, each with a correlation of 0.9 to the others, an allocation of one-third and a volatility of 20%. We would expect a portfolio like this to generate 4% excess returns (hence the implied returns must be 4% each as the three assets do not differ in terms of risk characteristics). We are positive about asset one (+5%) and negative about assets two and three (both −1%). We also assume that our forecast errors are independent (though this is not always realistic if forecasts are derived from a common macroeconomic scenario). Assuming our forecasts are 6% for each asset and that forecast errors are the same size as asset volatilities, we get

$$
\frac{\begin{pmatrix} 400 & 0 & 0 \\ 0 & 400 & 0 \\ 0 & 0 & 400 \end{pmatrix}^{-1}}{\begin{pmatrix} 400 & 0 & 0 \\ 0 & 400 & 0 \\ 0 & 0 & 400 \end{pmatrix}^{-1} + \tau^{-1}\begin{pmatrix} 400 & 360 & 360 \\ 360 & 400 & 360 \\ 360 & 360 & 400 \end{pmatrix}^{-1}} \begin{pmatrix} 5 \\ -1 \\ -1 \end{pmatrix}
$$

$$
+ \frac{\tau^{-1}\begin{pmatrix} 400 & 360 & 360 \\ 360 & 400 & 360 \\ 360 & 360 & 400 \end{pmatrix}^{-1}}{\begin{pmatrix} 400 & 0 & 0 \\ 0 & 400 & 0 \\ 0 & 0 & 400 \end{pmatrix}^{-1} + \tau^{-1}\begin{pmatrix} 400 & 360 & 360 \\ 360 & 400 & 360 \\ 360 & 360 & 400 \end{pmatrix}^{-1}} \begin{pmatrix} 4 \\ 4 \\ 4 \end{pmatrix} = \begin{pmatrix} 2.15 \\ 1.61 \\ 1.61 \end{pmatrix}
$$

Although the range of forecasts is high, this is not reflected in the predictive means. Forecasts are automatically compressed to reflect the high correlation between assets. Hence, return estimates come more into line with the covariance matrix of asset returns, which will allow more realistic asset allocations.

Suppose instead that we have little confidence in our forecast, ie, that we make the diagonal terms in the matrix of forecast errors large:

$$
\left(
\frac{
\begin{pmatrix} 10,000 & 0 & 0 \\ 0 & 10,000 & 0 \\ 0 & 0 & 10,000 \end{pmatrix}^{-1}
}{
\begin{pmatrix} 10,000 & 0 & 0 \\ 0 & 10,000 & 0 \\ 0 & 0 & 10,000 \end{pmatrix}^{-1} + \tau^{-1} \begin{pmatrix} 400 & 360 & 360 \\ 360 & 400 & 360 \\ 360 & 360 & 400 \end{pmatrix}^{-1}
}
\right)
\begin{pmatrix} 5 \\ -1 \\ -1 \end{pmatrix}
$$

$$
+ \left(
\frac{
\tau^{-1} \begin{pmatrix} 400 & 360 & 360 \\ 360 & 400 & 360 \\ 360 & 360 & 400 \end{pmatrix}^{-1}
}{
\begin{pmatrix} 10,000 & 0 & 0 \\ 0 & 10,000 & 0 \\ 0 & 0 & 10,000 \end{pmatrix}^{-1} + \tau^{-1} \begin{pmatrix} 400 & 360 & 360 \\ 360 & 400 & 360 \\ 360 & 360 & 400 \end{pmatrix}^{-1}
}
\right)
\begin{pmatrix} 4 \\ 4 \\ 4 \end{pmatrix}
=
\begin{pmatrix} 3.71 \\ 3.69 \\ 3.69 \end{pmatrix}
$$

In this case we find the refined forecasts to be very close to the equilibrium forecast, with effectively all their variation removed.

4.4.3 Effect of varying τ

Finally, we can look at the effect of variations in τ, the parameter that reflects the level of belief in the equilibrium returns. Suppose we forecast returns of 5% for asset one, 2% for asset two and −1% for asset three. Forecast errors are assumed to be uncorrelated and equal in size to asset volatility (20%).

Remember that if τ becomes smaller, this is equivalent to saying that our confidence in the equilibrium returns has increased as a reduced τ will scale down the covariance matrix of historical returns. In addition, as $\tau^{-1} \hat{\Omega}^{-1}$ becomes larger, the weight attached to the equilibrium returns and $\left(\Gamma^{-1} + \tau^{-1} \hat{\Omega}^{-1} \right)^{-1} \left(\tau^{-1} \hat{\Omega}^{-1} \right)$ also increases, approaching one. This effect is captured in Figure 4.5 for the 5%, 2% and −1% forecasts. As τ approaches zero, we arrive at the equilibrium forecasts of 4%. However, if our uncertainty about the equilibrium returns increases (ie, as τ approaches one), the spread between the three forecasts will rise once again. Reduced uncertainty about the historical data will not lead back to the sample data but back to the equilibrium returns. This is a crucial difference from the general multivariate case considered in Section 4.3.

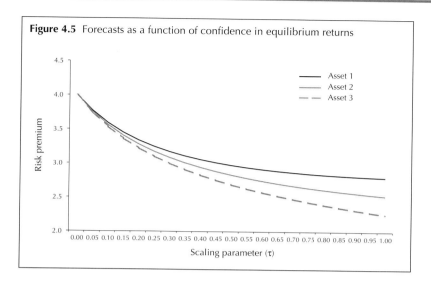

Figure 4.5 Forecasts as a function of confidence in equilibrium returns

4.4.4 Summary

The Black–Litterman model has proved popular with investors as it allowed them for the first time to separate forecast ("where will the market go?") from conviction ("how confident am I that my forecast is true?").[28] Additionally, it anchors the solution into the well-known market portfolio and creates consistency between raw forecasts and sample covariance matrices.

However, the B–L method will not use all the information available in historical means. It could well be argued that the model presented in this section puts an implicit prior (zero alpha with no uncertainty) on the capital asset pricing model (CAPM) as the true equilibrium model,[29] though this is not necessarily everybody's conviction.[30] Moreover, the model does not directly address parameter uncertainty, making Equation (4.10) a more complete model of reality as it incorporates the B–L model as a special case. Also, we have not yet dealt with problems arising from messy data. For example, how do we optimally combine time series with different starting and ending periods? The next section addresses this problem.

4.5 TIME SERIES OF DIFFERENT LENGTHS

Asset allocation and portfolio construction exercises are based on the use of historical data. Typically, however, the availability of these data differs across asset classes:[31] return series for developed equity markets reach back to the early 1970s (MSCI data); data on government bonds (Salomon Brothers data) and emerging market equities (IFC data) date back to the mid-1980s; data on emerging market debt reach back to the early 1990s

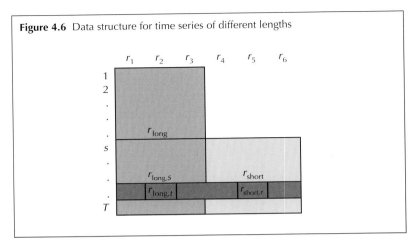

Figure 4.6 Data structure for time series of different lengths

(JPM data); and data on corporate debt only go back to the mid-1990s (Merrill Lynch data).[32] Asset allocators attempting to deal with combinations of these asset classes face the problem of how to handle return series of differing lengths. Should they estimate means and volatilities separately (using the maximum number of observations for each series) and calculate correlations on the overlapping data set? Or should they truncate the longer series to the length of the shortest so that a rectangular data matrix can be generated? How can we apply Bayesian analysis dealing with estimation risk to return series of different lengths? This section looks at these issues in detail.[33]

Suppose we have a non-rectangular data matrix of risk premia (one with time series of differing lengths) like that in Figure 4.6. We see three long series (T observations reaching from time 1 to T) and three short series (S observations, where $S = T - s + 1$ observations reaching from s to T). Long and short series are combined in $T \times 3$ and $S \times 3$ data matrices called $\mathbf{r}_{long}$ and $\mathbf{r}_{short}$. It is assumed that the overlapping S data points come from a joint multivariate normal distribution (indicated by S). Hence, $\mathbf{r}_{long, S}$ ($S \times 3$ data matrix) denotes the overlapping part of $\mathbf{r}_{long}$. An estimator that uses only the overlapping data (the rectangular data set that stretches from s to T and $\mathbf{r}_1$ to $\mathbf{r}_6$) is called a truncated estimator. These are just the normal sample estimators applied to the overlapping data set, and they can be written as follows:

$$\hat{\boldsymbol{\mu}}_{long}^{truncated} = \frac{1}{S} \mathbf{r}'_{long, s} \mathbf{1}_S$$

$$\hat{\boldsymbol{\mu}}_{short}^{truncated} = \frac{1}{S} \mathbf{r}'_{short} \mathbf{1}_S$$

$$\hat{\Omega}_{\text{long, long}}^{\text{truncated}} = \frac{1}{S}\left(\mathbf{r}_{\text{long, }S} - \hat{\boldsymbol{\mu}}_{\text{short}}^{\text{truncated}}\mathbf{1}_S\right)'\left(\mathbf{r}_{\text{long, }S} - \hat{\boldsymbol{\mu}}_{\text{short}}^{\text{truncated}}\mathbf{1}_S\right)$$

$$\vdots$$

$$\hat{\Omega}_{\text{short, short}}^{\text{truncated}} = \frac{1}{S}\left(\mathbf{r}_{\text{short, }S} - \hat{\boldsymbol{\mu}}_{\text{short}}^{\text{truncated}}\mathbf{1}_S\right)'\left(\mathbf{r}_{\text{short, }S} - \hat{\boldsymbol{\mu}}_{\text{short}}^{\text{truncated}}\mathbf{1}_S\right)$$

(4.17)

where $\mathbf{1}_S$ denotes an $S \times 1$ vector of ones. The truncated-sample estimator ignores the information available in the non-overlapping part of the longer time series.

4.5.1 Combined-sample estimate

How would a combined-sample maximum-likelihood (ML) estimator use the available information? First we have to recognise the dependencies between the long and the short series. Zero correlation between these series would imply that there is no information in the long series that could be used to estimate moments for the short series. Each of the short series is regressed against all of the three long series to capture dependencies:

$$r_{4,t} = \alpha_4 + \beta_{41}r_{1,t} + \beta_{42}r_{2,t} + \beta_{43}r_{3,t} + \varepsilon_{4,t}, \quad \forall t = s, \dots, T$$

$$r_{5,t} = \alpha_5 + \beta_{51}r_{1,t} + \beta_{52}r_{2,t} + \beta_{53}r_{3,t} + \varepsilon_{5,t}, \quad \forall t = s, \dots, T$$

$$r_{6,t} = \alpha_6 + \beta_{61}r_{1,t} + \beta_{62}r_{2,t} + \beta_{63}r_{3,t} + \varepsilon_{6,t}, \quad \forall t = s, \dots, T \quad (4.18)$$

The regression coefficients are then summarised in a matrix we will call B, all the elements of which are βs:

$$\mathbf{B}_{3\times3} = \begin{bmatrix} \hat{\beta}_{41} & \hat{\beta}_{51} & \hat{\beta}_{61} \\ \hat{\beta}_{42} & \hat{\beta}_{52} & \hat{\beta}_{62} \\ \hat{\beta}_{43} & \hat{\beta}_{53} & \hat{\beta}_{63} \end{bmatrix} \quad (4.19)$$

while the covariance of the residual terms (ie, the covariation between short series not explained by long series) is given as

$$\hat{\Omega}_{\varepsilon\varepsilon} = \begin{bmatrix} \text{cov}(\hat{\varepsilon}_4, \hat{\varepsilon}_4) & \text{cov}(\hat{\varepsilon}_4, \hat{\varepsilon}_5) & \text{cov}(\hat{\varepsilon}_4, \hat{\varepsilon}_6) \\ \text{cov}(\hat{\varepsilon}_5, \hat{\varepsilon}_4) & \text{cov}(\hat{\varepsilon}_5, \hat{\varepsilon}_5) & \text{cov}(\hat{\varepsilon}_5, \hat{\varepsilon}_6) \\ \text{cov}(\hat{\varepsilon}_6, \hat{\varepsilon}_4) & \text{cov}(\hat{\varepsilon}_6, \hat{\varepsilon}_5) & \text{cov}(\hat{\varepsilon}_6, \hat{\varepsilon}_6) \end{bmatrix} \quad (4.20)$$

These data can be used to decompose the total volatility of the short series into a part of total volatility explained by the long series (which can later be used to transform information from the long to the short series) and a part attributable only to the short series:

$$\hat{\mathbf{\Omega}}_{\text{short, short}}^{\text{truncated}} = \hat{\mathbf{\Omega}}_{\varepsilon\varepsilon}^{\text{truncated}} + \mathbf{B}\hat{\mathbf{\Omega}}_{\text{long, long}}^{\text{truncated}}\mathbf{B} \qquad (4.21)$$

$$\underbrace{\hphantom{\hat{\mathbf{\Omega}}_{\varepsilon\varepsilon}^{\text{truncated}}}}_{\substack{\text{Unexplained}\\ \text{variation}}} \qquad \underbrace{\hphantom{\mathbf{B}\hat{\mathbf{\Omega}}_{\text{long, long}}^{\text{truncated}}\mathbf{B}}}_{\substack{\text{Explained}\\ \text{variation}}}$$

The maximum-likelihood estimates for mean and variance for the long series should cause little surprise, being just the normal sample estimates applied to the complete history as these series contain the most information anyway:

$$\hat{\boldsymbol{\mu}}_{\text{long}}^{\text{ML}} = \frac{1}{T}\mathbf{r}_{\text{long}}' \, \mathbf{1}_S \qquad (4.22)$$

$$\hat{\mathbf{\Omega}}_{\text{long, long}}^{\text{ML}} = \frac{1}{T}\left(\mathbf{r}_{\text{long}} - \hat{\boldsymbol{\mu}}_{\text{long}}^{\text{ML}} \, \mathbf{1}_T\right)' \left(\mathbf{r}_{\text{long}} - \hat{\boldsymbol{\mu}}_{\text{long}}^{\text{ML}} \, \mathbf{1}_T\right) \qquad (4.23)$$

As a direct effect of using more data the sample error decreases but, as already mentioned in the previous chapter, this will only be of any help if the data are drawn from a stationary process; it is the mean and variance estimators for the shorter series that change. The maximum-likelihood estimator for the short series, $\hat{\boldsymbol{\mu}}_{\text{short}}^{\text{ML}}$, allocates the difference in the mean estimates of maximum-likelihood and truncated estimator for the long series. This difference is due to sample error as the longer-series estimate is assumed to be closer to the true mean, and it is distributed according to the respective βs.

$$\hat{\boldsymbol{\mu}}_{\text{short}}^{\text{ML}} = \hat{\boldsymbol{\mu}}_{\text{short}}^{\text{truncated}} + \hat{\mathbf{B}}\left(\hat{\boldsymbol{\mu}}_{\text{long}}^{\text{ML}} - \hat{\boldsymbol{\mu}}_{\text{long}}^{\text{truncated}}\right) \qquad (4.24)$$

If, for example, two series have a β of 0.5, only 50% of this difference is added to the truncated estimator (see example below). The same logic applies to the updated variance estimate:

$$\hat{\boldsymbol{\mu}}_{\text{short, short}}^{\text{ML}} = \hat{\mathbf{\Omega}}_{\varepsilon\varepsilon}^{\text{truncated}} + \mathbf{B}\hat{\mathbf{\Omega}}_{\text{long, long}}^{\text{ML}}\mathbf{B}' \qquad (4.25)$$

The maximum likelihood adds the explained variation in short-series movements to the unexplained variation but uses the whole data set to produce an estimate for the explained variation. Comparing Equations (4.21) and (4.25) shows this directly. This also extends to the covariance of long and short series:

$$\hat{\mathbf{\Omega}}_{\text{long, short}}^{\text{ML}} = \mathbf{B}\hat{\mathbf{\Omega}}_{\text{long, long}}^{\text{ML}} \qquad (4.26)$$

If volatility has been unusually low in the recent past (and short as well as long series show too little risk) but much higher over the longer historical record, this method will leverage up the volatility estimates according to the co-movements with the longer series. We can summarise by saying that that the use of a broader set of historical information not only improves the estimation of moments of the longer series (less sampling error), but it also changes the mean estimates for the shorter series.[34]

4.5.2 Introducing estimation error

So far we have just used sample information, but how would our estimates change if we were to use a non-informative prior? As we know from Section 4.1, the maximum-likelihood mean estimates will not change. However, in that instance we included the case of unequal time-series lengths because the maximum-likelihood estimator differs from the truncated estimator (usually used in Markowitz applications), and this difference will change the optimal allocations. The Bayesian covariance matrix will simply be a leveraged version of the maximum-likelihood estimates (compare with Section 4.5.1):

$$\hat{\Omega}^{predictive}_{long,\ long} = \frac{T+1}{T-k-2} \hat{\Omega}^{ML}_{long,\ long}$$

$$\hat{\Omega}^{predictive}_{long,\ short} = \frac{T+1}{T-k-2} \hat{\Omega}^{ML}_{long,\ short} \tag{4.27}$$

The more data are available for T, the smaller the difference between sample estimate (historical covariance) and predictive covariance. A slightly more complicated expression must be used to generate an expression for the covariance matrix of short series. However, in this expression, given below, both matrices are leveraged up again:

$$\hat{\Omega}^{predictive}_{short,\ short} = \Delta \hat{\Omega}^{truncated}_{\varepsilon\varepsilon} + \frac{T+1}{T-N-2} \mathbf{B}\hat{\Omega}^{ML}_{long,\ long}\mathbf{B}' \tag{4.28}$$

$$\Delta = \left(\frac{S}{S-k_{short}-2}\right) \times$$

$$\left(1+\frac{1}{S}\left[1+\frac{T+1}{T-k-2}\ \text{trace}\left(\hat{\Omega}^{truncated\ -1}_{long,\ long}\hat{\Omega}^{ML}_{long,\ long}\right)+\right.\right.$$

$$\left.\left.\left(\hat{\mu}^{ML}_{long}-\hat{\mu}^{truncated}_{long}\right)'\hat{\Omega}^{-1}_{long,\ long,S}\left(\hat{\mu}^{ML}_{long}-\hat{\mu}^{truncated}_{long}\right)\right]\right) \tag{4.29}$$

Table 4.1 Data for missing return series example

Quartal	European equities (%)	Latin American equities	Quartal	European equities (%)	Latin American equities (%)
Q3 93	8.21	—	Q2 97	8.44	20.7
Q4 93	9.01	—	Q3 97	7.81	4.2
Q1 94	−1.99	—	Q4 97	−0.36	−10.2
Q2 94	−1.86	—	Q1 98	19.84	0.2
Q3 94	3.71	—	Q2 98	4.75	−18.4
Q4 94	0.36	—	Q3 98	−14.77	24.4
Q1 95	5.55	—	Q4 98	18.26	6.9
Q2 95	5.69	—	Q1 99	−2.49	7.5
Q3 95	3.62	—	Q2 99	0.70	16.9
Q4 95	2.84	—	Q3 99	0.76	−9.4
Q1 96	3.15	—	Q4 99	16.97	35.6
Q2 96	2.06	—	Q1 00	−0.26	8.7
Q3 96	3.24	—	Q2 00	−3.50	−6.4
Q4 96	9.02	—	Q3 00	−7.63	−6.7
Q1 97	4.37	—	Q4 00	1.61	−9.2

Table 4.2 Results for data in Table 4.1

	Truncated-sample estimator		Maximum likelihood		Bayesian estimates	
	European equities	Latin American equities	European equities	Latin American equities	European equities	Latin American equities
μ	12.99%	4.27%	14.10%	5.26%	14.10%	5.26%
σ	19.34%	31.44%	14.26%	29.14%	15.28%	35.43%
SR_i	0.67	0.14	0.99	0.18	0.92	0.15

Figure 4.7 Scatter plot for overlapping data points

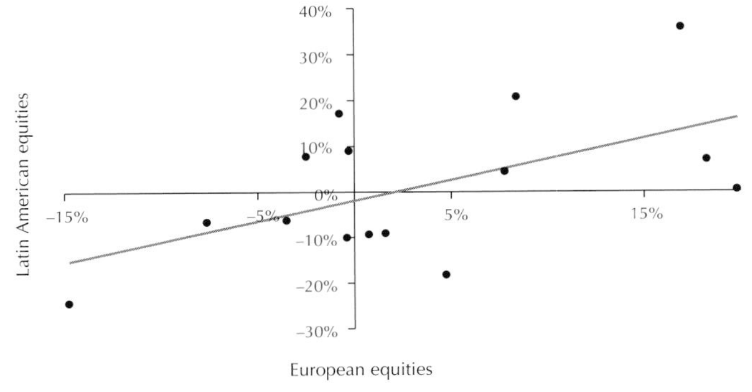

Although the mathematics is straightforward, it should be stressed once more that we assume a constant marginal distribution of the long-history assets and constant correlation.

A simple two-asset example will illustrate the core principles. Return data for European and Latin American equities are set out in Table 4.1. There are 30 quarters of data for the former but only 15 quarters for the emerging market (Latin American) equities. We can first calculate the truncated-sample estimator (Table 4.2). In this case, we only use the data from Q2 1997 to Q4 2000.

We see that the maximum-likelihood results lead to an upward revision on the emerging market returns as these are highly correlated with the developed market returns (see Figure 4.7). Thus, part of the return differential between the full-sample and the short-sample periods will be added to the average return of the shorter series.

The most dramatic impact arises from the upward revision of the volatility estimate for emerging market equities, which is the direct effect of a much higher estimation error than for developed markets.

APPENDIX A: DERIVATION OF UNIVARIATE EXAMPLE
From Equation (4.6) we already know that

$$p(\mu|r) \propto \exp\left\{-\frac{1}{2}\left(\frac{(\mu-\mu_{prior})^2}{\varphi^2} + \frac{\sum_{i=1}^{T}(r_i-\mu)^2}{\sigma^2}\right)\right\} \quad (A1)$$

Expanding the term in the main set of inner brackets on the right-hand side, we get

$$\mu^2\left(\frac{1}{\varphi^2}+\frac{T}{\sigma^2}\right)-2\mu\left(\frac{T\hat{\mu}}{\sigma^2}+\frac{\mu_{prior}}{\varphi^2}\right)+\frac{\sum_{i=1}^{T}r_i^2}{\sigma^2}+\frac{\mu_{prior}^2}{\varphi^2}$$

$$=\left(\mu-\frac{\left(\frac{T\hat{\mu}}{\sigma^2}+\frac{\mu_{prior}}{\varphi^2}\right)}{\left(\frac{1}{\varphi^2}+\frac{T}{\sigma^2}\right)}\right)^2 \times$$

$$\left(\frac{1}{\varphi^2}+\frac{T}{\sigma^2}\right)+\frac{\sum_{i=1}^{T}r_i^2}{\sigma^2}+\frac{\mu_{prior}^2}{\varphi^2}-\frac{\left(\frac{T\hat{\mu}}{\sigma^2}+\frac{\mu_{prior}}{\varphi^2}\right)}{\left(\frac{1}{\varphi^2}+\frac{T}{\sigma^2}\right)} \quad (A2)$$

It then follows that

$$\mu_{\text{predictive}} = \left(\frac{1}{\varphi_n^2} \mu_{\text{prior}} + \frac{T}{\sigma^2} \hat{\mu} \right) \left(\frac{1}{\varphi_T^2} + \frac{T}{\sigma^2} \right)^{-1}$$

$$\varphi_T = \left(\frac{1}{\varphi^2} + \frac{T}{\sigma^2} \right)^{\frac{1}{2}} \qquad\qquad (A3)$$

This technique is also known as completing the square.[35]

Instead of going through the analytics, we could also simulate the posterior distribution. We know that the posterior distribution can be written as $p(\theta|r) \propto p(r|\theta)p(\theta)$. All we have to do is to simulate from the prior distribution $p(\theta)$ and substitute this draw in the likelihood function $p(r|\theta)$. Multiplying both results and repeating these steps many times gives us the unnormalised posterior. We then add the realisations up and divide each realisation by the sum to get the normalised posterior.

APPENDIX B: ESTIMATION ERROR AND VOLATILITY FORECASTS

Risk arises from unpredictable variations; variations that can be forecast do not expose investors to risk. Suppose we employ a standard autoregressive approach, using dividend yields to forecast future equity returns as in the equation below:[36]

$$\begin{pmatrix} r_{t+1} \\ dy_{t+1} \end{pmatrix} = \begin{pmatrix} a_1 \\ a_2 \end{pmatrix} + \begin{pmatrix} b_1 \\ b_2 \end{pmatrix} dy_t + \begin{pmatrix} \varepsilon_{1,t} \\ \varepsilon_{2,t} \end{pmatrix}$$

$$\mathbf{z}_{t+1} = \mathbf{a} + \mathbf{b}x_t + \boldsymbol{\varepsilon}_t \qquad\qquad (B1)$$

where returns are denoted by r and dividend yields are expressed as dy, $\mathbf{z}_{t+1} = (r_{t+1}, dy_{t+1})'$, $\boldsymbol{\varepsilon}_t = (\varepsilon_{1t}, \varepsilon_{2t})'$ and $x_t = dy_t$. Equation (B1) describes the relationship for a single time period, whereas we are interested in the average relationship over many periods. Rewriting this equation for all data points ("stacking") gives us

$$\underbrace{\begin{pmatrix} r_2 & dy_2 \\ \vdots & \vdots \\ r_t & dy_t \end{pmatrix}}_{Z} = \underbrace{\begin{pmatrix} 1 & dy_1 \\ \vdots & \vdots \\ 1 & dy_{t-1} \end{pmatrix}}_{X} \underbrace{\begin{pmatrix} a_1 & a_2 \\ b_1 & b_2 \end{pmatrix}}_{C} + \underbrace{\begin{pmatrix} \varepsilon_{12} & \varepsilon_{22} \\ \vdots & \vdots \\ \varepsilon_{1t} & \varepsilon_{2t} \end{pmatrix}}_{E} \qquad (B2)$$

or in matrix form

$$\mathbf{Z} = \mathbf{XC} + \mathbf{E} \qquad\qquad (B3)$$

We recognise this as a simple regression model that can be estimated using ordinary least squares (OLS), giving the well-known solution[37]

$$\hat{C} = (X'X)^{-1} X'Z \qquad (B4)$$

The 2×2 covariance matrix of error terms (regression residuals) can be calculated in the usual way:

$$\hat{\Sigma} = \frac{(Z - X\hat{C})'(Z - X\hat{C})}{T} = \frac{\hat{E}'\hat{E}}{T} \qquad (B5)$$

where T is the number of observations.

We will use sample data from Table B1 to estimate our simple model. The matrix of regression coefficients shows the high persistency of dividend yields (shown by an autocorrelation of 0.79):

$$\hat{C} = \begin{pmatrix} a_1 & a_2 \\ b_1 & b_2 \end{pmatrix} = \begin{pmatrix} -14.89 & 0.87 \\ 4.3 & 0.79 \end{pmatrix} \qquad (B6)$$

while the covariance matrix of regression residuals exhibits a negative correlation between shocks to the system in Equation (B1):

$$\hat{\Sigma} = \begin{pmatrix} \text{cov}(\hat{\varepsilon}_1, \hat{\varepsilon}_1) & \text{cov}(\hat{\varepsilon}_1, \hat{\varepsilon}_2) \\ \text{cov}(\hat{\varepsilon}_2, \hat{\varepsilon}_1) & \text{cov}(\hat{\varepsilon}_2, \hat{\varepsilon}_2) \end{pmatrix} = \begin{pmatrix} 100.01 & -4.9 \\ -4.9 & 0.27 \end{pmatrix} \qquad (B7)$$

The correlation between ε_1 and ε_2 amounts to -0.94 and can be calculated from

$$-4.9 \times \frac{1}{\sqrt{100.01}} \times \frac{1}{\sqrt{0.27}}$$

Our simple regression model contains all information on the time-variable investment opportunities that are available. Out-of-sample forecasts (in per cent) for the next two quarters (Q2 and Q3) in 2001 for the UK equity market are

$$r_{Q2} = -14.89 + 4.3 \cdot 2.5 = -4.14$$

$$r_{Q3} = -14.89 + 4.3 \cdot (0.87 + 0.79 \cdot 2.5) = -2.66$$

We are now in a position to generate forecasts for returns in period $t + n$:

$$z_{t+1} = a + Bz_t + \varepsilon_t, \quad B = \begin{bmatrix} 0 & b_1 \\ 0 & b_2 \end{bmatrix}, \quad a = \begin{bmatrix} a_1 \\ a_2 \end{bmatrix}, \quad \varepsilon_t = \begin{bmatrix} \varepsilon_{1t} \\ \varepsilon_{2t} \end{bmatrix} \qquad (B8)$$

We will start with a simple two-period example. Knowing the return-generating process for $t+1$ and $t+2$,

$$z_{t+1} = \hat{a} + \hat{B}z_t + \varepsilon_t \tag{B9}$$

$$z_{t+2} = \hat{a} + \hat{B}z_{t+1} + \varepsilon_{t+1} \tag{B10}$$

Table B1 Monthly risk premium (RP) and dividend yield (DY) for UK equities

Quartal	RP	DY	Quartal	RP	DY	Quartal	RP	DY
Q1 75	−4.9	9.9	Q4 83	−1.5	5.2	Q3 92	−5.1	5.0
Q2 75	73.2	5.9	Q1 84	15.2	4.6	Q4 92	3.1	4.8
Q3 75	8.7	5.5	Q2 84	6.5	4.6	Q1 93	11.0	4.4
Q4 75	9.5	5.2	Q3 84	−8.9	5.2	Q2 93	4.4	4.0
Q1 76	12.3	4.7	Q4 84	13.9	4.9	Q3 93	1.7	4.0
Q2 76	0.0	4.8	Q1 85	16.3	4.4	Q4 93	11.1	3.7
Q3 76	−1.7	5.1	Q2 85	2.9	4.6	Q1 94	10.8	3.3
Q4 76	−20.8	6.8	Q3 85	−3.9	4.9	Q2 94	−5.2	3.6
Q1 77	26.2	5.5	Q4 85	7.1	4.7	Q3 94	−3.4	3.9
Q2 77	11.0	5.2	Q1 86	4.7	4.6	Q4 94	1.2	3.9
Q3 77	8.4	5.1	Q2 86	20.3	3.9	Q1 95	−0.6	4.0
Q4 77	12.0	4.7	Q3 86	−3.1	4.2	Q2 95	3.3	4.0
Q1 78	−5.2	5.2	Q4 86	1.3	4.2	Q3 95	8.0	3.8
Q2 78	−3.4	5.5	Q1 87	12.7	3.9	Q4 95	3.5	3.8
Q3 78	11.3	5.1	Q2 87	9.5	3.6	Q1 96	4.5	3.8
Q4 78	4.2	5.1	Q3 87	27.5	3.0	Q2 96	5.4	3.7
Q1 79	0.4	5.2	Q4 87	−5.7	3.3	Q3 96	−4.0	4.0
Q2 79	19.9	4.6	Q1 88	−22.7	4.3	Q4 96	10.4	3.7
Q3 79	−8.0	5.8	Q2 88	0.4	4.4	Q1 97	5.2	3.6
Q4 79	5.0	5.8	Q3 88	5.1	4.3	Q2 97	2.1	3.6
Q1 80	−2.3	6.1	Q4 88	−1.2	4.5	Q3 97	12.7	3.3
Q2 80	1.7	6.7	Q1 89	2.4	4.6	Q4 97	7.7	3.1
Q3 80	15.1	6.0	Q2 89	10.7	4.4	Q1 98	−0.3	3.1
Q4 80	5.3	5.8	Q3 89	10.7	4.1	Q2 98	14.4	2.7
Q1 81	−3.5	6.1	Q4 89	−7.5	4.7	Q3 98	2.6	2.7
Q2 81	12.5	5.5	Q1 90	8.9	4.5	Q4 98	−17.0	3.2
Q3 81	−0.7	5.7	Q2 90	−5.7	5.0	Q1 99	14.7	2.9
Q4 81	−10.8	6.6	Q3 90	8.0	4.7	Q2 99	10.4	2.4
Q1 82	10.2	6.1	Q4 90	−13.4	5.6	Q3 99	3.1	2.4
Q2 82	1.9	6.2	Q1 91	−1.3	5.7	Q4 99	−9.5	2.7
Q3 82	5.2	6.1	Q2 91	24.1	4.7	Q1 00	13.7	2.5
Q4 82	15.6	5.4	Q3 91	1.0	4.8	Q2 00	−6.4	2.5
Q1 83	3.7	5.3	Q4 91	2.2	4.8	Q3 00	5.1	2.3
Q2 83	12.8	4.8	Q1 92	−1.7	4.9	Q4 00	−2.5	2.4
Q3 83	−1.0	5.0	Q2 92	5.3	4.7	Q1 01	−2.2	2.5

Source: Datastream.

we can use substitution from Equations (B9) and (B10) to generate a two-period forecast:

$$\mathbf{z}_{t+2} = \hat{\mathbf{a}} + \hat{\mathbf{B}}\mathbf{z}_{t+1} + \boldsymbol{\varepsilon}_{t+1} = \hat{\mathbf{a}} + \hat{\mathbf{B}}\underbrace{\left(\hat{\mathbf{a}} + \hat{\mathbf{B}}\mathbf{z}_t + \boldsymbol{\varepsilon}_t\right)}_{z_{t+1}} + \boldsymbol{\varepsilon}_{t+1}$$

$$= \hat{\mathbf{a}} + \hat{\mathbf{a}}\hat{\mathbf{B}} + \hat{\mathbf{B}}^2\mathbf{z}_t + \hat{\mathbf{B}}\boldsymbol{\varepsilon}_t + \boldsymbol{\varepsilon}_{t+1}$$

Generalisation yields the return for period $t+n$:

$$\mathbf{z}_{t+n} =$$

$$\hat{\mathbf{a}} + \hat{\mathbf{B}}\hat{\mathbf{a}} + \hat{\mathbf{B}}^2\hat{\mathbf{a}} + \cdots + \hat{\mathbf{B}}^{n-1}\hat{\mathbf{a}} + \hat{\mathbf{B}}^n\mathbf{z}_t + \boldsymbol{\varepsilon}_{t+n} +$$

$$\hat{\mathbf{B}}\boldsymbol{\varepsilon}_{t+(n-1)} + \cdots + \hat{\mathbf{B}}^{n-1}\boldsymbol{\varepsilon}_{t+1} \qquad \text{(B11)}$$

Equation (B11) allows us to forecast any point in the future; note that, as the expected value of a residual is zero, all residual terms drop out – ie, become zero – if we take expectations. In the case of no forecasting power (where $\hat{\mathbf{B}} = 0$), our forecast coincides with the unconditional mean ($\hat{a}_1$ in $\hat{\mathbf{a}}$). The remaining step is to write down the conditional forecast (conditional on information known at t) and calculate the covariance matrix for the n-period returns ($\mathbf{z}_{t+1} + \ldots + \mathbf{z}_{t+n}$). This is done in Equation (B12):

$$\hat{\boldsymbol{\Sigma}}(n) = \hat{\boldsymbol{\Sigma}}$$

$$+ (\mathbf{I} + \hat{\mathbf{B}})\hat{\boldsymbol{\Sigma}}(\mathbf{I} + \hat{\mathbf{B}})'$$

$$+ \left(\mathbf{I} + \hat{\mathbf{B}} + \hat{\mathbf{B}}^2\right)\hat{\boldsymbol{\Sigma}}\left(\mathbf{I} + \hat{\mathbf{B}} + \hat{\mathbf{B}}^2\right)'$$

$$+ \cdots$$

$$+ \left(\mathbf{I} + \hat{\mathbf{B}} + \hat{\mathbf{B}}^2 + \cdots + \hat{\mathbf{B}}^{n-1}\right)\hat{\boldsymbol{\Sigma}}\left(\mathbf{I} + \hat{\mathbf{B}} + \hat{\mathbf{B}}^2 + \cdots + \hat{\mathbf{B}}^{n-1}\right)' \qquad \text{(B12)}$$

Admittedly this formula looks very unfriendly, but we will justify it using a two-period example. We first apply the variance operator to

$$\mathbf{z}_{t+1} + \mathbf{z}_{t+2} = \underbrace{\hat{\mathbf{a}} + \hat{\mathbf{B}}\mathbf{z}_t + \boldsymbol{\varepsilon}_t}_{z_{t+1}} + \underbrace{\hat{\mathbf{a}} + \hat{\mathbf{a}}\hat{\mathbf{B}} + \hat{\mathbf{B}}^2\mathbf{z}_t + \hat{\mathbf{B}}\boldsymbol{\varepsilon}_t + \boldsymbol{\varepsilon}_{t+1}}_{z_{t+2}}$$

However, uncertainty arises only from the residual terms as the model parameters are assumed to be fully known in t (no estimation error). We then get

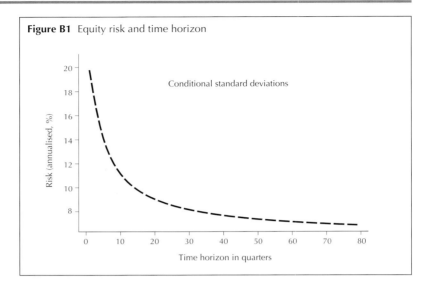

Figure B1 Equity risk and time horizon

$$\hat{\boldsymbol{\Sigma}}(2) = \mathrm{var}\left(\mathbf{z}_{t+1} + \mathbf{z}_{t+2}\right) = \mathrm{var}\left(\boldsymbol{\varepsilon}_t + \hat{\mathbf{B}}\boldsymbol{\varepsilon}_t + \boldsymbol{\varepsilon}_{t+1}\right)$$

$$= \mathrm{var}\left(\boldsymbol{\varepsilon}_t\left(\mathbf{I} + \hat{\mathbf{B}}\right) + \boldsymbol{\varepsilon}_{t+1}\right)$$

$$= (\mathbf{I} + \hat{\mathbf{B}})\hat{\boldsymbol{\Sigma}}(\mathbf{I} + \hat{\mathbf{B}})' + \hat{\boldsymbol{\Sigma}} \tag{B13}$$

We assume here that the residual terms are stationary (covariance in period two is the same as in period one) and uncorrelated across time. For a better understanding of Equation (B13), we can again investigate the no-information case ($\hat{\mathbf{B}} = \mathbf{0}$). In this circumstance, we get the familiar "square root of time" rule:

$$\hat{\boldsymbol{\Sigma}}(n) = \hat{\boldsymbol{\Sigma}} + \cdots + \hat{\boldsymbol{\Sigma}} = n\hat{\boldsymbol{\Sigma}}$$

Decomposing Equation (B13) further, we get

$$\hat{\boldsymbol{\Sigma}}(2) = \hat{\boldsymbol{\Sigma}} + (\mathbf{I} + \hat{\mathbf{B}})\hat{\boldsymbol{\Sigma}}(\mathbf{I} + \hat{\mathbf{B}})'$$

$$= \begin{bmatrix} \sigma_{11} & \sigma_{12} \\ \sigma_{21} & \sigma_{22} \end{bmatrix} + \left(\begin{bmatrix} 1 & 0 \\ 0 & 1 \end{bmatrix} + \begin{bmatrix} 0 & b_1 \\ 0 & b_2 \end{bmatrix}\right)\begin{bmatrix} \sigma_{11} & \sigma_{12} \\ \sigma_{21} & \sigma_{22} \end{bmatrix}\left(\begin{bmatrix} 1 & 0 \\ 0 & 1 \end{bmatrix} + \begin{bmatrix} 0 & b_1 \\ 0 & b_2 \end{bmatrix}\right)'$$

$$= \begin{bmatrix} 2\sigma_{11} + 2b_1\sigma_{12} + b_1^2\sigma_{22} & \cdots \\ \cdots & \cdots \end{bmatrix}_{2\times 2} \tag{B14}$$

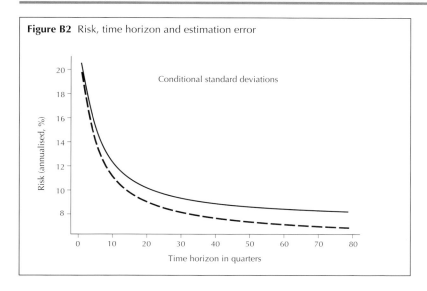

Figure B2 Risk, time horizon and estimation error

Only in the case of no forecasting opportunities (where $b = 0$) will the variance of the two-period returns equal twice the variance of the one-period returns. If $2b_1\sigma_{12} + b_1^2\sigma_{22} < 0$, we see that the conditional variance of the two-period returns is less than twice the variance of one-period returns. Substituting our estimated parameters, it is easy to see that these conditions are satisfied. The important term is the covariance between the residuals in Equation (B1). If they are sufficiently negative, shocks on dividend yields will be compensated by shocks on returns with the opposite sign. The more pronounced the impact of dividend yields (b_1) on tomorrow's returns, the stronger this effect will be.

Figure B1 plots the relationship between time horizon and conditional volatility (annualised) for up to 80 quarters (20 years). This is done using Equation (B12) for varying horizons. Time-variable investment opportunities (good when dividend yields are high and bad when they are low) result in good years followed by bad years and, hence, to a decrease in the unexplained volatility. Remember, it is only unexplained volatility (unexplained with respect to information at t) that exposes investors to risk; movements that can be anticipated are not a source of risk.

So far, we have accepted point forecasts from OLS as 100% true; uncertainty arose from the volatility in the residual terms, not from estimation error. However, we know that our model forecasts are affected by uncertainty.

To reflect estimation error in our return-generating model (B1), we will use the procedure already described in Section 4.1. Here the parameters of concern are $\boldsymbol{\theta} = (\mathbf{C}, \boldsymbol{\Sigma})$.

Step 1 Draw a new variance–covariance matrix from an inverted Wishart distribution. The inverse Wishart is a multidimensional extension of χ^2:

$$\Sigma^{-1} \sim \text{Wishart}\left(\text{no of data points} - \text{no of coefficients} - 2, \hat{\Sigma}^{-1}\right)$$

As a result, we get a new covariance matrix of residuals which generates new model parameters according to

$$\begin{pmatrix} a_1 \\ b_1 \\ a_2 \\ b_2 \end{pmatrix} \sim N\left(\begin{pmatrix} \hat{a}_1 \\ \hat{b}_1 \\ \hat{a}_2 \\ \hat{b}_2 \end{pmatrix}, \Sigma \otimes (\mathbf{X}'\mathbf{X})^{-1} \right)$$

Repeating this procedure 100,000 times produces 100,000 coefficient vectors, which will all be different. However, the average of all the samplings will be the same as the estimated parameters. Uncertainty only increases the dispersion of parameters, not the average parameter estimate.

Step 2 For each parameter vector from Step 1, simulate the multiperiod returns of our system, Equation (B1). The result is plotted in Figure B2. Introducing estimation error reduces the impact of forecastability on long-term equity risk without over-compensating forecastability. This is not a general result as it has been shown that estimation error can dominate the influence of forecastability.

1   Markowitz (1987, p. 57).
2   It has been argued that this judgmental part of traditional statistics already uses non-sample information and therefore that even frequentists implicitly use prior information.
3   $p(\mathbf{r}, \boldsymbol{\theta}) = p(\mathbf{r}|\boldsymbol{\theta})\, p(\boldsymbol{\theta})$ means that the probability of getting $\mathbf{r}$ and $\boldsymbol{\theta}$ is the same as drawing $\mathbf{r}$ conditional on a particular realisation on $\boldsymbol{\theta}$ times the probability of arriving at this realisation of $\boldsymbol{\theta}$ called $p(\boldsymbol{\theta})$.
4   See Klein and Bawa (1976) for an application in a two-asset context.
5   See Green (2000) or Borse (1997) for a discussion of Monte Carlo integration.
6   The example is taken from Barberis (1999).
7   See Kritzman (2000) for an overview of the time-diversification arguments.
8   The estimation error on the mean return is given by $\sigma/\sqrt{T}$, where T denotes the number of observations. Figure 4.2 plots the distribution of estimated mean returns for T equal to 60,120 and 240.
9   Conjugate priors have the same functional form (belong to the same family of distributions) as the likelihood function. This class of priors will be used throughout this chapter. See Morris (1983) for the exponential family of distributions. Conjugate priors are used for mathematical convenience as well as giving the prior a sample interpretation.
10 See Verbeek (2000, Chapter 6).
11 See Theil (1971). A prerequisite of this interpretation is that we use a conjugate prior.

12 We use an example similar to that in the book by Rudd and Clasing (1988).

13 See Grinold and Kahn (2000) for a review of the literature.

14 See Sharpe (1991) for an exposition on the arithmetic of active management.

15 This section follows O-Cinneide (2001). Other expositions using a similar set-up can be found in Frost and Savarino (1986) or Jorion (1986).

16 Turner and Hensel (1993) found that average returns within asset groups (bonds, equities, cash) were statistically undistinguishable between countries. Deriving priors of this form would be called empirical Bayes.

17 The parameters of the prior distribution are also called hyper-parameters. They are assumed to be known with no uncertainty.

18 Note that this does not mean it is normal. In fact, it has been shown by Barry (1974) that if there is uncertainty about both mean returns and the covariance matrix, the predictive distribution is t-distributed. Technically, this would require the investor to possess quadratic utility in order to rescue mean–variance-based portfolio selection.

19 Note that Equation (4.10) is very similar to Equation (4.7) where precision is now captured by the inverse on a variance–covariance matrix. Since Ψ_{prior}^{-1} contains estimation errors rather than asset variances, the elements in $\hat{\Omega}^{-1}$ have to be adjusted to arrive at the same order of magnitude. Note that $T\hat{\Omega}^{-1} = (1/T)^{-1}\hat{\Omega}^{-1}$, which corrects for different orders of magnitude.

20 See Jeffreys (1961).

21 See also Barry (1974) or Frost and Savarino (1986).

22 See Frost and Savarino (1986, p. 296).

23 A slight modification of this is the case of uninformative priors, where return series exhibit different lengths. Stambaugh (1997) shows that not only is estimation error higher for shorter series than for longer ones, but additionally that means change as long as assets are not completely uncorrelated. The mean difference between the overlapping parts of two series is pulled to the mean of a similar but longer return series (a correlated series with less estimation error).

24 We have already shown that non-informative priors do not change the set of efficient solutions.

25 The model described below is the Black–Litterman model (Black and Litterman, 1992). An excellent review can be found in Satchell and Scowcroft (1998) or Lee (2000).

26 See Black and Litterman (1992, p. 43, Equation 8).

27 See the experience report from Bevan and Winkelmann (1998).

28 A review of the CAPM can be found in Cuthbertson (1996, Chapter 3).

29 See Pastor (2000) for more on this.

30 This is also the case for multiple managers. See Chapter 7 for a more detailed discussion.

31 Longer series are available for the US from Ibbotson Associates, Chicago. Recently, Dimson, Marsh and Staunton (2001) recovered historical time series for all major stock and bond markets for the last 101 years.

32 The reader is referred to Stambaugh (1997) for a complete derivation of the methodology borrowed above.

33 Reassuringly, the maximum-likelihood estimator ensures that the covariance matrix of returns is still positive-definite. Other estimators – such as the use of long history on long series and short history on short series, including co-movements between long and short series – do not necessarily have these characteristics.

34 See Chiang (1984), p. 42.

35 See for example Cochrane (2001), Fama and French (1988), Shiller (1996) or Goetzmann and Jorion (1993) on this approach.

36 Readers are referred to Lütkepohl (1991) as the standard reference on vector autoregressive modelling.

37 See Comon (2001) for a similar study on emerging market equities.

BIBLIOGRAPHY

Barberis, N., 2000, "Investing for the Long Run when Returns are Predictable", *Journal of Finance* 45, pp. 225–64.

Barry, C., 1974, "Portfolio Analysis Under Uncertain Means", *Journal of Finance* 29, pp. 515–22.

Bevan, A., and K. Winkelmann, 1998, "Using the Black-Litterman Global Asset Allocation Model: Three Years of Experience", Working Paper (New York: Goldman Sachs).

Black, F., and R. Litterman, 1992, "Global Portfolio Optimization", *Financial Analysts Journal* 48, pp. 28–43.

Borse, G., 1997, *Numerical Methods with Matlab* (Boston: Thomson).

Chiang, A., 1984, *Fundamental Methods of Mathematical Economics*, Third Edition (New Jersey: McGraw-Hill).

Cochrane, J. H., 2001, *Asset Pricing* (Princeton University Press).

Comon, E., 2001, "Essays on Investment and Consumption Choice", Ph.D. thesis, Harvard University.

Cuthbertson, K., 1996, *Quantitative Financial Economics* (Chichester: Wiley & Sons).

Dimson, E., P. Marsh and M. Staunton, 2001, *Millennium Book II: 101 Years of Investment Returns* (London: ABN AMRO).

Fama, E., and K. French, 1988, "Dividend Yields and Expected Stock Returns", *Journal of Financial Economics* 24, pp. 23–49.

Frost, P., and J. Savarino, 1986, "An Empirical Bayes Approach to Efficient Portfolio Selection", *Journal of Financial and Quantitative Analysis* 21, pp. 293–305.

Goetzmann, W., and P. Jorion, 1993, "Testing the Predictive Power of Dividend Yields", *Journal of Finance* 48, pp. 663–79.

Green, W., 2000, *Econometric Analysis*, Fourth Edition (New Jersey: Prentice-Hall).

Grinold, R., and R. Kahn, 2000, *Active Portfolio Management*, Second Edition (New York: McGraw-Hill).

Jeffreys, H., 1961, *Theory of Probability*, Third Edition (Oxford University Press).

Jorion, P., 1986, "Bayes–Stein Estimation for Portfolio Analysis", *Journal of Financial and Quantitative Analysis* 21, pp. 279–92.

Klein, R., and S. Bawa, 1976, "The Effect of Estimation Risk on Optimal Portfolio Choice", *Journal of Financial Economics* 3, pp. 215–31.

Kritzman, M. P., 2000, *Puzzles of Finance* (New York: John Wiley & Sons).

Leonard, T,. and J. Hsu, 1999, *Bayesian Methods, An Analysis for Statisticians and Interdisciplinary Researchers* (Cambridge University Press).

Lütkepohl, H., 1991, *Introduction to Multiple Time Series Analysis* (Heidelberg: Springer-Verlag).

Markowitz, H., 1987, *Mean–Variance Analysis in Portfolio Choice and Capital Markets* (Blackwell).

Morris, C., 1983, "Natural Exponential Families with Quadratic Variance Functions: Statistical Theory", *The Annals of Statistics* 11, pp. 519–29.

O-Cinneide, C., 2001, *A Bayesian Approach to Portfolio Selection* (New York: Deutsche Asset Management).

Pastor, L., 2000, "Portfolio Selection and Asset Pricing Models", *Journal of Finance* 55, pp. 179–221.

Rudd, A., and H. K. Clasing Jr., 1988, *Modern Portfolio Theory: The Principles of Investment Management* (Irwine: Dow Jones).

Satchell, S., and A. Scowcroft, 1998, "A Demystification of the Black Litterman Model, Managing Quantitative and Traditional Portfolio Construction", Working Paper (Cambridge: Judge Institute).

Sharpe, W., 1991, "The Arithmetic of Active Management", *The Financial Analysts Journal* 47(1), January/February, pp. 7–9.

Shiller, R. J., 1996, "Price-Earnings Ratios as Forecasters of Returns: The Stock Market Outlook in 1996", Working Paper, Yale University.

Stambaugh, R., 1997, "Analysing Investments whose Histories Differ in Length", *Journal of Financial Economics* 45, pp. 285–331.

Theil, H., 1971, *Principles of Econometrics* (Amsterdam: John Wiley & Sons).

Turner, A., and C. Hensel, 1993, "Were the Returns from Stocks and Bonds of Different Countries Really Different in the 1980s", *Management Science* July, pp. 835–44.

Verbeek, M., 2000, *A Guide to Modern Econometrics* (Chichester: John Wiley & Sons).

Zellner, A., 1971, An Introduction to Bayesian Inference in Econometrics (New York: Wiley).

Scenario Optimisation

Scenario optimisation is used where the parameters of a mathematical model (asset returns over the next year, for example) are subject to randomness. One way to solve these stochastic programmes is to solve a deterministic problem with many different scenarios assumed for the uncertain inputs – in our case, returns. We can, for example, sample 100,000 scenarios for five assets from the predictive distribution (see Chapter 4) to arrive at a $100,000 \times 5$ cell matrix. After the draws have been made, uncertainty is removed and we are left with the deterministic problem of which asset weights to choose in order to maximise the objective, taking into account what can happen in all 100,000 scenarios. We will see later that for many objectives this can be written as a linear program.[1]

Scenario optimisation investigates how well feasible solutions perform in different scenarios (using an objective function to evaluate the solution for each scenario) and then tries to find the optimal solution. Although future asset returns are uncertain, scenario optimisation attempts to draw representative scenarios that could happen in the future. Scenario optimisation that is based on only a few scenarios may overadjust to the data, providing too optimistic an assessment of what can be achieved, while scenario optimisation with a very large set of scenarios can be computationally infeasible.[2]

The first section focuses on utility-based models, while the second section reviews basic issues in scenario generation. The remainder of the chapter focuses on risk perceptions that are widely used in asset management applications and can only be tackled using scenario optimisation.[3] All examples in this chapter are based on a set of return data given in Appendix A, and before proceeding further readers are advised to refer to the accompanying brief description of this data set on page 152.

5.1 UTILITY-BASED SCENARIO OPTIMISATION
Utility-based models have a strong foundation in decision theory as they directly maximise expected utility rather than relying on approximations (see Chapter 1). Expected utility allows us to deal with arbitrarily shaped distributions rather than forcing us to deal with mean and variance only.[4]

We define expected utility, EU, as

$$EU(W) = \sum_{i=s}^{S} p_s U(1+R_{ps}) = \frac{1}{S}\sum_{i=s}^{S} U(1+R_{ps})$$

$$= \frac{1}{S}\sum_{i=s}^{S} U\left(1+\sum_{i=1}^{k} w_i R_{is}\right) \tag{5.1}$$

where W denotes end-of-period wealth and R_{is} is the return of asset i in scenario s. Equation (5.1) states that expected utility is calculated for $s = 1,\dots,S$ scenarios. Each scenario is drawn with probability $p_s = 1/S$ and gives a portfolio return of R_{ps}. Utility is specified as a utility function with constant relative risk-aversion:

$$U(1+R) = \begin{cases} \dfrac{(1+R)^{1-\gamma}}{1-\gamma}, & \gamma \geq 0 \\ \ln(1+R), & \gamma = 1 \end{cases} \tag{5.2}$$

where γ is the risk-aversion coefficient. Any series of historic (or simulated) excess returns can be rewritten as

$$R_{is} = c + \mu_i + \sigma_i z_{is} \tag{5.3}$$

where c is the return of a risk-free alternative, μ_i is the expected unconditional excess return of the ith of $i = 1,\dots,k$ assets and σ_i is the ith asset's volatility. With z_{is} we describe the standardised random part of the excess returns, ie, we take the original series of excess returns, subtract its mean and divide the result by its volatility. Thereby we create a series with a mean of zero and a volatility of one that retains all non-normality in the data – standardisation does not change the shape of a distribution. However Equation (5.3) helps us to control the first two moments, ie, we can change the location (mean) and the dispersion parameter (volatility) as we like – for example, to allow for expectations of lower risk premia in the future – without changing the degree of non-normality in the data. If we wished we could also input a new risk-free rate, a new expected return or a new forward-looking volatility figure.

A similar decomposition is readily available for benchmark (portfolio) returns, R_{bs}:

$$R_{bs} = c + \mu_b + \sum_{i=1}^{k} w_i \sigma_i z_{is} \tag{5.4}$$

where μ_b is the expected risk premium on a given portfolio and $\sum_{i=1}^{k} w_i \sigma_i z_{is}$ describes the innovations (deviations from the expected benchmark return) as a sum of shocks on all k assets. If we regard these benchmark portfolio positions as optimal (zero alpha) – ie, we assume that Equation (5.1) has been optimised – we can find a valuation model from Equation (5.1) that equalises all expected returns under a set of modified probabilities, p_s^*:[5]

$$p_s^* = \frac{p_s \dfrac{\mathrm{d}U}{\mathrm{d}(1+R_{bs})}}{\sum_{i=1}^{S} p_s \dfrac{\mathrm{d}U}{\mathrm{d}(1+R_{bs})}} = \frac{p_s(1+R_{bs})^{-\gamma}}{\sum_{i=1}^{S} p_s(1+R_{bs})^{-\gamma}} \tag{5.5}$$

so that

$$\sum_{s=1}^{S} p_s^* R_{is} = \sum_{s=1}^{S} p_s^* R_{bs} \tag{5.6}$$

Substituting Equations (5.3) and (5.4) into Equation (5.6), we arrive at the utility-based version of "grapes from wine", ie, we arrive at the implied returns a scenario-based utility maximiser must have used to find the current portfolio weights optimal:[6]

$$\sum_{s=1}^{S} p_s^*(c + \mu_i + \sigma_i z_{is}) = \sum_{s=1}^{S} p_s^*\left(c + \mu_b + \sum_{i=1}^{k} w_i \sigma_i z_{is}\right)$$

Recalling that $\sum_{s=1}^{S} p_s^* = 1$, we can solve for μ_i to get

$$\mu_i = \mu_b + \sum_{s=1}^{S} p_s^*\left(\sum_{i=1}^{k} w_i \sigma_i z_{is}\right) - \sum_{s=1}^{S} p_s^*(\sigma_i z_{is}) \tag{5.7}$$

for all $i = 1,\ldots,k$. Changing the risk-aversion parameter will change marginal utility and, hence, p_s^* and the required implied returns.

Let us illustrate the procedure with the data tabulated in Appendix A. To obtain enough data points to span the sample space meaningfully, we bootstrap 500 annual excess returns from the raw data. This exercise yields the distributional characteristics for the sampled excess returns summarised in Table 5.1.[7] We also assume benchmark weights of 40% for the UK, 30% for Japan, 10% for Europe and 20% for the US.

Next we want to calculate the modified probabilities for different risk-aversions as described in Equation (5.5). Figure 5.1 presents the results for two different risk-aversions.

Higher risk-aversions lead to a significant increase in modified probability for negative market returns (remember that Figure 5.1 plots $1 + R$ rather than R alone). The more risk-averse an investor is, the more weight (higher adjusted probability) will be given to the left tail of the

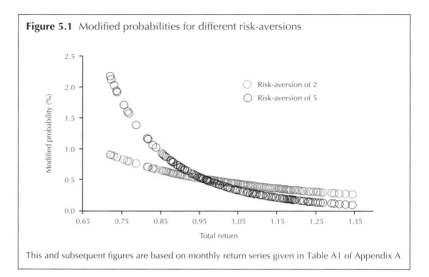

Figure 5.1 Modified probabilities for different risk-aversions

This and subsequent figures are based on monthly return series given in Table A1 of Appendix A

distribution. If assets show non-normality, the returns required to accept a given portfolio as optimal will change. This, in turn, will lead to changed implied returns, as calculated in the second and third terms of Equation (5.7). While the second term looks at the required risk premium that can be attributed to the benchmark return distribution, the third term catches the effect that can be attributed to the ith asset itself. Implied returns (returns that are required to compensate for risk-aversion and, in this case, also non-normality) will rise if, on average, deviations from expected returns, z_{is}, are highly negative when p_s^* is also high. Recall that p_s^* is high if marginal utility is high and, hence, deviations from expected benchmark returns, z_b, are low. This will be the case if z_i and z_b are positively correlated (or, in some states, negatively).

Table 5.1 Distributional characteristics of sampled excess returns for monthly return series given in Appendix A

Correlation

	UK	Japan	Europe	US
UK	1.00			
Japan	0.22	1.00		
Europe	0.72	0.32	1.00	
US	0.59	0.26	0.58	1.00

Distribution

	UK	Japan	Europe	US
Volatility (%)	14.99	19.58	17.51	15.46
Skewness	0.11	0.79	0.27	0.12
Kurtosis	0.29	1.86	−0.16	−0.16

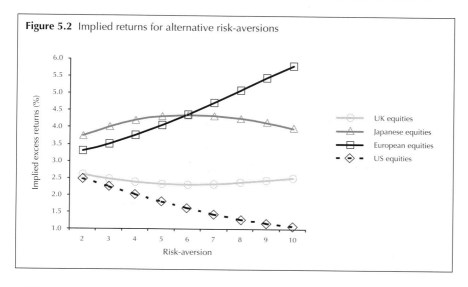

Figure 5.2 Implied returns for alternative risk-aversions

We can now look directly at how implied returns (obtained using Equation (5.2)) change as we alter risk-aversions. The results are summarised in Figure 5.2. We assume a risk premium of 3% for the optimal portfolio together with a risk-free rate of 3.5%.

As risk-aversion rises, the required returns for the most risky assets (Japanese and European equities) also increase, though not in a linear fashion (as would be the case for ordinary implied excess returns if we used a Markowitz framework). For example, we see that the implied excess return for UK equities – the asset with the lowest volatility – falls for intermediate risk-aversions but that, as risk-aversion increases further, it rises again. The reason for this is that UK equities are also the asset with the least positive skewness. For rising risk-aversions we have to expect considerable return differences to justify the current portfolio holdings.

In this section we have seen that implied returns can be backed out from actual allocations even in a utility-based scenario optimisation framework. However, as most investors feel somewhat uncomfortable specifying their utility functions (most readers will find it difficult to find a value of γ that suits them in Equation (5.2)), we will move away from utility-based to risk-based models for the remainder of this chapter.

5.2 SCENARIO GENERATION

Scenario optimisation techniques turn a stochastic problem into a deterministic problem by simulating future scenarios for all assets.[8] The problem becomes deterministic as soon as the simulation stops and all scenarios have been generated. In this form the problem can now be solved using mathematical (mostly linear) programming techniques.

Key to the quality of the solution we get is the quality of the sampled scenarios. In particular, scenarios must be:

❑ *parsimonious* – one should use a relatively small number of scenarios to save computing time;
❑ *representative* – scenarios must offer a realistic description of the relevant problem and not induce estimation error; and
❑ *arbitrage-free:* scenarios should not allow the optimiser to find highly attractive solutions that make no economic sense.

Before we look at scenario optimisation techniques we will therefore concentrate for a few pages on scenario generation.

Scenario generation can draw on an array of proven methods. First, we could use Bayesian methods as described in Chapter 4 to model the predictive distribution. Theoretically, the predictive distribution is ideal as it is exactly this distribution – which incorporates uncertainty about estimated parameters as well as prior knowledge about the future – that defines expected utility. In practice, however, investors might find Bayesian methods technically challenging, and priors always leave the impression of arbitrariness and are difficult to formulate, particularly as one also always needs to specify the degree of belief. Furthermore, the predictive distributions of Chapter 4 will be close to a normal distribution and so might not reflect the level of non-normality in the data.

A second method is to use bootstrapping to generate future scenarios, calculating annual returns from 12 bootstrapped monthly returns and repeating this procedure 1,000 times to get a distribution of future annual returns.[9] Although bootstrapping leaves correlations unchanged, it will, by construction (as it imposes the independence assumption of the central limit theorem on the resampled data), destroy all dependencies between two return realisations, such as autocorrelation in returns, Garch effects, etc. Recall that bootstrapping is done by repeated independent draws, with replacement.[10] The data will therefore look increasingly normal after a bootstrapping exercise even if they were not normally distributed in the first place.

Instead of bootstrapping from the empirical distribution, we could use Monte Carlo simulation, ie, draw from a parametric distribution. This can be done by fitting a distribution to each asset under consideration and then generating a multivariate distribution by sampling from the individual distributions separately, while gluing distributions together according to a correlation matrix using rank correlations.

Alternatively, we could estimate a vector–autoregressive model of the form[11]

$$\mathbf{r}_t = \boldsymbol{\mu} + \boldsymbol{\Theta}(\boldsymbol{\mu} - \mathbf{r}_{t-1}) + \boldsymbol{\epsilon}_t, \qquad \boldsymbol{\epsilon}_t \sim N(\mathbf{0}, \boldsymbol{\Omega}) \qquad (5.8)$$

where $\mathbf{\Theta}$ is the matrix of autoregressive parameters, $\mathbf{\mu}$ defines mean returns, $\mathbf{r}_{t-1}$ defines lagged returns and and $\mathbf{\Omega}$ describes the covariance structure of the error terms, $\mathbf{\epsilon}$. While Equation (5.8) is mainly used to develop multiperiod scenarios for multiperiod optimisation (not dis-cussed here but standard in the asset–liability modelling literature) because it introduces path-dependency into asset returns, it also proves useful in one-period models where significant path-dependence has considerable influence on the riskiness of different assets even over one period.[12] It has been shown that as long as the covariance matrix from which we sample is non-singular, the conditional variance of any asset with respect to all other assets is positive.[13] This is the same as saying that no asset can be perfectly explained (replicated) by a combination of the other assets, and it therefore rules out arbitrage.

5.2.1 Eliminating arbitrage

An important consideration in generating scenarios is to reduce or eliminate the possibility of arbitrage. Suppose we used one of the above methods to generate $s = 1, \ldots, S$ scenarios for k assets. All scenarios are summarised in a scenario matrix, $\mathbf{S}_{S \times k}$, that contains $S \times k$ asset returns:

$$\mathbf{S} = \begin{bmatrix} 1+c+r_{11} & 1+c+r_{12} & \cdots & 1+c+r_{1k} \\ 1+c+r_{21} & 1+c+r_{22} & \cdots & 1+c+r_{2k} \\ \vdots & \vdots & \ddots & \vdots \\ 1+c+r_{S1} & 1+c+r_{S1} & \cdots & 1+c+r_{Sk} \end{bmatrix} \qquad (5.9)$$

For notational convenience in later equations we let $\mathbf{R}'_s = (c + r_{s1} \cdots c + r_{sk})$ denote the vector of returns across all k assets in scenario s. Although arbitrage is ruled out if we sample from a non-singular covariance matrix, this is strictly true only for a large number of drawings as sampling error for a small number of drawings might result in arbitrage. To test for arbi-trage opportunities – which the optimiser will certainly find and will leverage on – we have first to understand what arbitrage means in the context of our scenario matrix, $\mathbf{S}_{S \times k}$. Suppose that we live in a world with two assets and two scenarios. $\mathbf{S}^1$ and $\mathbf{S}^2$, below, are examples of two scenario matrices:

$$\mathbf{S}^1 = \begin{bmatrix} 1+10\% & 1+8\% \\ 1+6\% & 1+5\% \end{bmatrix}, \quad \mathbf{S}^2 = \begin{bmatrix} 1+10\% & 1+8\% \\ 1+4\% & 1+5\% \end{bmatrix}$$

Both scenarios in each matrix are equally likely. An arbitrage opportunity can be loosely defined as a portfolio that is guaranteed not to lose money at the end of the investment period in any scenario but which generates a positive cashflow at the beginning (the investor receives money by cleverly setting up that arbitrage portfolio by selling and buying both assets).[14] To find arbitrage mathematically, we solve

$$\min_{\mathbf{w}} \mathbf{w1}, \quad \mathbf{S}^1 \mathbf{w} \geq \mathbf{0} \tag{5.10}$$

where **1** is a vector of ones. The minimisation objective in Equation (5.10) expresses the prize of an arbitrage portfolio. All assets are assumed to cost one monetary unit. If the objective is negative, the investor receives money. The constraints apply to the payoffs in both scenarios. Solving Equation (5.10) for both scenario matrices we see that the first scenario matrix, $\mathbf{S}^1$, incorporates an arbitrage opportunity in that the optimiser will not converge, while the second, $\mathbf{S}^2$, does not. This is not surprising, as it is clear that in scenario matrix $\mathbf{S}^1$ trivially asset one dominates asset two in both scenarios, giving higher returns in both states of the world; hence, long asset one and short asset two will do the trick. However, as the number of assets and scenarios rises, situations like this become more difficult to pick out, so we will settle for Equation (5.10) to test for arbitrage opportunities.[15] The likelihood of encountering arbitrage opportunities increases as the number of scenarios decreases, but this problem can be eliminated by sampling additional states of the world until arbitrage opportunities disappear. Basically, adding additional columns to the scenario matrix will make it unlikely that we will find a combination of assets that allows arbitrage. Also, limiting ourselves to long-only portfolios – as they apply to most institutional investors – will avoid unbounded solutions (in the presence of arbitrage the arbitrage profit becomes infinite) but will still result in solutions where some assets are overrepresented.

5.3 MEAN–ABSOLUTE DEVIATION

The first scenario-based alternative to Markowitz optimisation we will consider is the mean–absolute deviation model (MAD).[16] This measures risk as an absolute deviation from the mean rather than squared deviation as in the case of variance. We can define MAD as

$$MAD = \sum_{s=1}^{S} p_s \left| \mathbf{w}' \left[\mathbf{R}_s - \overline{\mathbf{R}} \right] \right| \tag{5.11}$$

where p_s denotes the probability of scenario s, **w** is the vector of portfolio weights (in all scenarios), $\mathbf{R}_s$ is the vector of k asset returns in scenario s and $\overline{\mathbf{R}}$ is the vector of asset means across all scenarios. As we work with simulated scenarios with equal probability, we will always set $p_s = 1/S$. Whereas in variance-based methods the property of the square penalises larger deviations at an increasing rate, this is not the case with MAD. In fact MAD implies that a further unit of underperformance relative to the mean creates the same disutility no matter how big the loss already is.

However, one advantage of MAD is that we can specify the costs of deviations above and below the mean differently, putting greater weight (costs) on underperformance than on outperformance. A second advantage is its computational ease. We can minimise MAD using a linear program, ie, minimise[17]

$$\frac{1}{S} \sum_{s=1}^{S} MAD_s \qquad (5.12)$$

with respect to MAD_s, $s = 1, \ldots, S$, and $\mathbf{w}$ subject to the constraints

$$MAD_s - c_d \mathbf{w}'(\mathbf{R}_s - \overline{\mathbf{R}}) \geq 0, \qquad s = 1, \ldots, S$$

$$MAD_s - c_u \mathbf{w}'(\mathbf{R}_s - \overline{\mathbf{R}}) \geq 0, \qquad s = 1, \ldots, S$$

$$\mathbf{w}'\overline{\mathbf{R}} \geq r_{target}$$

$$\mathbf{w}'\mathbf{1} = 1$$

$$w_i \geq 0 \qquad (5.13)$$

where c_d measures the costs of underperforming the portfolio mean, c_u measures the costs of outperforming the portfolio mean and r_{target} is the targeted portfolio return.

The computational mean–absolute deviation-based portfolio selection method described here offers a range of appealing properties compared to variance-based models:

1. There is no need to calculate a covariance matrix. However, this is only true if we rely on historical data for scenario generation; simulated scenarios from a parametric distribution have to be drawn using a covariance matrix.
2. Solving linear programs is much easier than mean–variance optimisation. The number of constraints ($2S + 2$ in the case of mean–absolute deviation) depends on the number of scenarios, not on the number of assets.
3. The upper bound on the number of assets in the optimal solution is related to the number of scenarios ($2S + 2$ in the case of mean–absolute deviation).

We can now use the scenarios in Table A1 of Appendix A to create an efficient frontier in mean–absolute deviation return space. Figure 5.3 plots three efficient frontiers for $c_d = 1, 3, 5$ and $c_u = 1$. Higher costs for underperformance will shift the frontiers to the right. This must be so by definition, but how much will the underlying portfolio weights change? Isolating the risk aspect, we will focus on the minimum-risk portfolios in Figure 5.3.

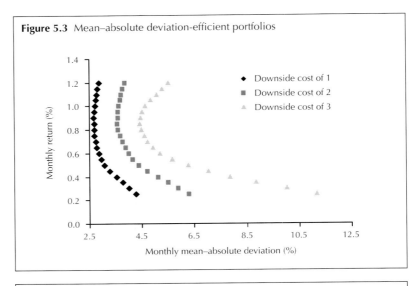

Figure 5.3 Mean–absolute deviation-efficient portfolios

Table 5.2 Minimum-risk portfolios for different deviation costs, c_d

	Weights (%)			
	w_1	w_2	w_3	w_4
$c_d = 1$	39.44	17.55	0.00	43.01
$c_d = 3$	40.50	22.24	3.09	34.17
$c_d = 5$	47.72	19.40	2.89	30.00

Assets 1–4 are, respectively, UK, Japanese, European and US equities. Results calculated for return data in Table A1 of Appendix A1.

Table 5.2 shows that the optimal position in asset 4 becomes smaller as deviation costs rise. This is not surprising as we know from Table 5.1 that US equities exhibit the most negative skewness and the highest excess kurtosis. However, as we have only 120 scenarios for our optimisation exercise, the reader will appreciate that a few observations might change the picture completely.

5.4 MINIMUM REGRET

The second objective we want to deal with is minimum regret. Suppose we obtain the scenario matrix **S**, either from historical returns or from a scenario simulation exercise. As in basic decision theory, we could choose a minimax criterion, ie, we might want to minimise the maximum port-folio loss, referred to as "minimising regret".[18] This could be the optimal strategy for investors who have to ensure that under all means (scenarios) they never experience a particular size of loss. Focusing on extreme events has its merits if returns deviate substantially from normality or if

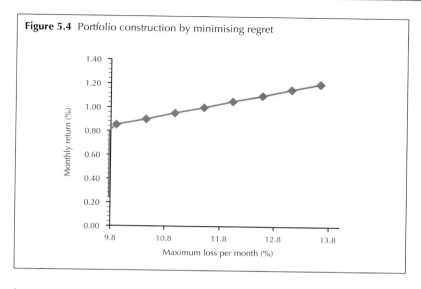

Figure 5.4 Portfolio construction by minimising regret

investors are extremely risk-averse.[19] Minimising the maximum loss can also be written as a linear program, ie, we maximise

$$R_{min} \tag{5.14}$$

with respect to $\mathbf{w}$ and R_{min} (minimum portfolio return) subject to the following set of constraints

$$\underbrace{\mathbf{w}'\mathbf{R}_s - R_{min}}_{\sum_{i=1}^k w_i(1+c+r_{is}) - R_{min}} \geq 0, \quad s = 1, \ldots, S$$

$$\mathbf{w}'\overline{\mathbf{R}} - R_{min} \geq R_{target}$$

$$\mathbf{w}'\mathbf{1} = 1$$

$$w_i \geq 0 \tag{5.15}$$

where we use the same notation as in Section 5.3. The efficient frontier – in this case the geometric location of minimum regret for a given return target – is plotted in Figure 5.4.

It can be seen from the figure that the maximum loss remains constant for a wide range of return requirements. The reason for this is that the optimal solution is concentrated in 100% of asset 1 (UK equities) up to a return requirement of 0.8% per month. This in turn results from the fact that asset 1 is the asset with the smallest minimum loss in the whole sample (as the reader can see from Table A1 in Appendix A). However, this on its own would not be enough to give the above result as diversification can reduce the maximum portfolio loss if it is possible to add assets that perform well if asset 1 performs badly. Looking at the scenarios in Table A1 we see that all assets performed very poorly in August 1998, when all assets lost about 10% or more, leaving no room for diversification. Although a scenario-based approach allows for the fact that all assets tend to do poorly in down markets and, hence, concentrates on the least volatile asset, few practitioners would feel happy with this extreme allocation as it will maximise the regret of having chosen the wrong asset class. Portfolios with higher return requirement are constructed by shifting out of asset 1 into asset 4 (US equities), which has an average return almost as high as asset 3 (European equities) but a lower minimum return. Again, for practical purposes the extremeness of the chosen portfolios will prove to be a serious limitation.

5.5 CONDITIONAL VALUE-AT-RISK

As investors come to recognise (unfortunately, often through bitter experience – ie, unexpected losses) that risk management is an integral part of portfolio management, there is an increasing interest in value-at-risk (VAR) as a measure of investment risk. Calculations of VAR help one to assess what maximum loss – either as an absolute monetary value or in terms of return – an investment portfolio might experience with confidence β over a prespecified time period. We need to specify a level of confidence (typically 0.95, ie, 95%) as the maximum possible loss will always be 100%. Interest in VAR as a risk measure is driven by regulatory frameworks, widespread popularity and intuitive appeal. However, the last is often ill-founded, as can be seen from the following list of serious shortcomings:

1. Investors subscribing to VAR implicitly state that they are indifferent between very small losses in excess of VAR and very high losses – even total ruin. This is hardly a realistic position.
2. VAR is not sub-additive, ie, we might find that the portfolio VAR is higher than the sum of the individual asset VARs. Suppose that we invest in a corporate bond with a 2% probability of default. With this default probability the VAR at the 95% confidence level is zero. However, if we move to a diversified bond portfolio (with zero default correlation) containing 100 bonds, the probability of at least one loss is 87% $(1 - 0.98^{100})$. Hence, portfolio optimisation using VAR would result in concentrated portfolios as the VAR measure would indicate that the concentrated portfolio was less risky.
3. VAR also has serious mathematical drawbacks. It is a non-smooth, non-convex and multi-extremum (many local minima) function that makes it difficult to use in portfolio construction. We therefore have to rely on heuristics and can never be 100% sure that the optimal solution has been found. As VAR-based scenario optimisation effectively has to

count all losses higher than a moving threshold, keeping track of this changing tail, while at the same time maximising VAR, is a complicated, mixed-integer problem. Little commercially available software is available to overcome this problem.

Despite these drawbacks, investors display an astonishing interest in VAR.[20] However, there is a close relative of value-at-risk known as "conditional value-at-risk" (CVAR).[21] CVAR provides information which is complementary to that given by plain VAR in that it measures the expected excess loss over VAR if a loss larger than VAR actually occurs. Hence, it is the average of the worst $(1 - \beta)$ losses. CVAR must, by definition, be larger than VAR as it provides information about what kind of losses might hide in the tail of the distribution (hence its alternative name of "tail VAR"). Whereas VAR is a quantile, CVAR is a conditional tail expectation – ie, an expected value for those realisations that fall below the VAR threshold. Also in contrast to VAR, CVAR is sub-additive and can easily be implemented using linear programming, making it computationally very attractive. CVAR can be written as

$$R_{CVAR}(\mathbf{w}, \beta) = R_{VAR} + \frac{\overbrace{\frac{1}{S}\sum_{s=1}^{S}\max[R_{VAR} - \mathbf{w}'\mathbf{R}_s, 0]}^{\text{average excess loss over all scenarios}}}{\underbrace{1-\beta}_{\substack{\text{probability of}\\\text{excess loss}}}} \tag{5.16}$$

where R_{VAR} is the return VAR – the maximum percentage loss with confidence β. It has been shown that we can write portfolio construction by scenario optimisation using CVAR as risk measure as the linear program below,[22] where we minimise

$$R_{VAR} + \frac{1}{S}\frac{1}{1-\beta}\sum_{s=1}^{S}d_s \tag{5.17}$$

with respect to d_s, $\mathbf{w}$ and R_{VAR} under the constraints

$$d_s \geq R_{VAR} - \mathbf{w}'\overline{\mathbf{R}}_s, \quad s=1,\ldots,S$$
$$d_s \geq 0, \quad s=1,\ldots,S$$
$$\mathbf{w}'\overline{\mathbf{R}} \geq R_{target}$$
$$\mathbf{w}'\mathbf{1} = 0 \tag{5.18}$$

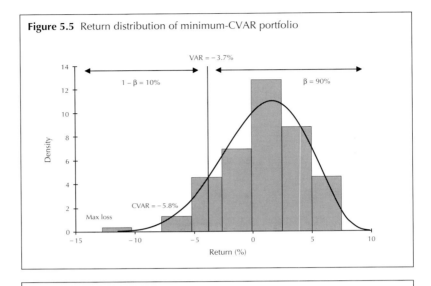

Figure 5.5 Return distribution of minimum-CVAR portfolio

Table 5.3 Minimum-CVAR portfolios for different confidence levels

		Confidence level				
		0.75	**0.8**	**0.85**	**0.9**	**0.95**
	w_1	43.7	49.3	23.2	23.3	25.7
Weights (%)	w_2	14.0	9.6	14.9	18.5	21.6
	w_3	2.8	0.0	0.0	0.0	0.0
	w_4	39.5	41.0	61.9	58.2	52.8
Risk (%)	VAR	0.93	1.7	2.73	3.7	5.20
	CVAR	3.65	4.3	4.94	5.8	6.86

Assets 1–4 are, respectively, UK, Japanese, European and US equities. Results calculated for return data in Table A1 of Appendix A1.

Suppose we use the data in Appendix A as a description of a finite set of scenarios. We will examine a particular problem in which the objective is to minimise CVAR for $\beta = 0.9$.[23] The solution is given in Table 5.3, where we see that an allocation of 23.3% to asset 1, 18.5% to asset 2 and the remaining 58.2% to asset 4 yields the minimum CVAR of 5.8%. The corresponding VAR is 3.7%. The distribution of portfolio returns corresponding to this allocation and the scenario matrix **S** is plotted in Figure 5.5 along with the best-fitting distribution (in this case a general beta distribution) imposed on the graph. Figure 5.5 shows the maximum loss, CVAR and VAR, and it splits the distribution into those returns smaller than VAR and those higher than VAR. It should be noted that VAR calculated from the procedure above is not the minimum VAR for a

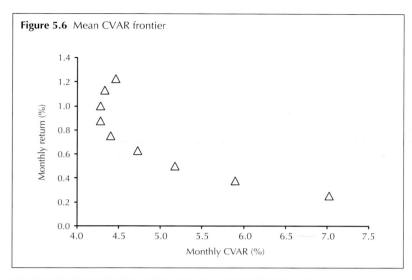

Figure 5.6 Mean CVAR frontier

Table 5.4 Portfolios along mean CVAR frontier

	Return (%)								
	0.25	**0.38**	**0.50**	**0.63**	**0.75**	**0.88**	**1.00**	**1.13**	**1.23**
Weights (%)									
w_1	1.46	22.41	43.35	45.12	47.45	46.87	34.91	8.02	0.00
w_2	98.54	77.59	56.65	43.25	29.63	17.16	9.26	7.30	0.31
w_3	0.00	0.00	0.00	0.00	0.00	0.00	8.41	22.61	29.79
w_4	0.00	0.00	0.00	11.63	22.91	35.96	47.41	62.07	69.90
Risk (%)									
VAR	4.37	3.30	2.52	2.04	1.76	1.49	1.75	2.03	2.16
CVAR	7.03	5.89	5.17	4.73	4.40	4.28	4.27	4.33	4.46

Assets 1–4 as in previous tables.

given confidence level (though in most cases it is not far from it). It is also easy to see that portfolio returns are not normally distributed, which is why we might want to use scenario optimisation. CVAR (−5.8%) is higher than VAR (−3.7%) as CVAR adds the expected excess losses to VAR. The relationship between VAR and CVAR for various confidence levels can be judged from Table 5.3. The more we move into the tail of the distribution, the closer the results both risk measures give.[24]

VAR and CVAR only coincide if the tail of the distribution is cut off. Although for a normal distribution it is generally true that the two risk measures become increasingly similar as we move into the tail of a distribution (because the likelihood of large losses becomes small very fast), this is not necessarily true for non-normal distributions. There was convergence in our example as we had a limited data set that eventually truncated itself. Applying the same logic as before, we can calculate the geometric location of all mean CVAR-efficient portfolios as in Figure 5.6. Note that only a few of these portfolios are truly efficient as is the case for the other two objectives. Data for the underlying portfolios are given in Table 5.4.

As with the techniques described earlier in the chapter, linear programming tends to produce portfolios that are concentrated in a few holdings. However, the computational ease and theoretical superiority of CVAR as a risk measure make CVAR optimisation an interesting alternative to traditional portfolio construction methods.

5.6 CONCLUSION

Scenario optimisation demands considerably more effort from investors than traditional Markowitz optimisation with its widely available mean–variance optimisation software solutions. Nevertheless, scenario optimisation is worth the effort if returns are non-normally distributed or if options are involved. However, most users of scenario optimisation take a very naive approach, calculating the option payoff for a given strike using the simulated asset price for that scenario. This allows only the option weight as a choice variable, whereas, for example, the value of the option strike is equally important. Moreover, this approach might generate arbitrage opportunities if the option is priced under a different distribution to that used for scenario generation. This is likely to be the case if option prices are taken from current market prices.

APPENDIX A: DATA SET FOR SCENARIO OPTIMISATION

So that the reader can replicate the calculations in this chapter, the data set on which they are based is provided in Table A1. The data set is a 10-year time series of monthly hedged returns (hedged into US dollars) for the four major equity markets (Europe, UK, US and Japan) plus a time series for one-month US Treasury bills, which represent the risk-free security in our analysis. The data can be viewed as a time series of returns or, alternatively, if we believe the data are drawn from a stationary distribution, we could also interpret each monthly row as a new scenario. The reader may care to check for himself that the returns are non-normally distributed, exhibiting skewness and excess kurtosis. While not a prerequisite for scenario optimisation, this nevertheless makes the technique more interesting as it can explicitly address non-normality.

Table A1 10-year time series of monthly hedged returns for major equity markets and one-month US Treasury bills (%)

Date	UK	Japan	Europe	US	US bills
30 April 1991	0.47	−0.35	0.60	0.40	0.47
31 May 1991	0.14	0.32	4.15	4.16	0.47
28 June 1991	−3.72	−7.65	−3.77	−4.58	0.47
31 July 1991	7.48	2.89	0.25	4.69	0.47
30 August 1991	2.23	−6.16	0.97	2.43	0.45
30 September 1991	−0.74	5.57	−2.45	−1.69	0.45
31 October 1991	−2.21	2.97	−1.26	1.73	0.41
29 November 1991	−6.59	−8.09	−3.56	−4.04	0.37
31 December 1991	2.14	−1.03	0.10	11.43	0.32
31 January 1992	2.76	−4.45	5.45	−1.66	0.32
28 February 1992	−0.06	−5.38	2.72	1.15	0.33
31 March 1992	−4.97	−7.97	−1.98	−1.84	0.35
30 April 1992	9.42	−6.03	1.54	2.93	0.31
29 May 1992	1.95	3.52	1.92	0.41	0.32
30 June 1992	−8.24	−10.57	−6.21	−1.52	0.30
31 July 1992	−5.36	−0.25	−7.25	4.17	0.27
31 August 1992	−4.21	14.30	−5.54	−2.39	0.27
30 September 1992	8.13	−5.11	−0.50	1.09	0.23
30 October 1992	3.51	−1.91	1.66	0.61	0.24
30 November 1992	4.39	3.62	3.12	3.33	0.28
31 December 1992	3.43	−1.33	2.17	1.11	0.26
29 January 1993	−0.97	−0.41	1.16	0.88	0.24
26 February 1993	2.06	−1.35	5.85	1.32	0.23
31 March 1993	1.09	11.37	1.46	2.06	0.25
30 April 1993	−1.63	14.19	−1.42	−2.20	0.25
31 May 1993	1.03	−0.80	1.38	2.56	0.25
30 June 1993	2.10	−2.78	3.20	0.31	0.26
30 July 1993	1.39	5.34	4.70	−0.10	0.25
31 August 1993	6.05	2.29	6.41	3.62	0.26
30 September 1993	−1.89	−3.71	−2.91	−0.98	0.25
29 October 1993	4.35	1.95	6.68	1.76	0.26
30 November 1993	0.23	−15.86	−2.12	−0.67	0.27
31 December 1993	7.90	5.60	7.80	1.22	0.26
31 January 1994	2.98	13.85	4.72	3.64	0.25
28 February 1994	−4.27	−0.01	−4.67	−2.80	0.29
31 March 1994	−6.73	−5.52	−2.93	−4.32	0.30
29 April 1994	1.36	3.22	3.51	1.43	0.33
31 May 1994	−5.02	5.38	−4.30	1.68	0.36
30 June 1994	−1.82	−0.95	−4.88	−2.80	0.35
29 July 1994	5.78	−1.84	5.06	3.39	0.38
31 August 1994	5.64	0.89	1.14	3.95	0.39
30 September 1994	−7.27	−3.47	−5.80	−2.10	0.40
31 October 1994	2.38	0.91	0.91	2.32	0.43
30 November 1994	−0.37	−2.77	0.74	−3.39	0.48
30 December 1994	0.20	2.32	−0.13	1.49	0.47

Table A1 (*continued*)

Date	UK	Japan	Europe	US	US bills
31 January 1995	−3.01	−6.31	−2.02	2.78	0.50
28 February 1995	1.01	−6.85	0.93	3.97	0.49
31 March 1995	4.46	−2.37	−3.01	2.70	0.49
28 April 1995	2.59	2.47	5.11	3.16	0.49
31 May 1995	3.57	−5.05	3.33	3.93	0.48
30 June 1995	−0.05	−4.05	−0.33	2.48	0.46
31 July 1995	4.96	11.98	4.04	3.42	0.47
31 August 1995	0.76	6.59	0.62	0.03	0.45
29 September 1995	0.78	2.00	−0.12	4.51	0.45
31 October 1995	0.13	−1.55	−1.62	−0.03	0.46
30 November 1995	3.60	5.71	2.80	4.42	0.46
29 December 1995	1.12	7.18	2.40	1.53	0.42
31 January 1996	2.47	2.67	5.07	3.59	0.42
29 February 1996	−0.58	−3.01	1.07	1.06	0.42
29 March 1996	−0.34	5.47	2.29	1.03	0.43
30 April 1996	3.60	4.15	3.45	1.50	0.43
31 May 1996	−2.16	−1.61	0.58	2.69	0.43
28 June 1996	−0.92	2.39	1.60	0.61	0.43
31 July 1996	0.45	−6.81	−4.97	−4.38	0.44
30 August 1996	4.77	−2.29	2.33	2.26	0.44
30 September 1996	2.26	6.38	4.87	5.62	0.42
31 October 1996	0.51	−4.15	0.69	2.58	0.43
29 November 1996	2.44	2.38	6.78	7.58	0.43
31 December 1996	1.57	−4.46	2.01	−1.87	0.43
31 January 1997	3.39	−6.04	7.88	6.87	0.43
28 February 1997	1.25	2.15	3.94	0.73	0.44
31 March 1997	0.36	−0.33	3.22	−4.46	0.44
30 April 1997	2.99	6.51	2.00	6.61	0.44
30 May 1997	3.69	2.59	2.52	5.68	0.41
30 June 1997	−0.40	6.16	8.95	4.58	0.43
31 July 1997	6.20	0.79	9.65	7.93	0.44
29 August 1997	−0.78	−6.66	−9.37	−5.92	0.44
30 September 1997	8.94	−0.71	8.28	5.24	0.43
31 October 1997	−7.74	−9.22	−7.98	−2.71	0.43
28 November 1997	−0.11	0.07	4.62	4.86	0.43
31 December 1997	6.00	−3.30	5.91	1.50	0.45
30 January 1998	5.34	6.85	5.72	1.31	0.43
27 February 1998	6.08	0.56	7.77	7.03	0.44
31 March 1998	3.42	−1.08	10.17	5.20	0.43
30 April 1998	0.21	−0.85	0.12	1.19	0.42
29 May 1998	−1.36	−0.37	4.07	−1.99	0.42
30 June 1998	−0.74	2.01	2.53	4.31	0.42
31 July 1998	−0.21	3.04	2.47	−0.97	0.42
31 August 1998	−9.77	−13.21	−15.48	−13.90	0.41
30 September 1998	−3.69	−6.01	−9.85	6.59	0.36
30 October 1998	7.38	0.41	8.04	7.76	0.36
30 November 1998	5.74	10.22	8.09	6.81	0.38
31 December 1998	2.25	−4.58	3.76	5.91	0.37

Table A1 (*continued*)

Date	UK	Japan	Europe	US	US bills
29 January 1999	0.08	4.15	2.55	4.32	0.37
26 February 1999	4.64	0.17	−1.10	−2.79	0.39
31 March 1999	2.29	14.11	2.00	4.16	0.38
30 April 1999	4.10	5.42	4.92	3.62	0.38
31 May 1999	−5.15	−3.22	−2.92	−2.32	0.39
30 June 1999	1.86	9.26	3.69	5.38	0.40
30 July 1999	−1.24	4.97	−2.84	−3.24	0.40
31 August 1999	0.36	−4.91	3.25	−0.63	0.41
30 September 1999	−4.00	3.79	−0.92	−2.97	0.40
29 October 1999	3.29	2.74	5.61	6.54	0.42
30 November 1999	4.17	2.62	7.75	2.15	0.44
31 December 1999	4.59	6.93	12.96	6.98	0.45
31 January 2000	−9.71	0.56	−3.57	−5.35	0.47
29 February 2000	−0.78	0.43	10.26	−2.37	0.48
31 March 2000	6.31	1.66	1.06	9.98	0.49
28 April 2000	−2.26	−1.84	0.24	−3.23	0.49
31 May 2000	1.07	−4.92	−0.99	−2.64	0.47
30 June 2000	−0.30	5.69	−0.52	2.40	0.49
31 July 2000	1.81	−7.47	1.02	−1.79	0.52
31 August 2000	3.97	4.34	2.10	5.20	0.53
29 September 2000	−4.31	−3.14	−4.68	−5.44	0.52
31 October 2000	2.56	−4.16	2.67	−0.71	0.53
30 November 2000	−3.43	−2.16	−5.39	−7.90	0.52
29 December 2000	1.56	−2.55	−0.33	−0.15	0.49
31 January 2001	0.61	1.13	1.96	3.66	0.42
28 February 2001	−5.34	−3.24	−8.27	−8.94	0.40
30 March 2001	−3.11	3.96	−4.84	−6.37	0.36

APPENDIX B: SCENARIO OPTIMISATION WITH S-PLUS

We assume in this appendix that the reader is familiar with the basics of S-PLUS and NUOPT for S-PLUS.[25] If not, there are many excellent textbooks on this exciting modelling language that allows one to deal with complex financial modelling problems.[26] Here we will focus on mean–absolute deviation (MAD, discussed in Section 5.3) as an objective. The web page that accompanies this book offers downloads of further S-PLUS functions that perform sophisticated portfolio construction and data modelling operations. Programs will include (among others) optimisations based on lower partial moments and semivariance as well as portfolio resampling. The functions will create single portfolios as well as tracing out efficient frontiers.

We start with the usual housekeeping operations – that is, we clear the workspace, include the NUOPT module, load the data, check for missing observations and store the asset names for further usage. To do this, key in the following instructions, highlight them and press F10 to execute the command.

```
remove(ls(""))
module(nuopt)
import.data(FileName=scenarios.xls",FileType="Excel",
  DataFrame="scenarios")
if(any(is.na(scenarios))==T) stop("no missing data are
  allowed")
asset.names<-c(dimnames(scenarios)[[2]])
```

The data frame "scenarios" contains the scenario matrix **S**. The expected format is a rectangular data matrix that contains as many columns as assets and as many rows as scenarios. The scenario matrix is assumed to be arbitrage-free. This is the only set of information we need, together with inputs for the costs of up- and downside deviations from the portfolio mean.

In the next step we write a function that defines the MAD model for NUOPT. We start by defining this function and its inputs:

```
MAD.model<-function(scenarios, cost.up, cost.dn,
  r.target){}
```

The function "MAD.model" expects a scenario matrix, inputs for upside and downside deviation costs as well as a target return for the MAD optimisation. We can now start to insert the code within the { } brackets. We first calculate asset means for all assets –

```
rbar<-apply(scenarios, 2, mean)
```

– and count the number of scenarios:

```
n.obs<-nrow(scenarios)
```

We then set up indices to define assets and scenarios. Use "j" to index assets and "t" to index scenarios:

```
asset<-Set()
period<-Set()
j<-Element(set=asset)
t<-Element(set=period)
```

Having done that, we define parameters (which remain fixed in the optimisation, ie, they are not choice variables):

```
R<-Parameter(scenarios, index=dprod(t,j))
rbar<-Parameter(as.array(rbar), index=j)
r.target<-Parameter(r.target, changeable=T)
cost.up<-Parameter(cost.up, changeable=T)
cost.dn<-Parameter(cost.dn, changeable=T)
```

Now we need to define the variables. As in the main text, we use weights as well as upside and downside deviations as variables:

```
x<-Variable(index=j)
up<-Variable(index=t)
dn<-Variable(index=t)
up[t]>=0
dn[t]>=0
```

The last is defined implicitly using the identity

```
up[t]-dn[t]==Sum((R[t,j]-rbar[j])*x[j],j)
```

as "up[t]" and "dn[t]" are constrained to be non-negative. Finally, we set our objective:

```
risk<-Objective(type="minimize")
risk~Sum((cost.up*up[t]+cost.dn*dn[t]),t)/(n.obs-1)
```

as well as the relevant constraints:

```
Sum(rbar[j]*x[j],j)>=r.target
Sum(x[j],j)==1
x[j]>=0
```

We now use the function MAD.model to set up a system that can be solved:

```
MAD.system<-System(MAD.model, scenarios, cost.up,
    cost.dn, r.target)
```

At this stage we can use the show.model() command to view the model we have just defined.

The last step is to solve the model, calculate weights as well as the value of the objective, and set up a correctly labelled weight vector:

```
solution<-solve(MAD.system, trace=T)
weight<-matrix(round(solution$variable$x$current,
   digit=2)*100, ncol=1)
risk<-solution$objective
dimnames(weight)<-list(asset.names, "weight")
```

The downloadable codes on the website will also contain a function –

```
MAD.frontier<-function(scenarios, cost.up, cost.dn,
   n.pf){...}
```

– that allows the tracing out of a complete efficient frontier.

1 See Dembo (1991) as the classic reference for scenario optimisation.
2 See Mak, Morton and Wood (1999) for a simple method for deriving confidence bands for a particular solution to a stochastic programme.
3 See Pflug (1996) for a taxonomy of stochastic optimisation problems.
4 We follow Grinold (1999) for the remaining part of this section. The author is indebted to R. Grinold for providing the return data set used in this chapter.
5 See Cochrane (2001) or Bossaerts (2002) on pricing kernels.
6 See Grinold (1996).
7 Note that we do not report the sample means as we do not intend to rely on them.
8 An intuitive description of this process is found in Dembo and Freeman (1998).
9 Supposing that we have 10 years of monthly data for four time series, we can then draw random numbers from a uniform distribution ranging from one to 120. If we sample n, we take the return of the nth month across all our assets. Repeatedly sampling (with replacement, ie, August 1998 could be sampled several times within a year) and compounding returns gives us resampled multiperiod returns.
10 Bootstrapping bond returns should therefore be applied with caution as bond yields exhibit mean-reversion and duration is also a function of the interest level. (For a brief explanation of resampling, see Note 9.)
11 See Lütkepohl (1991).
12 See Ziemba and Mulvey (1998).
13 See Dert (1995, p. 60).
14 See Pliska (1997) for a complete definition of arbitrage opportunities.
15 The reader should note that we would also find arbitrage where $\mathbf{w1} = 0$, $\mathbf{S}^1\mathbf{w} \geq 0$ and at least one of the inequalities holds strictly. The dual problem to Equation (5.10) is $\min \mathbf{0}'\mathbf{w}$ subject to $\mathbf{S}^1\boldsymbol{\pi} = 1$, $\boldsymbol{\pi} \geq 0$. If the dual has a solution, then $\mathbf{w1}$ cannot be negative.
16 This model was introduced into the literature by Konno and Yamazaki (1991).
17 See Feinstein and Thapa (1993) or Speranza (1993) on linear optimisation in portfolio construction. It is sometimes argued that linear transaction cost constraints help to mitigate the error maximisation properties of portfolio optimisers. While it will certainly be true that the range of solutions becomes smaller, it is not clear at all how one should deal with the inherent arbitrariness in this kind of portfolio optimisation heuristic.
18 See Young (1998).
19 However, if returns are multivariate normal or investors' preferences are closely approximated by mean–variance objectives, mean–variance-based investing will show superior results.
20 See Jorion (2001) or Pearson (2002) for the application of VAR in investment management.

21 See Pflug (2000) on the relationship between VAR and CVAR.
22 See Larsen, Mausser and Uryasev (2001).
23 The calculations have been performed using the NUOPT optimiser under SPLUS. However, they can easily be replicated using EXCEL. For EXCEL to be able to deal with the large number of constraints, the box linear problem within Solver must be ticked.
24 See also Pflug (2000) for the relationship between VAR and CVAR.
25 Extensive information on S-PLUS can be found on MathSoft's home page, http://www.mathsoft.com/splus/.
26 See Krause and Olson (2000) or Venables and Ripley (1997).

BIBLIOGRAPHY

Bossaerts, P., 2002, *The Paradox of Asset Pricing* (Princeton University Press).

Cochrane, J., 2001, *Asset Pricing* (Princeton University Press).

Dembo, R., 1991, "Scenario Optimization", *Annals of Operations Research* 30, pp. 63–80.

Dembo, R., and A. Freeman, 1998, *The Rules of Risk* (New York: John Wiley & Sons).

Dert, C., 1995, "Asset Liability Management for Pension Funds: A Multistage Chance Constrained Programming Approach", Ph.D. Thesis, Erasmus University Rotterdam.

Feinstein, C., and M. Thapa, 1993, "A Reformulation of Mean Absolute Deviation Portfolio Optimization Model", *Management Science* 39, pp. 1552–3.

Grinold, R., 1996, "Domestic Grapes from Imported Wine", *Journal of Portfolio Management* 22, pp. 29–40.

Grinold, R., 1999, "Mean–Variance and Scenario-Based Approaches to Portfolio Selection", *Journal of Portfolio Management* 25, pp. 10–22.

Jorion, P., 2001, *Value at Risk*, Second Edition (New York: McGraw-Hill).

Krause, A., and Olson M., 2000, *The Basics of S and S-Plus*, Second Edition (New York: Springer).

Konno, H., and H. Yamazaki, 1991, "Mean Absolute Deviation Portfolio Optimization Model and its Application to Tokyo Stock Market", *Management Science* 37, pp. 519–31.

Larsen, N., H. Mausser and S. Uryasev, 2001, "Algorithms for Optimization of Value at Risk", Research Report no. 2001-9, University of Florida; http://www.ise.ufl.edu/uryasev.

Lütkepohl, H., 1991, *Introduction to Multiple Time Series Analysis* (Berlin: Springer Verlag).

Mak, W., D. Morton and R. Wood, 1999, "Monte Carlo Bounding Techniques for Determining Solution Quality in Stochastic Programs", *Operations Research Letters* 24, pp. 47–56.

Mulvey, W., and J. Ziemba, 1998, *Worldwide Asset Liability Management* (Cambridge University Press).

Pearson, N., 2002, *Risk Budgeting* (New York: John Wiley & Sons).

Pliska, S., 1997, *Introduction to Mathematical Finance* (Oxford: Blackwell Publishers).

Pflug, G., 1996, *Optimization of Stochastic Models* (Boston: Kluwer Academic Publishers).

Pflug, G., 2000, "Some Remarks on the Value at Risk and the Conditional Value at Risk", in S. Uryasev (ed.), *Probabilistic Constrained Optimization: Methodology and Applications* (Amsterdam: Kluwer Academic Publishers), pp. 272–81.

Speranza, M., 1993, "Linear Programming Models for Portfolio Optimization", *Journal of Finance*, 14, pp. 107–23.

Venables, W., and B. Ripley, 1997, *Modern Applied Statistics with S-PLUS*, Third Edition (New York: Springer-Verlag).

Young, M., 1998, "A Minimax Portfolio Selection Rule with Linear Programming Solution", *Management Science* 44, pp. 673–83.

Ziemba, W., and J. Mulvey, 1998, Worldwide Asset and Liability Modelling (Cambridge University Press).

Benchmark-Relative Optimisation

6.1 TRACKING ERROR: SELECTED ISSUES

Tracking error measures the dispersion (volatility) of active returns (portfolio return minus benchmark return) around the mean active return. It is designed as a measure of relative investment risk and was introduced into the academic arena in the early 1980s.[1] Since then it has become the single most important risk measure in communications between asset manager, client and consultant.

Benchmark-relative investment management has often been rationalised from either a risk perspective (a benchmark anchors the portfolio in risk–return space and thus gives sponsors confidence in what their money is invested in and what risk this investment carries), or a return perspective (claiming that it is easier to forecast relative returns than total returns). However, the return argument looks spurious; to say that forecasting relative distances is possible whereas forecasting absolute distances is not ignores the fact that the two are closely related: a total distance is the same as the benchmark distance times a relative distance. A more plausible argument that is made is that the estimation error is smaller for relative than for absolute return forecasts.

6.1.1 Tracking error and time aggregation

Assume that decisions on the weight of asset i relative to the benchmark b are made on the basis of relative risk premia, $r_i - r_b$. It can then be shown that the volatility of relative returns will be smaller than the volatility of absolute returns of asset i if[2]

$$\text{var}(r_i - r_b) < \text{var}(r_i) \Leftrightarrow \sigma_i^2 + \sigma_b^2 - 2\rho\sigma_i\sigma_b < \sigma_i^2 \Leftrightarrow \rho > \frac{1}{2}\left(\frac{\sigma_b}{\sigma_i}\right)$$

Tracking error (TE) is calculated in its simplest standard deviation-based *ex-post* form as

$$\sigma_a = \sqrt{\frac{1}{T-1}\sum_{t=1}^{T}\left(r_{at} - \bar{r}_a\right)^2} \tag{6.1}$$

Small deviations from the mean active return, $\bar{r}_a$, carry little weight, while large deviations are increasingly punished as a result of the square function.[3] This is also called a "return-based" estimate. The *ex-ante* TE is calculated using the familiar quadratic form

$$\sigma_a = \sqrt{\mathbf{w}_a' \, \boldsymbol{\Omega} \, \mathbf{w}_a} \qquad (6.2)$$

where $\mathbf{w}_a$ denotes a $k \times 1$ vector of active positions. It is therefore also called a "weight-based" estimate.

Now suppose that we construct monthly portfolios with the same *ex-ante* expected TE as in Equation (6.2) in each month. How can we aggregate this into an annual number? Assuming for simplicity that annual returns are additive ($r_{a,12} = \sum_{t=1}^{12} r_{a,t}$), we can calculate the volatility of annual active returns from[4]

$$\text{var}\left(\sum_{t=1}^{12} r_{a,t} \right) = \text{var}(r_{a,1}) + \cdots + \text{var}(r_{a,12}) = 12\,\sigma_a^2 \qquad (6.3)$$

Suppose we have calculated the *ex-ante* TE for each month to be $1\%/\sqrt{12}$ and assume also that, even though we made no forecast error for the monthly TE, the realised TE is still different from 1%. What could have caused this discrepancy? How realistic is the above procedure? Essentially, Equation (6.3) assumes period-by-period active returns to be serially independent. However, as most tactical positions tend to stay on an account for a prolonged time and as factors driving active returns tend to be trending (serially correlated), this will also cause active return to be autocorrelated.[5] This means that every negative (positive) active return is now more likely to be followed by another negative (positive) active return, which creates more dispersion in cumulative active returns than if they were not autocorrelated. At this point we can borrow from the logic of variance ratio tests, which test for serial correlation in asset returns.[6] If the "true" annual TE is higher than the annualised TE and the variance ratio

$$\frac{(\text{true tracking error})^2}{(\text{annualised tracking error})^2} = \frac{\text{var}\left(\sum_{i=1}^{12} r_i \right)}{12\,\sigma_a^2} = \text{variance ratio}$$

is significantly greater than one, we could conclude that returns show positive serial correlation. Now we can turn the idea around and calculate a leverage factor (variance ratio) that has to be applied to single-period volatilities if returns over multiple periods are autocorrelated:

$$\underbrace{\text{var}\left(\sum_{1}^{12} r_{a,t} \right)}_{\substack{\text{actual annual} \\ \text{volatility}}} = \underbrace{\left(1 + 2\sum_{i=1}^{11} \left(1 - \frac{i}{12} \right) \rho_i \right)}_{\text{variance ratio}} \underbrace{12\,\sigma_a^2}_{\substack{\text{naive} \\ \text{annual} \\ \text{volatility}}} \qquad (6.4)$$

where ρ_i is the ith-order autocorrelation coefficient. If autocorrelations were zero, we could simply multiply the monthly volatility by 12 to arrive at annual volatility. We can use Equation (6.4) first to calculate the "fudge factor" and then to adjust the naive volatility estimate. Though it might look tempting to use this fudge factor, it should also be kept in mind that autocorrelations are not easier to forecast than TE – in fact they are notorious for their variability.

It is important to note that TE has no link with performance.[7] It would be incorrect to conclude that a fund with a TE of 0.5% per annum would (assuming normality) have a one in six chance of underperformance by more than 0.5%. The obvious example is a fund that underperforms/out-performs its benchmark by exactly 10 basis points (bp) every month: as the volatility of a constant is zero, we would find that the fund and benchmark drifted apart considerably over the long run, yet the TE using the conventional calculation given above would remain zero.[8] This is equivalent to saying that one cannot have an educated discussion about a normal distribution by considering only the dispersion parameter.[9] The core problem is that TE is used to calculate performance ranges under the silent assumption that average active performance is zero, while at the same time realised TE is measured and estimated using the non-zero sample mean. It would be more realistic to reconcile both assumptions by also basing TE estimates on the zero-mean assumption. The average of squared active returns would yield a higher TE and yet be more consistent with the assumption of zero active return.

6.1.2 Mis-estimation of tracking error

Ex-ante TE (usually weight-based estimates calculated from multifactor risk models) is an estimate of the volatility of future active returns around the mean expected active return. It is heavily used in determining the relative riskiness of active strategies by managers who are given client-specific risk limits. However, if *ex-ante* TE is compared with its *ex-post* counterpart (the volatility of historic active returns), the measures are usually found to differ. There are many reasons why Equation (6.2) might provide a poor forecast for Equation (6.1), and it is not possible (or advisable) to counter every one of them. It should be emphasised that although TE underestimation has been the main focus of recent interest, overestimation is in many cases almost equally likely. In this section we review the main causes of TE mis-estimation, the four most important of which are as follows.

1. *Sampling error* (too few data).[10] As the true TE is unknown, we have to rely on realised historical data, but since historical data are by definition limited, we will (under the assumption that model parameters do not change) always mis-estimate the true TE. However, the usual

maximum-likelihood methods will yield unbiased estimates, so we cannot claim that sampling error leads to over- or underestimation of TE. This will change for optimised portfolios, where estimation error always leads to underestimation of expected TE (see Chapter 3).

2. *Modelling error* (non-stationary data, or wrong process assumptions).[11] TE estimates based on the stationarity assumption will fail if volatilities or correlations are time-varying.[12] Although conditional risk (multifactor) models are certainly more suited to dealing with time-varying moments, over- or underestimation is equally likely. Rising correlations lead – other things being equal – to lower TEs, whereas falling correlations result in increased ones. As sudden changes in correlation are often the result of exogenous shocks (for example, the increased correlation between all bond markets after the surprise Federal Reserve interest rate hike in early 1994 and the reduced correlation between high- and low-grade fixed-income instruments after the Russian crisis of 1998), they are by definition difficult to forecast. Modelling error also arises if we assume uncorrelated period-by-period returns (in individual time series or risk factors) when in fact they are not uncorrelated. The most prominent example here is the autocorrelation in growth-style factor returns during the TMT (technology, media and telecom) bubble. Attempts to fix this problem by estimating the correlation structure should be treated with caution as this calls for forecastability of returns, making risk management a secondary issue. The additional noise from ill-suited forecasts will increase mis-estimation rather than reducing it.

3. *In-sample optimisation.*[13] Portfolio optimisation using historical data is essentially an in-sample optimisation exercise. As portfolio optimisers "over-adjust" to the data – exploiting every minor, statistically insignificant and economically implausible opportunity – they will be disappointed by out-of-sample performance.[14]

4. *Constant weight assumption.*[15] TE estimates are based on the assumption that portfolio weights stay fixed, while in fact they do not. Adding uncertainty about weights will unambiguously tend to an underestimation of TE.[16] However, the importance of this effect is considered differently.[17]

6.1.3 Tracking error optimisation

TE optimisation can be solved within the framework already set out in Chapter 1. We set $\mathbf{A} = \mathbf{1}'$ and $\mathbf{b} = \mathbf{0}$ in Equation (1.3), where $\mathbf{1}$ is a $k \times 1$ vector of ones. The utility maximisation now becomes

$$Utility \approx \mathbf{w}'\boldsymbol{\mu} - \frac{1}{2\lambda}\,\mathbf{w}'\boldsymbol{\Omega}\mathbf{w} \quad \text{subject to} \quad \mathbf{1}'\mathbf{w} = \mathbf{0} \qquad (6.5)$$

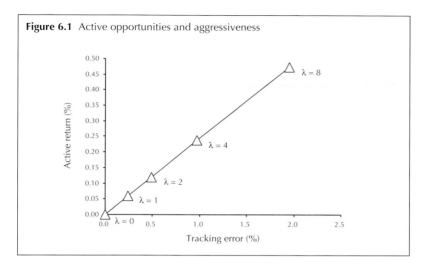

Figure 6.1 Active opportunities and aggressiveness

with the familiar-looking solution

$$\mathbf{w}_a^* = \lambda \mathbf{\Omega}^{-1} \left(\mathbf{\mu} - \mathbf{1}(\mathbf{1}'\mathbf{\Omega}^{-1}\mathbf{1})^{-1} \mathbf{1}'\mathbf{\Omega}^{-1}\mathbf{\mu} \right) \qquad (6.6)$$

Note that it is the self-financing constraint (over- and underweights must sum to zero) that gives the vector of portfolio weights a new interpretation. A change in aggressiveness (λ) will scale the optimal weights up or down, but it will leave the slope of the TE-efficient frontier unchanged. Again, we will use a simple numerical example to illustrate this. Suppose we are given expected returns, covariance matrix and benchmark weights on a given asset universe as

$$\mathbf{\Omega} = \begin{bmatrix} 0.04 & 0.0252 & 0.0036 & 0.0024 \\ 0.0025 & 0.0441 & 0.0038 & 0.0025 \\ 0.0036 & 0.0038 & 0.0036 & 0.0014 \\ 0.0024 & 0.0025 & 0.0014 & 0.0016 \end{bmatrix}, \quad \mathbf{\mu} = \begin{bmatrix} 4 \\ 3 \\ 2 \\ 1 \end{bmatrix} \qquad (6.7)$$

For a risk tolerance of one we optimally invest into

$$\mathbf{w}_a^* = \mathbf{\Omega}^{-1} \left(\mathbf{\mu} - \mathbf{1}(\mathbf{1}'\mathbf{\Omega}^{-1}\mathbf{1})^{-1} \mathbf{1}'\mathbf{\Omega}^{-1}\mathbf{\mu} \right) = \begin{bmatrix} 0.65\% \\ -0.008\% \\ 3.92\% \\ -4.58\% \end{bmatrix} \qquad (6.8)$$

The active frontier (geometric location of active opportunities) is plotted in Figure 6.1; it starts at the origin, where a zero tolerance for active risk implies zero active weights and, hence, a 100% investment in the passive benchmark.

All portfolios along the active frontier are perfectly correlated as the active portfolio weights differ only by a linear scaling, which depends on the investor's aggressiveness. This also means that all portfolios contain exactly the same information. Note that so far, no information on benchmark weights has been needed. As long as we can go short (and face no additional constraints), the optimal active portfolio is independent of a particular benchmark. This results in perfect scalability (an investment process is deemed scalable if a given set of active positions – ie, the model portfolio – can be implemented on various client benchmarks with little or no effort), which is a necessary requirement for modern investment processes as it allows new business to be managed at low marginal cost, the marginal costs of transforming an already produced model portfolio to a different benchmark being almost zero.

6.2 TRACKING ERROR EFFICIENCY VERSUS MEAN–VARIANCE EFFICIENCY

Most practitioners feel uncomfortable with benchmark portfolios and TE constraints as they feel that the TE straightjacket is detrimental to overall portfolio efficiency. Despite long being scorned, academia finally provided help.[18] Suppose that a manager is given a benchmark and he/she forecasts that over the next year some assets will deliver the same return as the benchmark but at significantly reduced total risk (this is the same as saying that the benchmark is not efficient). While this is an attractive opportunity in total risk–return space, it is much less so in TE–active return space. The investment is expected to yield no return in excess of the benchmark return but would expose the portfolio manager to active risk. A fixed-income investor with a domestic government bond benchmark has no incentive to invest into currency-hedged international fixed-income instruments (which give the same expected return under the assumption of negligible transaction costs and a zero risk premium on currency risk) as he would take on TE without compensation in the form of increased returns. This leads to a paradox. Plan sponsors hire a manager precisely because they think he or she has better information, but the manager cannot exploit this information advantage under the imposed TE constraint.

We will now look more formally at the key question considered in this section: how do TE-efficient portfolios compare with Markowitz-efficient portfolios in mean–variance space, ie, are TE-efficient portfolios also mean–variance-efficient? Optimal active portfolios were constructed in Section 6.1. In this section these active portfolios will be added to a given benchmark portfolio and the resulting long portfolios in mean–variance space will be compared.

Suppose that the benchmark portfolio is given as $\mathbf{w}_b = (0.25\ 0.1\ 0.55\ 0.1)'$. We can now add the active (zero-investment portfolios) from Figure 6.1 to this benchmark portfolio and compare mean–variance-efficient portfolios

Are Tracking Error efficient portfolios also MV efficient?

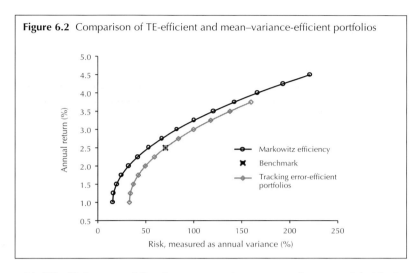

Figure 6.2 Comparison of TE-efficient and mean–variance-efficient portfolios

with TE-efficient portfolios in mean–variance space. In general (with the exception of a mean–variance-efficient benchmark, in which case the equality sign would hold) we can write

$$\mathbf{w}_{te} = \mathbf{w}_b + \lambda \mathbf{w}_a^* \neq \mathbf{w}_{mv}^* \tag{6.9}$$

Portfolios constructed according to Equation (6.9) are plotted in Figure 6.2. The frontier of all TE-efficient portfolios passes through the (inefficient) benchmark and at all levels of return is dominated by the mean–variance-efficient frontier. Even though, in our setting, the portfolio manager has all the information required to reach the Markowitz-efficient frontier, the imposed TE constraint makes doing so unattractive to him. Every TE-efficient portfolio will lie exactly the same distance away from a mean–variance-efficient portfolio with the same expected return as the benchmark portfolio itself.[19]

It would appear, then, that there is an independent portfolio that, if added to a TE-efficient portfolio, would result in a Markowitz-efficient portfolio. We see from Figure 6.2 that this portfolio would have to have the following properties (among others):[20]

❑ *Zero-investment portfolio.* This is necessary to guarantee 100% investment (weights in a zero-investment portfolio sum to zero and the portfolio's variance equals the distance between the two frontiers);

❑ *Zero return.* Adding the independent portfolio to a TE-efficient portfolio must leave the return expectation constant; and

❑ *Zero covariance with Markowitz-efficient portfolios.* If this were not so the distance would not remain constant as the covariance terms would destroy additivity.

Assuming TE optimisation under an add-up constraint, weights for this add-on portfolio, $\mathbf{w}_z$, can in general be derived as

$$\mathbf{w}_z = \frac{1}{d}\left[(be-af)\,\boldsymbol{\Omega}^{-1}\mathbf{1} + (bf-ce)\,\boldsymbol{\Omega}^{-1}\boldsymbol{\mu} + d\boldsymbol{\Omega}^{-1}\boldsymbol{\Gamma}\right] \qquad (6.10)$$

where $a = \boldsymbol{\mu}'\boldsymbol{\Omega}^{-1}\boldsymbol{\mu}$, $b = \boldsymbol{\mu}'\boldsymbol{\Omega}^{-1}\mathbf{1}$, $c = \mathbf{1}'\boldsymbol{\Omega}^{-1}\mathbf{1}$, $d = ac - b^2$, $e = \boldsymbol{\mu}'\boldsymbol{\Omega}^{-1}\boldsymbol{\Gamma}$, $f = \mathbf{1}'\boldsymbol{\Omega}^{-1}\boldsymbol{\Gamma}$ and $\boldsymbol{\Gamma}$ is the $k \times 1$ vector of asset covariances with the benchmark assets (for all k assets). Using the data in our example, we obtain

$$\mathbf{w}_z = \frac{1}{d}\left[(be-af)\,\boldsymbol{\Omega}^{-1}\mathbf{1} + (bf-ce)\,\boldsymbol{\Omega}^{-1}\boldsymbol{\mu} + d\boldsymbol{\Omega}^{-1}\begin{bmatrix}147\\130\\34\\18\end{bmatrix}\right] = \begin{bmatrix}0.09\\0.12\\-0.52\\0.31\end{bmatrix}$$

$$(6.11)$$

We can now use $\mathbf{w}_z$ to check whether the data fulfil the three requirements outlined above. As required, the return of $\mathbf{w}_z$ is equal to

$$\begin{bmatrix}0.09\\0.12\\-0.52\\0.31\end{bmatrix}\begin{bmatrix}4\\3\\2\\1\end{bmatrix} = 0.09\cdot 4 + \cdots + 0.31\cdot 1 = 0$$

with covariance of zero with respect to all benchmark portfolios:

$$\begin{bmatrix}0.09\\0.12\\-0.52\\0.31\end{bmatrix}\begin{bmatrix}0.04 & 0.0252 & 0.0036 & 0.0024\\0.0025 & 0.0441 & 0.0038 & 0.0025\\0.0036 & 0.0038 & 0.0036 & 0.0014\\0.0024 & 0.0025 & 0.0014 & 0.0016\end{bmatrix}\begin{bmatrix}-0.015\\-0.018\\0.082\\0.095\end{bmatrix} = 0$$

and variance (equal to the distance between the frontiers) of

$$\begin{bmatrix}0.09\\0.12\\-0.52\\0.31\end{bmatrix}\begin{bmatrix}0.04 & 0.0252 & 0.0036 & 0.0024\\0.0025 & 0.0441 & 0.0038 & 0.0025\\0.0036 & 0.0038 & 0.0036 & 0.0014\\0.0024 & 0.0025 & 0.0014 & 0.0016\end{bmatrix}\begin{bmatrix}0.09\\0.12\\-0.52\\0.31\end{bmatrix} = 17.35$$

In general we can express the relationship between Markowitz-efficient portfolios and mean–variance-efficient portfolios with equal return as

$$\mathbf{w}'_{mv}\,\boldsymbol{\Omega}\,\mathbf{w}_{mv} - \mathbf{w}'_{te}\,\boldsymbol{\Omega}\,\mathbf{w}_{te} = \mathbf{w}'_z\,\boldsymbol{\Omega}\,\mathbf{w}_z \qquad (6.12)$$

In practice, however, some institutional portfolios also include so-called "beta" constraints into TE optimisation, ie, plan sponsors constrain the sensitivity of portfolio returns with respect to benchmark returns. They do this in an attempt to avoid leverage (or deleverage) as part of portfolio construction, setting the sensitivity to one. This is also called "beta neutrality". Effectively, this will destroy the scalability of an investment process as the optimal active positions now depend on the benchmark, whereas previously they did not.[21] This analysis shows that, if TE optimisation is imposed on the active manager, setting the appropriate benchmark is important because there is no room to improve on an inefficient benchmark later.

6.3 BENCHMARK-RELATIVE PORTFOLIO CONSTRUCTION: PRACTICAL ISSUES

Practitioners who undertake benchmark-relative portfolio construction will almost always face two questions:

1. What exactly should they be forecasting – should they attempt to forecast risk premia or deviations from equilibrium returns?
2. Does portfolio optimisation really add anything? Is it not enough just to have good forecasts?

We address the first question with an example. Suppose that equities offer a fair risk premium (equilibrium risk premium) of 5% per annum over cash with a volatility of 20% and cash yields of 5%. Assume we have varying skill with an information coefficient, IC, ranging from 0.0 to 0.2. The information coefficient captures the correlation between forecast return and return realisation.[22] An asset manger can forecast total returns, R_i, with an expected mean of 10%; risk premia, $R_i - c$, with an expected mean of 5%; or deviations from the fair risk premium, $R_i - c - \pi_i$, with an expected mean of 0%. Each time the forecast variable is positive, equities are overweighted by 50% relative to cash. What are the expected active returns (portfolio return minus benchmark return) from these strategies? Monte Carlo simulation yields the results given in Table 6.1, where active returns are measured in basis points (bp).

Table 6.1 Skill, forecast and performance

Forecast	Skill, measured as information coefficient		
	$IC = 0$	$IC = 0.1$	$IC = 0.2$
R_i	100	160	240
$R_i - c$	50	120	200
$R_i - c - \pi_i$	0	80	160

The data, obtained by Monte Carlo simulation, are returns expressed as basis points.

We would expect a manager with no skill to achieve a mean active return of zero. However, even a manager with no information could outperform the benchmark by about 100bp per year. Why should this be? Forecasting total returns and overweighting them each time they are positive would yield a structural long equity bias (overweight equities on average) as total returns can be expected to be positive in about 70% of all cases in our example. Being long equity 70% of the time would in turn allow him to collect parts of the equity risk premium. The effect is less pronounced for risk premia (positive 60% of the time) and disappears for deviations from the fair equilibrium risk premium (positive deviations are as likely as negative deviations, ie, 50%). Structural biases should be avoided as they offer rewards for taking on structural risks – effectively, the collection of a risk premium – rather than for skill. In order to avoid a structural bet we could:

❑ Forecast deviations from the fair risk premium. This requires an estimate of the equilibrium risk premium. In the simplest case we take the CAPM (capital asset pricing model) and calculate $\pi_i = \beta_i \pi_m$, where π_m is the market risk premium and β_i reflects systematic risk.[23]

❑ Forecast whatever we like, but run the portfolio optimisation under a factor-neutrality constraint. Again, in a CAPM world this would require a portfolio beta of one with respect to the benchmark.

Both approaches should theoretically result in the same portfolios. In practice, however, they differ as this would require that we use exactly the same model for return refinement and risk decomposition. The example also shows that active return is a flawed concept. Essentially, it is a return figure with no adjustment for systematic risk, and it can easily be gamed. Adding a small to medium allocation of corporate bonds to a government bond fund will, in the long run, increase mean active return without any need for skill. As long as clients and consultants are unwilling to discourage this behaviour and euphemistically call it "style", it makes business sense for investment managers to engage in theses practices as it is a source of return the manger can bank on in the long run.[24]

The second question we wish to address in this section is whether portfolio construction brings any benefit to the investment process. Again we will use an example to illustrate the issues. Let us suppose we have monthly total return data for emerging market bonds (EMBI series) for Argentina, Brazil, Bulgaria, Ecuador, Mexico, Morocco, Nigeria, Panama, Peru, Poland, Russia and Venezuela covering the time period between January 1994 and January 2001.

We simulate an asset manager who tries to forecast cross-sectional emerging market returns for alternative levels of skill measured, as before, through the information coefficient. First we standardise the cross section of returns to make them standard normal, subtracting the cross-

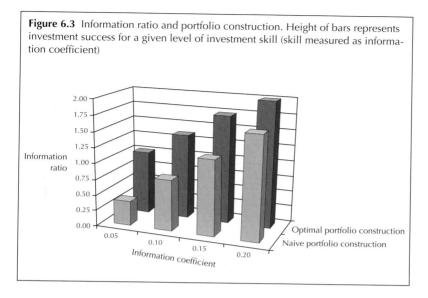

Figure 6.3 Information ratio and portfolio construction. Height of bars represents investment success for a given level of investment skill (skill measured as information coefficient)

sectional mean, $\bar{R}_t$, and dividing by cross-sectional volatility, σ_t.[25] Next we generate cross-sectional forecasts:

$$R_{i,t}^f \sim \underbrace{\left(IC \, \frac{R_i - \bar{R}_t}{\sigma_t} + \sqrt{1 - IC^2} \, z \right)}_{\text{bivariate standard normal}} \sigma_t + \bar{R}_t \qquad (6.13)$$

where $R_{i,t}^f$ denotes the simulated forecast for asset i in period t and z is a standard normal random variable for all assets and all time periods in our data sample, For each point in time we construct portfolios using two different portfolio construction methodologies:

1. *Optimal portfolio construction.* Use Equation (6.6) to construct TE-efficient portfolios that optimally trade off marginal risk against marginal return.
2. *Heuristic portfolio construction.* Overweight the top six countries and underweight the bottom six countries by equal amounts. Rankings are based on sorted forecast returns.

For the whole historical data set we generate a set of forecasts, calculate actual risk-adjusted performance (information ratio) for both portfolio construction methodologies and repeat history 1,000 times. The results are shown in Figure 6.3. For high information coefficients (an information coefficient of 0.2 is equivalent to an impressive R^2 of 0.44 in an out-of-sample backtest of a regression model), the choice of portfolio construction methodology makes little difference. This is no surprise as good return forecasts will dominate the portfolio construction process and risk management becomes increasingly less important for those who do have such forecasts. However, as the quality of the forecasts deteriorates, portfolio construction gains in importance. Although the level of information ratio falls for both methodologies, the spread increases for low to modest skill levels. Given that an information coefficient of 0.05 is regarded as good among active managers, it is not difficult to see why portfolio construction is considered important by institutional investors.

6.4 DUAL-BENCHMARK OPTIMISATION

So far we have assumed that investors have a single well-defined benchmark. Some investors, however, use more than one yardstick as a basis for measuring investment success. In most cases this practice is implicit rather than explicit – as in the case of a manager who is forced to manage relative risk but also needs to keep track of total risk to avoid blame for negative market returns as the plan sponsor will certainly not accept underperformance in a falling market.[26] Other examples are pension funds that have to follow peer benchmarks even though these are known to be inefficient in risk–return space, and plan sponsors who want to do well in terms of absolute return but at the same time want to beat a particular peer in their group.

Dual-benchmark optimisation requires finding the optimal portfolio weights, $\mathbf{w}_p$, relative to two benchmarks $\mathbf{w}_{b1}$ and $\mathbf{w}_{b2}$ – ie, aggregating (weighting) the two separate optimisation problems

$$Utility_i \approx \mathbf{w}'_{ai}\boldsymbol{\mu} - \frac{1}{2\lambda_i}\mathbf{w}'_{ai}\boldsymbol{\Omega}\,\mathbf{w}_{ai}, \qquad i = 1, 2 \qquad (6.14)$$

in a coherent way. Note that we write the active position against the ith benchmark as $\mathbf{w}_{ai} = \mathbf{w}_p - \mathbf{w}_{bi}$. If we set[27]

$$\theta = \frac{\dfrac{1}{2\lambda_1}}{\dfrac{1}{2\lambda_1} + \dfrac{1}{2\lambda_2}} \qquad (6.15)$$

and use the weighting factor θ to generate

$$\mathbf{w}_b = \theta\mathbf{w}_{b1} + (1-\theta)\mathbf{w}_{b2}$$

$$\frac{1}{2\lambda} = \theta\frac{1}{2\lambda_1} + (1-\theta)\frac{1}{2\lambda_1} \qquad (6.16)$$

we can solve the traditional Markowitz problem $Utility_{combined} = \mathbf{w}'_a\boldsymbol{\mu} - \frac{1}{2}\lambda\mathbf{w}'_a\boldsymbol{\Omega}\mathbf{w}_a$, where $\mathbf{w}_a = \mathbf{w}_p - \mathbf{w}_b$. All that is required is to redefine the new single benchmark as a weighted average (with weights given in

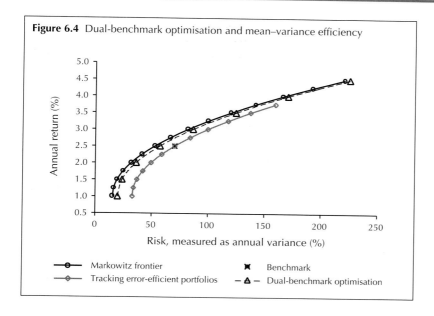

Figure 6.4 Dual-benchmark optimisation and mean–variance efficiency

Equation (6.15)) of the two previous benchmarks. A solution to this problem is given in Figure 6.4 for the example data set used in Section 6.2.

Moving away from the benchmark by introducing the objective of also beating cash – effectively the Markowitz objective – shifts the resulting frontier closer to the Markowitz frontier. The weightings will reflect the relative risk tolerance (importance) assigned to both objectives.[28] Any standard portfolio optimiser can be used for this. We do not have to worry about how to determine the risk tolerance parameter as we will vary this parameter anyway to trace out a new efficient frontier.

Alternatively, it has been suggested that the Pareto criterion can be applied to dual-benchmark optimisation.[29] This implies finding a solution such that it would be impossible to improve the risk-adjusted outperformance (utility) relative to benchmark one without losing utility from managing relative to benchmark two. Instead of weighting both utility functions we try to maximise, with respect to $\mathbf{w}_p$:

$$\min\left(Utility_1, Utility_2\right) \approx$$

$$\min\left(\mathbf{w}'_{a1}\boldsymbol{\mu} - \frac{1}{2\lambda_1}\mathbf{w}'_{a1}\boldsymbol{\Omega}\,\mathbf{w}_{a1},\ \mathbf{w}'_{a2}\boldsymbol{\mu} - \frac{1}{2\lambda_2}\mathbf{w}'_{a2}\boldsymbol{\Omega}\,\mathbf{w}_{a2}\right) \quad (6.17)$$

For simplicity we assume that $\lambda = \lambda_1 = \lambda_2$.[30] In case $\lambda \to \infty$, we will try to maximise the minimum of the two active utilities. Equation (6.17) can be solved by maximising

$$Utility_1 = \mathbf{w}'_{a1}\boldsymbol{\mu} - \frac{1}{2\lambda} \mathbf{w}'_{a1}\boldsymbol{\Omega}\,\mathbf{w}_{a1} \qquad (6.18)$$

adding a linear constraint to the usual optimisation problem:

$$\underbrace{(\mathbf{w}_{b1} - \mathbf{w}_{b2})'\boldsymbol{\Omega}\,\mathbf{w}_p}_{\text{covariance}} = \lambda\underbrace{(\mathbf{w}_{b1} - \mathbf{w}_{b2})'\boldsymbol{\mu}}_{\text{return difference}} + \underbrace{\frac{\mathbf{w}'_{b1}\boldsymbol{\Omega}\,\mathbf{w}_{b1} - \mathbf{w}'_{b2}\boldsymbol{\Omega}\,\mathbf{w}_{b2}}{2}}_{\text{risk difference}}$$

If we focus on risks only ($\boldsymbol{\mu} = 0$), the linear constraint forces the risk difference between the two benchmarks to equal the covariance between the benchmark returns and a misfit portfolio that fills the difference between the two benchmarks.

In practice, dual-benchmark optimisation is of little, if any, consequence to practitioners as there is a clear separation of roles: consultants and sponsors set benchmarks (ie, total returns), while relative returns are controlled by investment managers. Although theoretically compelling, practitioners feel they have little guidance on how to set relative weights for competing objectives.

6.5 TRACKING ERROR AND ITS FUNDING ASSUMPTIONS

This section shows that changing the funding assumptions in calculating marginal contributions to tracking error can significantly enhance the interpretation and acceptance of portfolio risk decomposition and implied alpha calculation.[31] A meaningful decomposition of risk is a prerequisite for risk budgeting techniques, which are at the heart of modern investment processes.

6.5.1 Scalability

Ex-ante TE is usually calculated using the well-known quadratic form of Equation (6.2).[32] In a world with no restrictions on short sales, benchmark and active positions can be perfectly separated. Active risk is generated by active positions, which can be overlaid on any benchmark. Each portfolio with a given TE (but possibly a different benchmark) has the same firm-specific alpha. Investment products differ only in their benchmark and level of aggressiveness. Varying levels of aggressiveness can be achieved through a linear scaling factor, ϕ, which leverages active positions according to the desired level of aggressiveness. A factor greater than unity gives a more aggressive portfolio than the model portfolio, and vice versa.[33] For example: doubling the scaling factor (doubling active positions) results in twice as much TE as before. The TE is also linear homogeneous in scaling factors and, hence, in active weights, as can be confirmed from the following equation:

$$\sigma_a \phi^k = \left(\mathbf{w}_a' \phi \, \Omega \, \mathbf{w}_a \phi \right)^{\frac{1}{2}} = \left(\phi^2 \, \mathbf{w}_a' \, \Omega \, \mathbf{w}_a \right)^{\frac{1}{2}}$$

$$= \phi \left(\mathbf{w}_a' \, \Omega \, \mathbf{w}_a \right)^{\frac{1}{2}} = \phi \sigma \qquad (6.19)$$

This means that to create more aggressive portfolios one does not have to set up a new model portfolio. Scalability is a key requirement in modern investment processes as it allows new business to be accepted at low marginal costs and, hence, enables the typically high fixed costs to be quickly proportionalised.

6.5.2 Decomposition

It is well known in mathematics that linear homogeneous functions can be expressed using an Euler equation.[34] Applying this to the TE function yields the following result:

$$\sigma_a = \mathbf{w}_a' \frac{d\sigma}{d\mathbf{w}_a} = \sum_i w_{ai} \frac{d\sigma}{dw_i}$$

Thus, TE can be decomposed into the summation of all marginal contributions to TE multiplied by active weights. Dividing both sides by TE yields the familiar result that all percentage contributions to risk (elasticity) have to sum to one. Again, a familiar property of linear homogeneous functions.

The implicit assumption in the above decomposition is that each position is funded from cash and, as cash has no volatility (at least not in a one-period framework), all risk comes from the asset positions. A problem of this assumption is that it does not reflect actual decision-making. Portfolio managers do not fund their positions from cash but, rather, from other markets (pairs or triplets of positions form one trade) or from benchmarks (an overweight in one asset is financed by equally weighted underweights in all other assets). An overweight in the long end of the US fixed-income market is not likely to be funded from cash but rather from the one- to three-year US government sector (intramarket spread trade), the long end in Canada (intermarket spread trade), the long end of the US corporate sector (credit spread trade), or from multiple positions in medium- and short-maturity assets (barbell trade). However, it should be noted that although the TE decomposition will change, the total TE stays the same irrespective of the funding assumption.

6.5.2.1 Trade funding

Suppose we have a matrix, $\mathbf{T}$, of l active trades in k assets, each row of which represents one trade (giving the approach we are about to consider its alternative name of "trade funding", as opposed to cash funding).

Positive entries, representing overweighted trade positions, are funded from negative (underweight) entries, as indicated below:

$$
\mathbf{T} = \begin{bmatrix} w_{a1} & 0 & \cdots & -w_{ak} \\ w_{a2} & -w_{a2} & -w_{a3} & 0 \\ \vdots & & & \vdots \\ & & \cdots & \end{bmatrix}_{l \times k}
\tag{6.20}
$$

It can be assumed that the positions in each row sum to zero (imposing a restriction that does not, however, change the mathematics involved).[35] The aggregate portfolio position is the sum of the individual trade positions. Equipped with $\mathbf{T}$ we can now calculate the variance–covariance matrix of trades, $\mathbf{\Omega}_{\text{trades}}$, which is of dimension l by l:

$$
\mathbf{\Omega}_{\text{trades}} = \mathbf{T}' \mathbf{\Omega} \, \mathbf{T}
\tag{6.21}
$$

Numbers on the main diagonal of $\mathbf{\Omega}_{\text{trades}}$ represent the TE of the lth trade. Covariances between trades are captured by the off-diagonal entries. The TE of the total portfolio can be calculated by summing the individual entries of the new variance–covariance matrix of trades[36]

$$
\sigma_a = \left(\mathbf{1}' \, \mathbf{\Omega}_{\text{trades}} \, \mathbf{1} \right)^{\frac{1}{2}}
\tag{6.22}
$$

In order to calculate the marginal contribution to TE from each single trade we just take the first derivative with respect to $\mathbf{1}$, defined to be an $l \times 1$ vector of ones, as below:

$$
\frac{d\sigma_a}{d\mathbf{1}} = \mathbf{\Omega}_{\text{trades}} \, \mathbf{1} \, \sigma_a^{-1}, \qquad \sigma = \mathbf{1} \frac{d\sigma_a}{d\mathbf{1}}
\tag{6.23}
$$

TE decomposition follows the Euler equation-based approach introduced above. It is a straightforward matter to slice the variance–covariance matrix further into types of trades and to calculate the TEs arising from different decision areas:

$$
\mathbf{\Omega}_{\text{trades}} = \begin{bmatrix} \mathbf{\Omega}_{DD} & \mathbf{\Omega}_{DC} & \cdots & \mathbf{\Omega}_{DCr} \\ \vdots & \mathbf{\Omega}_{CC} & & \vdots \\ & & \ddots & \\ & & & \mathbf{\Omega}_{CrCr} \end{bmatrix}
\tag{6.24}
$$

Along the main diagonal we find the variance–covariance sub-matrices for duration (D), currency (C) and credit (Cr), with the covariances between the different blocks of trade in off-diagonal positions.

Such decomposition becomes more important as TE budgeting is incorporated into investment processes.[37] If $\mathbf{T}$ becomes a diagonal matrix with active weights along the main diagonal and zero elsewhere, we get the same results as with the cash funding approach. Although this is certainly the most realistic approach, a risk management system using it will require additional information in the form of pairs, triplets and quadruplets of asset positions that form one trade. It becomes apparent that risk management tools have to reflect the respective investment process – which is why standard software suppliers do not offer risk decomposition by trades. Without knowledge of the portfolio manager's thoughts, any decomposition is impossible. Portfolios cannot simply be loaded from a fund accounting system into a risk management system as there is an infinity of trade decompositions that will deliver the same active weightings $\mathbf{w}_a' = \mathbf{1}'\,\mathbf{T}$.

6.5.2.2 Benchmark funding

Portfolio managers often think of the benchmark return as their cost of funding.[38] We can express a long active position in asset i as being funded from $k-1$ equal underweights in the remaining assets. Benchmark funding is actually a special case of trade funding and can be captured by the following trade matrix:

$$
\mathbf{T}_{I \times I} = \begin{bmatrix} w_{a1} & \dfrac{-w_{a1}}{k-1} & \cdots & \dfrac{-w_{a1}}{k-1} \\ w_{a2} & \dfrac{-w_{a2}}{k-1} & \cdots & \dfrac{-w_{a2}}{k-1} \\ \vdots & & & \vdots \\ & & \cdots & \end{bmatrix}
\tag{6.25}
$$

The same mathematics applies as for the trade funding matrix (6.20).

One advantage of benchmark funding is that percentage contributions to risk are less often negative (which can, for example, happen if assets have similar risks and high correlations, as is the case for fixed-income markets). Since this is easier for portfolio managers to understand, acceptance of the procedure should rise. Percentage contributions to TE generally become negative if an active position and its marginal contribution to risk are of different sign. Suppose that asset i is underweight. As can be seen below, there is a direct effect (due to asset volatility) and an indirect effect (covariances):

$$
\frac{d\sigma_a}{dw_{ai}} = \underbrace{2\,w_{ai}\,\sigma_i^2}_{\text{direct}} + \underbrace{2\sum_{i \neq j} w_{aj}\,\sigma_{ij}}_{\text{indirect}}
\tag{6.26}
$$

The direct effect on underweights will always be negative (negative active weight) as this implies that risk can be reduced by increasing the position towards zero. In most cases the marginal contribution for asset i will be negative unless there is, for example, a sizeable overweight in an asset with a high correlation with that asset. If the position in asset i is financed instead with $k-1$ overweights in the remaining benchmark assets, the percentage allocation of TE for asset i remains positive as long as

$$\sigma_i^2 - \sum_{i \neq j} \frac{\sigma_{ij}}{k-1} > 0 \qquad (6.27)$$

Expressed in words: the direct effect dominates the indirect effect provided that the variance is higher than the average covariance.[39] We can also use this approach to quantify correlation risk. Assuming equal correlation between asset i and all other assets j ($\rho_{ij} = \rho_i$), we get, for benchmark funding,

$$\frac{d\sigma_a^2}{d\rho_i} = \frac{w_{ai}^2 \sigma_i \left(\sum \sigma_j \right)}{k-1} \qquad (6.28)$$

Correlation risk rises with bet size and asset volatility. However, the benchmark funding approach is not recommended as it leads to flawed decision-making. This is because overweights do not have to beat the benchmark return. Positive alphas can also be generated by overweighting underperforming assets if the corresponding underweights are even stronger underperformers. Hence, the popular belief that it is difficult to outperform the benchmark if only a few assets are outperforming is, taken on its own, also not true.

6.5.2.3 Implied position analysis

For any active holding to be optimal the marginal contribution to risk and the marginal contribution to return (alpha) have to be equal to the information ratio.[40] This follows directly from optimality conditions. Improvements on the overall risk–return optimality could be achieved if the relationship between marginal risk and marginal return were not the same for all active positions. In the case of trade funding we get

$$\alpha = \frac{d\sigma_a}{d\mathbf{1}} IR \qquad (6.29)$$

where α is the $k \times 1$ vector of active returns and IR is the information ratio. All active positions would plot on a straight line where the x-axis represents marginal risk and the y-axis represents marginal return. Portfolios which do not show this feature are either not optimised or are subject to constraints.

This concept can easily be applied to calculate implied asset movements. In the case of fixed-income management this could, for example, be used to calculate implied yield curve changes. Suppose that a positively weighted duration deviation (a weight-adjusted duration overweight) has been implemented. The return of this position can be approximated by

$$\alpha_i = -w\,d\,d_i\,\mathrm{d}y_i \qquad (6.30)$$

Substituting this into the optimality condition for unconstrained optimal portfolios, we get

$$\mathrm{d}y_i = -\frac{IR\,\dfrac{\left(\sum_{j=1}^{m}\zeta_{ij}\right)}{\sigma_a}}{w\,d\,d_i} \qquad (6.31)$$

where ζ_{ij} refers to element i,j in the variance–covariance matrix of trades, Ω_{trades}. The marginal contribution to risk of the ith trade is calculated by summing the entries in the trade variance–covariance matrix along the ith row and dividing them by TE:

$$\frac{\mathrm{d}\sigma_a}{\mathrm{d}\mathbf{1}} = \frac{\mathrm{d}(\mathbf{1}'\Omega_{\text{trades}}\mathbf{1})}{\mathrm{d}\mathbf{1}} = \frac{1}{2}\frac{2\,\Omega_{\text{trades}}\mathbf{1}}{\sigma_a} = \begin{bmatrix} \dfrac{1}{\sigma_a}\sum_{j=1}^{m}\zeta_{1j} \\ \dfrac{1}{\sigma_a}\sum_{j=1}^{m}\zeta_{2j} \\ \dfrac{1}{\sigma_a}\sum_{j=1}^{m}\zeta_{mj} \end{bmatrix} \qquad (6.32)$$

We are now able to calculate the implied market movements from a given set of active positions (nominal weights, weighted duration deviations, trade matrix, etc). These implied forecasts can then be compared with the manager's forecasts (if they exist) or his/her market assessment. If implied movements and expected market movements differ considerably, portfolio managers should rethink their positions and adjust them accordingly. This iterative process is also called "view optimisation". The main advantages of this technique are twofold. Traditional mean–variance-optimised portfolios often show (unrealistically) high information ratios. This does not apply to reverse optimisation as the information ratio is held constant and all returns are scaled accordingly. It also works as a reality check – whether the views implied by the current positions correspond with the forecast returns and investors' views.

We could also use the decomposition above to identify "best hedges", ie, to identify the risk-minimising trades.[41] Suppose we engage in l trades and each trade is leveraged up or down according to ϕ_j, $j = 1, \ldots, l$. The leverage factor for, say, the fourth trade (ϕ_4) that minimises active portfolio risk (*ceteris paribus*) can be calculated from

$$\min \left(\sum_{i=1}^{l} \sum_{j=1}^{l} \phi_i \phi_j \zeta_{ij} + (\Delta \phi_4)^2 \zeta_{44} + \sum_{i=1}^{l} \phi_i \Delta \phi_4 \zeta_{i4} \right) \qquad (6.33)$$

where Δ indicates the change in the respective leverage factor. The solution to Expression (6.33) gives us

$$\Delta \phi_4^* = \frac{\sum_{i=1}^{l} \phi_i \zeta_{i4}}{\zeta_{44}} \qquad (6.34)$$

The right-hand side of Equation (6.34) contains the standardised covariance (beta) of the returns of the fourth trade with all other trades, including itself, which together make up active portfolio risk.

6.5.3 Summary
Tracking error is routinely used in modern asset management practice. At the same time risk budgeting techniques suggest that its decomposition (eg, what percentage of my TE comes from currency decisions?) is just as important as its size. In this section it has been shown that a more realistic decomposition of tracking error can enhance the understanding and acceptance of risk numbers. Employing this approach makes the thinking of portfolio managers more explicit and, thus, eases the task of portfolio construction with multiple benchmarks. Thinking of risk positions as trades allows portfolio managers to quickly monitor risk and the performance of trades.

6.6 TRADING BANDS FOR TACTICAL ASSET ALLOCATION
Trading bands are defined by the minimum and maximum allocations to a particular asset or asset class. Although they are a relic of a past in which TE calculations were not readily available, they are still required by consultants and plan sponsors. Their strength is the transparency they confer and the ease of legal action if broken; their weakness is their unreliability in achieving what they are supposed to do – control active risk. Trading bands that feel reasonable in times of high correlation will expose a fund to much higher active risk than planned if correlations break down. Conversely, rising correlations will reduce the dispersion of active returns around the benchmark but will also make it difficult to achieve the targeted active return for a given bet size (as defined by the trading bands). TE calculations are not immune to mis-estimation of active risks, but they will gradually pick up changes in the market environment.

Either trading bands must be changed in line with changes in the market-place (in which case they differ only philosophically from TE-based risk management) or they will fail to achieve their objective.

Every active fund can be written as the sum of all possible pairwise decisions. For example, in a fund containing four asset classes there are six pairwise asset allocation decisions: three decisions of the first asset against the other three assets, plus two decisions of the second asset against assets three and four, plus one decision of asset three against asset four. Although trading ranges mainly follow a risk objective, setting the ranges should also reflect the opportunity to add value. If an investment manager feels particularly confident about one of his decision pairs (for example, the balance decision in a balanced fund or a government bond/emerging market debt decision in a fixed-income product), this should be reflected in the trading bands.

Suppose we are developing the trading ranges for a global fixed-income product investing in government bonds and investment-grade, high-yield and emerging market debt. The development is a two-stage process. First we have to specify the maximum TE available for the tactical asset allocation decision layer. Assuming this to be 100bp, we then have to calculate the covariance matrix of active decisions by calculating the usual quadratic form using the trade matrix of all possible pairs. The next step is the most critical. We need to write down the information ratios for all pairwise decisions. It is assumed that the allocation decisions as between government bonds and all other asset classes are assigned an information ratio of 0.6, whereas it is considered that no skill is required to choose between high-yield and emerging market debt (EMD).

The process of actually deriving the optimal trading ranges is a quadratic optimisation problem in which optimal scaling factors ϕ_i (factors leveraging individual trade pairs) are derived and subsequently transformed into ranges:

$$\alpha = \sum IR_i \phi_i \zeta_i$$

$$\sigma_a = \left(\sum_i \sum_j \phi_i \phi_j \zeta_{ij} \right)^{1/2} \tag{6.35}$$

After we have found the optimal scaling factors ϕ_i^*, we use them to leverage up the positions underlying the individual trades and find the optimal trading range for the ith asset from

$$w_j \in \left[\sum_i w_{bi} + \phi_i^* \operatorname{abs}(w_{ai}), \ w_{bi} - \sum_i \phi_i^* \operatorname{abs}(w_{ai}) \right] \tag{6.36}$$

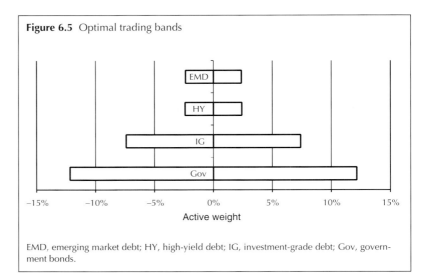

Figure 6.5 Optimal trading bands

EMD, emerging market debt; HY, high-yield debt; IG, investment-grade debt; Gov, government bonds.

For those who do not like theory, here is a practical solution to our example. It is apparent from Figure 6.5 that the more volatile decision areas (EMD, high-yield) are given tighter limits than the less volatile asset classes. This would only be reversed if one assumed unrealistically high information ratios for high-yield and emerging market debt. The main advantage of setting ranges as suggested above is that:

❏ All ranges are set simultaneously. Hence, any combination of active weights will yield a maximum TE of 100bp.
❏ The ranges reflect skill *and* risk.

This contrasts favourably with traditional techniques that define ranges in terms of risk only and limit the analysis to individual assets rather than looking at all ranges simultaneously.

APPENDIX A: GLOBAL FIXED-INCOME POLICY MODEL

A1 Basic issues in fixed-income risk management

Quantitative risk management, consistent forecasting and precise portfolio construction are central to any successful investment process. This appendix shows how to build an easily implemented fixed-income risk management and portfolio construction model for a benchmark-relative fixed-income investor.

Risk management models can only rarely be taken from the shelf. They have to be tailored to fit the specific underlying investment decision process. For volatility estimation it clearly makes a difference whether investment decisions are made frequently (volatility capture) or infrequently (structural alpha).[42] Whereas in the former process risk management has to capture changes in short-term volatility by using high-frequency data, in the latter it will rely more on structural relationships using low-frequency data. It has also to be decided whether the implementation of decisions is done on a "bucket" basis (the decision variable is the weighted duration deviation within a given bucket) or on an instrument-by-instrument basis (single bonds). As derivatives – the most efficient instrument for implementing portfolio allocation decisions – can deliver both linear and non-linear exposures, it should be decided whether portfolio construction will employ non-linear derivatives.

Our objective in this appendix is to model risk arising from macro-bets taken on a bucket basis. Buckets are defined in terms of time-to-maturity (eg, all bonds with less than three years to maturity form the one- to three-year bucket). Typically, buckets are one- to three-year, three- to five-year, five- to seven-year, seven- to ten-year and over ten-year. The view taken here is that yield curve movements are approximately parallel within buckets but less so between buckets. A duration-matched barbell (in which long- and short-maturity bonds are combined to match the duration of an intermediate-maturity bond) is not without interest rate risk as it certainly carries yield curve exposure. For benchmark-orientated investors this problem compounds as an active portfolio is equivalent to a leveraged investor.[43] The use of duration as a risk measure for international bond portfolios is even more flawed as it relies on the assumption of equal volatility and perfect correlation. Being overweight duration in Japan by one year against a one-year duration underweight in the US is certainly not a hedge against globally falling rates but is, rather, two separate duration positions.[44] Changes in bond yields across yield curve buckets are highly correlated within a given market, as can be seen from Figure A1. The bivariate scatter plots become cloudier as we move away from neighbouring buckets. This simply means that correlation is higher between the 1–3 year and 3–5 year buckets than between the 1–3 year and 10+ buckets.

Figure A1 Daily yield curve changes for the US

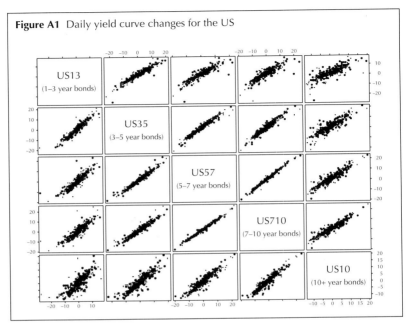

One of the best-known statistical techniques for dealing with highly correlated series is principal component analysis. This is basically a data reduction technique that, in our case, tries to capture most of the volatility in the original series by creating a new, wholly artificial set of orthogonal series. For fixed-income markets the first three artificially created time series (the so-called principal components) explain most of the variance. The obvious advantage of this approach is that the number of parameters to be estimated in a risk model is greatly reduced. But can we give an economic meaning to these principal components? To answer this question we have to look at the sensitivities (loading) of yield curve changes to these principal components as in Figure A2.

The sensitivity of yields along the curve to changes in the first principal component is very similar. If the first principal component moves, all yields will move by approximately the same extent. This is called a "parallel yield curve move". If the second principal component moves upward, the short end yield will fall (negative loading), while long end yields will rise (positive loading).[45] This is called a steepening of the curve. If the third principal component rises, yields in the middle sector of the curve will rise while yields at the ends will fall. This is called a change in curvature.

Let us consider a global bond portfolio. We want to know what the TE decomposition will look like if we assume a duration-neutral barbell position in the US (long one year-weighted duration deviation at the ends and short one year in the middle of the curve), a short-duration position in

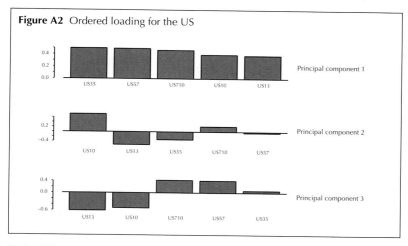

Figure A2 Ordered loading for the US

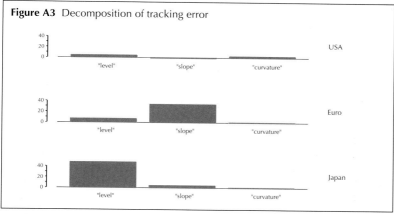

Figure A3 Decomposition of tracking error

Japan (short 1.5 year in the 10+ bucket) and a duration-neutral yield curve position in Europe (long one year in the 10+ bucket and short one year at the short end).

The contributions to overall TE from the different active positions are plotted in Figure A3. The barbell position in the US makes the smallest contribution as the weighted duration deviations are small and the volatility of yield curve reshaping is also small. The small exposure to shifts in the level of yields (despite being duration-neutral) arises from factor loadings that are slightly different from each other. The spread position in Europe contributes most of its risk via the exposure to changes in the yield curve slope. The biggest exposure, however, arises from the duration exposure in Japan as the duration factor is more volatile than the others and because Japan shows little correlation with other developed bond markets.

A2 Single-country model

At this stage we should become a little more formalistic in describing what is going on and how to replicate the suggested model. We start with decomposing the movements of the yield-to-maturity in the ith bucket of the jth country, Δy_i^j, into movements of $n_f = 3$ factors plus noise (unexplained variation):

$$\Delta y_i^j = \underbrace{\sum_{k=1}^{n_f} a_{i,k}^j \Delta f_k^j}_{\substack{\text{sensitivity-weighted} \\ \text{factor changes}}} + \underbrace{\epsilon_i^j}_{\text{noise}} \qquad (A1)$$

$\underbrace{}_{\substack{\text{yield} \\ \text{change}}}$

As we have seen in Figure A2, each factor can be interpreted as a change in the level, slope or curvature of the yield curve.[46] The loadings $a_{i,k}^j$ represent the sensitivity of the ith bucket in the jth country to changes in the kth country-specific factor.

Assume further that we model $n_b = 5$ yield curve buckets in n_c countries. The factors and loadings for each country are simultaneously extracted by using principal component analysis on the exponentially weighted covariance matrix of yield curve changes. The global variance–covariance matrix of principal components is then constructed from the time series of factor scores. The correlation structure of international bond markets can also be captured with principal component analysis. For example, the first components in the US and Canada are highly correlated but show only little correlation with Japan. Therefore, by employing principal component analysis we can not only reduce the number of parameters to be estimated but also put economic interpretations on the factors driving yield curve changes that are familiar to portfolio managers. This enhances both the power of the model and its acceptability to portfolio managers.

How can we translate yield change risk into return risk? It is well known that total returns for a given yield curve bucket can be approximated by

$$R_i^j \approx \underbrace{y_i^j}_{\text{carry}} - \underbrace{D_i^j \Delta y_i^j}_{\substack{\text{effect of} \\ \text{duration}}} + \underbrace{\tfrac{1}{2} C_i^j \left(\Delta y_i^j\right)^2}_{\substack{\text{convexity} \\ \text{adjustment}}} \qquad (A2)$$

Applying the variance operator we get

$$\text{var}\left(R_i^j\right) \approx \left(D_i^j\right)^2 \text{var}\left(\Delta y_i^j\right) \qquad (A3)$$

given the observation that yield and convexity effects are likely to be small. From principal component analysis we know that[47]

$$\text{var}\left(\Delta y_i^j\right) = \sum_{k=1}^{n_f} \left(a_{i,k}^j\right)^2 \text{var}\left(\Delta f_k^j\right) + \text{var}\left(\epsilon_i^j\right) \qquad (A4)$$

as the factor changes are independent by construction and not correlated with the error term. Taking the country-specific loading matrix and the variance–covariance matrix of factor movements, we get the covariance matrix of yield changes, $\mathbf{V}_j$,

$$\mathbf{V}_j = \mathbf{A}_j \, \boldsymbol{\Phi}_j \, \mathbf{A}_j' + \boldsymbol{\Theta}_j \qquad (A5)$$

where $\mathbf{A}_j$ and $\boldsymbol{\Theta}_j$ are, respectively, the matrices of loadings and of unexplained variations. The full matrices in (A5) are given below.

$$\mathbf{V}_j = \begin{bmatrix} \text{var}(\Delta y_1^j) & \text{cov}(\Delta y_1^j,\Delta y_2^j) & \cdots & \cdots & \text{cov}(\Delta y_1^j,\Delta y_5^j) \\ \text{cov}(\Delta y_2^j,\Delta y_1^j) & \text{var}(\Delta y_2^j) & & & \\ \vdots & & \ddots & & \\ \vdots & & & \ddots & \\ \text{cov}(\Delta y_5^j,\Delta y_1^j) & & & & \text{var}(\Delta y_5^j) \end{bmatrix}_{n_b \times n_b}$$

$$\mathbf{A}_j = \begin{bmatrix} a_{11}^j & a_{12}^j & a_{13}^j \\ a_{21}^j & a_{22}^j & a_{23}^j \\ \vdots & & \\ \vdots & & \\ a_{51}^j & a_{52}^j & a_{53}^j \end{bmatrix}_{n_b \times n_f}$$

$$\boldsymbol{\Phi}_j = \begin{bmatrix} \text{var}(\Delta f_1^j) & 0 & 0 \\ 0 & \text{var}(\Delta f_2^j) & 0 \\ 0 & 0 & \text{var}(\Delta f_3^j) \end{bmatrix}_{n_f \times n_f}$$

$$\boldsymbol{\Theta}_j = \begin{bmatrix} \text{var}(\varepsilon_1^j) & 0 & \cdots & \cdots & 0 \\ 0 & \text{var}(\varepsilon_2^j) & & & \\ \vdots & & \ddots & & \\ \vdots & & & \ddots & \\ 0 & & & & \text{var}(\varepsilon_5^j) \end{bmatrix}_{n_b \times n_b}$$

The variance of changes in the ith yield bucket not explained by the first three principal components is denoted as $\mathrm{var}(\varepsilon_i^j)$. From the variance–covariance matrix of yield changes it is only a small step to that of total returns:

$$\Omega_j = \underbrace{\mathbf{D}_j \, \mathbf{A}_j \, \mathbf{\Phi}_j \, \mathbf{A}'_j \, \mathbf{D}'_j}_{\substack{\text{variance–covariance} \\ \text{factors}}} + \underbrace{\mathbf{D}_j \, \mathbf{\Theta}_j \, \mathbf{D}'_j}_{\substack{\text{variance–} \\ \text{covariance} \\ \text{yield changes}}} = \underbrace{\mathbf{D}_j \, \mathbf{V}_j \, \mathbf{D}'_j}_{\substack{\text{variance–} \\ \text{covariance} \\ \text{total returns}}} \tag{A6}$$

where

$$\Omega_j = \begin{bmatrix} \mathrm{var}(R_1^j) & \mathrm{cov}(R_1^j, R_2^j) & \cdots & \cdots & \mathrm{cov}(R_1^j, R_5^j) \\ \mathrm{cov}(R_2^j, R_1^j) & \mathrm{var}(R_2^j) & & & \\ \vdots & & \ddots & & \\ \vdots & & & \ddots & \\ \mathrm{cov}(R_5^j, R_1^j) & & & & \mathrm{var}(R_5^j) \end{bmatrix}_{n_b \times n_b}$$

$$\mathbf{D}_j = \begin{bmatrix} D_1^j & 0 & \cdots & \cdots & 0 \\ 0 & D_2^j & & & \\ \vdots & & \ddots & & \\ \vdots & & & \ddots & \\ 0 & & & & D_5^j \end{bmatrix}_{n_b \times n_b}$$

and D_i^j denotes the duration of the ith bond bucket (the one- to three-year bucket if i equals 1) for the jth country. As most of the variance is explained by the first three principal components, the second term in (A6), $\mathbf{D}_j \mathbf{\Theta}_j \mathbf{D}'_j$, is often dropped. For ease of exposition we follow this convention here. The reader should however be warned that this assumption makes a significant difference for some countries – notably Japan and Switzerland. In order to calculate the portfolio total volatility we have to apply the vector of portfolio weights to the truncated Equation (A6):

$$\sigma_{\text{total}} = \left(\mathbf{w}'_j \, \mathbf{D}_j \, \mathbf{A}_j \, \mathbf{\Phi}_j \, \mathbf{A}'_j \, \mathbf{D}'_j \, \mathbf{w}_j \right)^{\frac{1}{2}}$$

$$\mathbf{w}'_j = \begin{bmatrix} w_1^j & w_2^j & \Lambda & w_5^j \end{bmatrix} \tag{A7}$$

Alternatively, we can write this using weighted duration (portfolio weight times portfolio duration):

$$\mathbf{wd}_j' = \mathbf{w}_j' \, \mathbf{D}_j = \left[w_1^j D_1^j \quad w_2^j D_2^j \quad \Lambda \quad w_5^j D_5^j \right]_{1 \times n_b}$$

and apply this to the variance–covariance matrix of yield changes:

$$\sigma = \left(\mathbf{wd}_j' \, \mathbf{A}_j \, \mathbf{\Phi}_j \, \mathbf{A}_j' \, \mathbf{wd}_j \right)^{\frac{1}{2}}$$

$$= \left(\mathbf{wd}_j' \, \mathbf{V}_j \, \mathbf{wd}_j \right)^{\frac{1}{2}} \tag{A8}$$

TE can now be easily calculated by using the vector of weighted duration deviations, **wdd**. Weighted duration deviation is calculated by multiplying the weight with which a portfolio is invested into the ith bucket by the portfolio duration in that bucket and subtracting its benchmark equivalent. Effectively, it is the weighted portfolio duration minus the weighted benchmark duration.

$$\mathbf{wdd}_j' = \left[w_1^j D_1^j - w_{1,B}^j D_{1,B}^j \quad \cdots \quad w_5^j D_5^j - w_{5,B}^j D_{5,B}^j \right]_{1 \times n_b} \tag{A9}$$

Again, TE is given by the usual quadratic form

$$\sigma_{\text{active}} = \left(\mathbf{wdd}_j' \, \mathbf{A}_j \, \mathbf{\Phi}_j \, \mathbf{A}_j' \, \mathbf{wdd}_j \right)^{\frac{1}{2}}$$

$$= \left(\mathbf{wdd}_j' \, \mathbf{V}_j \, \mathbf{wdd}_j \right)^{\frac{1}{2}} \tag{A10}$$

Alternatively, the TE can be calculated using duration-adjusted weights:

$$\omega_i^j = w_{\text{adj},i}^j - w_{i,B}^j = w_i^j \, \frac{D_i^j}{D_{i,B}^j} - w_{i,B}^j = \frac{wdd_i^j}{D_{i,B}^j} \tag{A11}$$

and applying them to the variance–covariance matrix of total returns:

$$\sigma_a = \left(\omega_j^T \, \mathbf{\Omega}_j \, \omega_j \right)^{\frac{1}{2}}$$

$$\omega_j' = \left[\omega_1^j \quad \omega_2^j \quad \Lambda \quad \omega_5^j \right] \tag{A12}$$

A3 Multi-country model

How does the preceding model change in a multi-country setting? Very little, as we shall now see. In principle, Equation (A5) remains much the same:

$$\mathbf{V}^* = \mathbf{A}^* \boldsymbol{\Phi}^* \mathbf{A}^{*'} + \boldsymbol{\Theta}^* \tag{A13}$$

where

$$\mathbf{A}^* = \begin{bmatrix} A_1 & 0 & & & \\ 0 & A_2 & & & \\ & & \ddots & & \\ & & & \ddots & \\ & & & & A_{n_c} \end{bmatrix}_{(n_c n_b) \times (n_c n_b)}$$

$$\boldsymbol{\Phi}^* = \begin{bmatrix} \Phi_{11} & \Phi_{12} & \cdots & \\ \Phi_{21} & \Phi_{22} & & \\ \vdots & & \ddots & \\ & & & \Phi_{n_c n_c} \end{bmatrix}_{(n_f n_c) \times (n_f n_c)}$$

$$\boldsymbol{\Theta}^* = \begin{bmatrix} \theta_1 & 0 & \cdots & \cdots & 0 \\ 0 & \theta_2 & & & \\ \vdots & & \ddots & & \\ \vdots & & & \ddots & \\ 0 & & & & \theta_{n_c} \end{bmatrix}_{(n_c n_b) \times (n_c n_b)}$$

It follows directly that $\boldsymbol{\Omega}^* = \mathbf{D}^* \mathbf{A}^* \boldsymbol{\Phi}^* \mathbf{A}^{*'} \mathbf{D}^{*'} + \mathbf{D}^* \boldsymbol{\Theta}^* \mathbf{D}^{*'}$, where

$$\mathbf{D}^* = \begin{bmatrix} D_1 & 0 & \cdots & \cdots & 0 \\ 0 & D_2 & & & \\ \vdots & & \ddots & & \\ \vdots & & & \ddots & \\ 0 & & & & D_{n_c} \end{bmatrix}_{(n_c n_b) \times (n_c n_b)}$$

All other calculations follow accordingly. Instead of using the local loading, factor correlation, weight and duration, we use their global counterparts – here labelled with a star. For example:

$$\sigma_{\text{active}} = \left(\mathbf{wdd}^{*'} \mathbf{A}^* \boldsymbol{\Omega}^* \mathbf{A}^{*'} \mathbf{wdd}^* \right)^{\frac{1}{2}}$$

$$= \left(\mathbf{wdd}^{*'} \mathbf{V}^* \mathbf{wdd}^* \right)^{\frac{1}{2}} \tag{A14}$$

A4 Including credit

A simple way of including corporate bonds is to model the investment-grade corporate bond market as a whole, not distinguishing between AAA and BBB ratings.[48] The corporate bond spread volatility arising from different maturity buckets is modelled directly as we recognise that movements in corporate bond yields, Δyc_i^j, can be decomposed into changes in government bond yields, Δy_i^j, and changes in the credit spread, Δs_i^j:

$$\Delta yc_i^j = \Delta y_i^j + \Delta s_i^j = \sum_{k=1}^{K} a_{i,k}^j \, \Delta f_k^j + \sum_{k=1}^{K} \underbrace{b_{i,k}^j}_{\substack{\text{spread} \\ \text{factor} \\ \text{loading}}} \underbrace{\Delta fc_k^j}_{\substack{\text{spread} \\ \text{factor}}} + e_i^j \qquad (A15)$$

Changes in credit spread are modelled using principal components, where the components can be interpreted as changes in level, slope and curvature of the credit curve with loading, $b_{i,k}^j$. For a one-country model including credit (along the five yield curve buckets), the matrices involved change as outlined below:

$$\mathbf{V}_j = \mathbf{A}_j \, \mathbf{\Phi}_j \, \mathbf{A}_j' + \mathbf{\Theta}_j \qquad (A16)$$

where the covariance matrix of yield changes can be decomposed into

$$\mathbf{V}_j = \begin{bmatrix} \mathbf{V}_j^{11} & \mathbf{V}_j^{12} \\ \mathbf{V}_j^{21} & \mathbf{V}_j^{22} \end{bmatrix}_{(2n_b) \times (2n_b)}$$

$$\mathbf{V}_j^{11} = \begin{bmatrix} \mathrm{var}(\Delta y_1^j) & \mathrm{cov}(\Delta y_1^j, \Delta y_2^j) & \cdots \\ \vdots & \ddots & \\ \mathrm{cov}(\Delta y_5^j, \Delta y_1^j) & & \mathrm{var}(\Delta y_5^j) \end{bmatrix}_{n_b \times n_b}$$

$$\mathbf{V}_j^{12} = \begin{bmatrix} \mathrm{cov}(\Delta y_1^j, \Delta yc_1^j) & \cdots & \mathrm{cov}(\Delta y_1^j, \Delta yc_5^j) \\ & \ddots & \\ & & \end{bmatrix}_{n_b \times n_b}$$

$$\mathbf{V}_j^{22} = \begin{bmatrix} \mathrm{var}(\Delta yc_1^j) & \cdots & \mathrm{cov}(\Delta yc_1^j, \Delta yc_5^j) \\ & \ddots & \\ & & \mathrm{var}(\Delta yc_5^j) \end{bmatrix}_{n_b \times n_b}$$

and the new matrix of factor loadings (yield curve and credit) is given as

$$
\mathbf{A}_j =
\left[
\begin{array}{ccc|ccc}
a^j_{11} & a^j_{12} & a^j_{13} & 0 & 0 & 0 \\
a^j_{21} & a^j_{22} & a^j_{23} & 0 & 0 & 0 \\
\vdots & & & \vdots & & \\
\vdots & & & \vdots & & \\
a^j_{51} & a^j_{52} & a^j_{53} & 0 & 0 & 0 \\
a^j_{11} & a^j_{12} & a^j_{13} & b^j_{11} & b^j_{12} & b^j_{13} \\
 & & & b^j_{21} & b^j_{22} & b^j_{23} \\
\vdots & & & \vdots & & \\
\vdots & & & \vdots & & \\
a^j_{51} & a^j_{52} & a^j_{53} & b^j_{51} & b^j_{52} & b^j_{53}
\end{array}
\right]_{2n_b \times 2 \times n_f}
$$

where the different parts of the matrix are, top left, the yield curve risk of government bonds, top right, the zero spread risk of government bonds, bottom left, government risk in corporates, and bottom right, spread factor risk. The combined matrix of factor volatilities is given as

$$
\boldsymbol{\Phi}_j =
\left[
\begin{array}{ccc|ccc}
\mathrm{var}(\Delta f^j_1) & 0 & 0 & \mathrm{cov}(\Delta f^j_1, \Delta fc^j_1) & \cdots & \\
0 & \mathrm{var}(\Delta f^j_2) & 0 & \vdots & \ddots & \\
0 & 0 & \mathrm{var}(\Delta f^j_3) & & & \\
\mathrm{cov}(\Delta f^j_1, \Delta fc^j_1) & \cdots & & \mathrm{var}(\Delta fc^j_1) & 0 & 0 \\
\vdots & \ddots & & 0 & \mathrm{var}(\Delta fc^j_2) & 0 \\
& & & 0 & 0 & \mathrm{var}(\Delta fc^j_3)
\end{array}
\right]_{2n_f \times 2n_f}
$$

Here the parts are government factors (top left), factor covariation (top right and bottom left) and spread factors (bottom right).

Apart from knowing the size of the TE taken it is vital for portfolio managers to know which positions are more diversifying than others and how much TE can be attributed to a specific factor, country or bucket:

$$
\frac{d\sigma_{\mathrm{active}}}{d\,\mathbf{wdd}} = \frac{\mathbf{V}^*\mathbf{wdd}^*}{\sigma_{\mathrm{active}}}
$$

$$
\frac{d\sigma_{\mathrm{active}}}{d\,\mathbf{f}} = \frac{\boldsymbol{\Omega}^*\mathbf{A}^{*\prime}\mathbf{wdd}^*}{\sigma_{\mathrm{active}}}
$$

Calculating the percentage contributions from here is a straightforward exercise. This approach can easily be overlaid with trade funding.

1 See Sharpe (1981).

2 See Roll (1992).

3 Alternatively, mean absolute deviation (MAD) has also been labelled as TE as in Rudolf, Wolter and Zimmermann (1999):

$$\sigma_{MAD} = \frac{1}{T-1} \sum_{t=1}^{T} \left| r_{at} - \bar{r}_a \right|$$

who claim that linear fee arrangements would make MAD better suited to capturing risk than Equation (6.1). We will ignore the latter definition because it has little impact on practitioners and also because the argument is not always convincing. Even if the fee arrangement is linear, the relationship between performance and fees will be non-linear as better performance leads to more assets under management and vice versa.

4 Alternatively, assume that we deal with log active returns.

5 The technology stock bubble of 2000 is a good example of this. Many fund managers engaged in very "sticky" bets (so termed because fund managers held them for a long time) while at the same time the trend in markets made historical volatility small. This led to a marked underestimation of weights-based TE versus return-based TE as the latter increased sharply upwards due to increased volatility and reduced correlation between stocks.

6 For a review of variance ratio tests, see Campbell, Lo and MacKinlay (1997).

7 See Satchell and MacQueen (1998).

8 For this reason some index trackers do not minimise TE but instead minimise transaction cost (return component) with a TE constraint.

9 Assuming that normality is another caveat when trying to link TE to performance. However, non-normality might be less of a problem for diversified active positions as a large number of over- and underweights would bring the central limit theorem into play. Skewness might diversify away much quicker than in long-only portfolios as the negative skewness of individual asset returns is transformed into a positive skewness for under-weights and, hence, over- and underweights quickly reduce portfolio skewness.

10 See Gardner et al. (2000).

11 See Fishwick (1999).

12 See Scowcroft and Sefton (2001).

13 See Michaud (1989).

14 See Muller (1993).

15 See Satchell and Hwang (2001).

16 Suppose we can express uncertainty in weights as $\mathbf{w}_a = \bar{\mathbf{w}}_a + \mathbf{v}$, where $\mathbf{w}_a \approx N(\mathbf{0}, \mathbf{\Sigma})$. We can then decompose the squared TE into $\sigma^2 = \bar{\mathbf{w}}_a \mathbf{\Omega} \bar{\mathbf{w}}_a + \mathbf{\mu}_a \mathbf{\Omega} \mathbf{\mu}_a + \text{tr}(\mathbf{\Omega}\mathbf{\Sigma})$. As the last two terms are always positive (positive-definite matrix and trace of a covariance matrix), this will always be higher than the conventional calculation.

17 See Hartmann (2002) versus Lawton (2001).

18 See Roll (1992) or Wilcox (1994, 2000).

19 This is only true as long as we measure risk as variance, as only variance is additive.

20 See Leupold (1996, pp. 99–100).

21 In practice, active positions and benchmark are much more difficult to separate as binding long-only constraints prohibit the effective use of short sales. As a reaction, asset managers cluster their books of business around a few model portfolios and in general become increasingly reluctant to accept non-standard ("odd" benchmark) business.

22 More on different aspects of the information coefficient can be found in Grinold and Kahn (2000).

23 The equilibrium risk premium is most likely not stable. Hence Lee (2000) suggests using a filter mechanism to take time variation into account.

24 Instead of defining $\bar{\alpha} = \bar{R}_i - \bar{R}_b$, we should estimate $\bar{\alpha} = (R_i - c) - \hat{\beta}(R_b - c)$. This would resolve the problem in a CAPM world.

25 Cross-sectional volatility is a function of correlation and volatility. It is, however, not true that a higher cross section of returns leads to more attractive risk/return opportunities for active management, ie, a higher information ratio. Even if assets were highly correlated or volatility were low, we could always leverage up all active positions to generate the appropriate active return (assuming leverage were possible). The information ratio stays constant and is a function of skill (information coefficient) and effort (number of bets) only.

26 See Kritzman and Rich (1998).

27 See Wang (1999).

28 The case $\theta = \frac{1}{2}$ does not mean that both benchmarks are tracked equally.

29 The Pareto solution was introduced by Shectman (2000).

30 General optimisers will find solutions to deviating cases also. We are, however, concerned with solutions that can be handled within the "normal" mean–variance framework.

31 See Scherer (2001).

32 Although the TE computation is similar to the calculation of portfolio volatility, it reacts differently to changes in market environment. Low-correlation assets reduce total risk but increase TE as active positions can drift apart more freely. Hence, rising correlations will tend to make long short positions better hedges, which will result in a drop in TE (unless overcompensated by rising volatility).

33 Scaling factors are restricted to being positive as negative numbers would result in a change in positions (overweights become underweights and vice versa).

34 See Berck and Sydsaeter (1991, p. 15, Equation (3.17)).

35 Active nominal weights have to sum to zero for portfolios which cannot use leverage. However, for fixed-income portfolios it makes more sense to describe active positions in terms of weighted duration deviations. These do not have to sum to one.

36 We could even generalise further at this stage and give weights different from unity to individual trades.

37 See Scherer (2000).

38 While this is not correct – as it is well known that active positions are independent of benchmarks (this argument is weakened for high-TE products or narrow benchmarks) – it still appears to be widespread.

39 Inserting $w_{aj} = w_{ai}/(k-1)$ into the definition of the marginal contribution to risk yields the result in the text.

40 The information ratio shows the relationship between excess return and TE. The higher the information ratio, the more favourable this trade-off becomes. However, very high information ratios are hardly credible as an information ratio of 1.96 implies only a 2.5% probability of underperforming with respect to a given benchmark.

41 Litterman and Winkelmann (1996).

42 Structural alphas arise from a systematic bias in portfolio construction. These biases could arise from being structurally long equities in a balanced fund, constantly overweighting credit or constantly underweighting Japan. Along this structural position the investor tries to capture the volatility in the according asset. The higher the volatility, the longer the distance the investor can capture and the higher the potential out (under)performance from volatility capture. See Lee (2000).

43 An active portfolio is effectively a zero-investment long short portfolio.

44 Statistical analysis shows that a global interest rate factor explains only about 50% of the variance in global yield changes as opposed to about 90% for national yield changes.

45 It should be noted that the exposures are ordered by absolute size.

46 Instead of using principal component analysis – which has the disadvantage that the principal components are orthogonal by construction – one might want to define the corresponding yield curve movements. Define yield curve factors according to

$$\Delta l = level_t - level_{t-1}$$

$$= \frac{1}{5} \sum_i y_{i,t}^j - \frac{1}{5} \sum_i y_{i,t-1}^j$$

$$\Delta s = slope_t - slope_{t-1}$$

$$= \left(y_{5,t}^j - y_{1,t}^j \right) - \left(y_{5,t-1}^j - y_{1,t-1}^j \right)$$

$$\Delta c = curvature_t - curvature_{t-1}$$

$$= \left(y_{5,t}^j + y_{1,t}^j - 2 y_{2,t}^j \right) - \left(y_{5,t-1}^j + y_{1,t-1}^j - 2 y_{2,t-1}^j \right)$$

and run OLS regression to calculate the specific loading (exposure):

$$\Delta y_i^j = \alpha_i^j + \alpha_{i,l}^j \Delta l^j + \alpha_{i,s}^j \Delta s^j + \alpha_{i,c}^j \Delta c^j + \varepsilon_i^j$$

47 For an application of principal component analysis to fixed-income markets, see Golub and Tilman (2000).

48 Rather than modelling the credit spread using principal component analysis, we might want to try swap spreads:

$$\Delta s_{i,\,rating}^j = \beta_0 + \beta_1 \Delta s_{swap}^j + \upsilon_{i,\,rating}^j$$

However, the number of parameters being estimated here may be too high to ensure sufficient accuracy in the results.

BIBLIOGRAPHY

Berck, P., and K. Sydsaeter, 1991, *Economists Mathematical Manual*, Second Edition (Berlin: Springer).

Campbell, J., A. Lo and A. MacKinlay, 1997, *The Econometrics of Financial Markets* (Princeton University Press).

Fishwick, E., 1999, "Unexpectedly Large or Frequent Extreme Returns in Active TE Portfolios", Franklin Portfolio Associates.

Gardner, D., D. Bowie, M. Brooks and M. Cumberworth, 2000, "Predicted TEs: Fact or Fantasy", Working Paper, Faculty and Institute of Actuaries.

Golub, B., and M. Tilman, 2000, *Risk Management* (New York: John Wiley & Sons).

Grinold, R., and R. Kahn, 2000, *Active Portfolio Management*, Second Edition (New York: McGraw-Hill).

Hartmann, S., 2002, "Laying the Foundations", ABN AMRO Research Paper, January.

Kritzman, M., and D. Rich, 1998, "Risk Containment for Investors with Multivariate Utility Functions", *Journal of Derivatives* 5, pp. 178–470.

Lawton, C., 2001, "An Alternative Calculation of TE", *Journal of Asset Management* 2, pp. 223–34.

Lee, W., 2000, *Theory and Methodology of Tactical Asset Allocation* (New Hope: Fabozzi Associates).

Leupold, T., 1996, *Benchmarkorientierte Portfoliooptimierung* (Bern: Haupt Verlag).

Litterman, R., and K. Winkelmann, 1996, "Managing Market Exposure", *Journal of Portfolio Management* 22, pp. 32–49.

Michaud, R., 1989, "The Markowitz Optimization Enigma: Is Optimized Optimal?", *Financial Analysts Journal* 45, pp. 31–42.

Muller, P., 1993, "Empirical Tests of Biases in Equity Portfolio Optimization", in: S. Zenios, *Financial Optimization* (Cambridge University Press).

Roll, R., 1992, "A Mean Variance Analysis of TE", *Journal of Portfolio Management* 18, pp. 13–22.

Rudolf, M., H. Wolter and H. Zimmermann, 1999, "A Linear Model for Tracking Error Minimisation", *Journal of Banking and Finance* 23, pp. 85–103.

Satchell, S., and S. Hwang, 2001, "TE: Ex Ante Versus Ex Post Measures", *Journal of Asset Management* 2, pp. 241–6.

Satchell, S., and J. MacQueen, 1998, "Why Forecast TE Seem Sometimes Inconsistent With Actual Performance", Working Paper, Alpha Strategies Ltd.

Scherer, B., 2000, "Preparing the Best Risk Budget", *Risk* 13, pp. 3–32.

Scherer, B., 2001, "A Note on TE Funding Assumptions", *Journal of Asset Management* 2, pp. 235–40.

Scowcroft, A., and J. Sefton, 2001, "Do TEs Reliably Estimate Portfolio Risk?", *Journal of Asset Management* 2, pp. 205–22.

Sharpe, W., 1981, "Decentralised Investment Management", *Journal of Finance* 36, pp. 217–34.

Shectman, P., 2000, "Multiple Benchmarks and Multiple Sources of Risk", Working Paper, Northfields.

Wang, M., 1999, "Multiple-Benchmark and Multiple Portfolio Optimization", *Financial Analysts Journal* 55, pp. 63–72.

Wilcox, J., 1994, "EAFE is for Wimps", *Journal of Portfolio Management* 20, pp. 68–75.

Wilcox, J., 2000, *Investing by the Numbers* (New Hope: Fabozzi Associates).

7

Core–Satellite Investing:
Budgeting Active Manager Risk

The central objective of this chapter is to show pension fund trustees how they can optimally combine the skills of both index-tracking and active fund managers. It is the most important decision after the strategic asset allocation has been derived, given the increasingly competitive nature of the pension fund market. Current practice is to use weight allocation to choose among managers (well performing managers get higher weights while others are terminated). This chapter will show that this can be considerably more inefficient than the risk allocation method, where well performing managers are allowed to become more aggressive, while less successful managers are moved into passive management. Instead of using the weight allocation method, the suggestion ventured is to efficiently use all available information on managers showing return histories of different lengths as truncation would lead to an increase of estimation error and hence to allocations of little practical use. Finally, the chapter offers an estimate of the loss in efficiency if the correlation structure between managers and asset classes is not properly taken into account.

Core–satellite investing is the division of funds into a passive part (the core) and an active part (one or more satellites of active managers). The main reason for this separation lies in fee arbitrage.[1] Suppose a pension fund targets 1% tracking error versus its liability-driven long-term policy benchmark. Additionally, suppose that, for the sake of simplicity, currently 100% of the pension assets are invested with a single active manager. Instead of paying active fees on 100% of its assets managed by a low (1%) tracking error manager, the pension fund could achieve the same active risk budget of 1% by investing 50% in indexed funds and 50% in a more active manager with 2% tracking error. The pension fund could then afford to pay twice as much for the more aggressive manager and still break even on fee expenditures. The idea is that while asset managers charge fees on the total volume, the biggest part of the fund is effectively indexed (dead weight).[2]

However, this often-quoted calculation relies on two assumptions, which are addressed in detail later in the chapter. The first assumption is that aggressive managers can maintain the same information ratios as their less aggressive counterparts. The second is that fees are calculated as asset-based fees (current practice). If fees were calculated as lump sum payments (a fixed US$ amount, independent of fund volume or tracking error size), mandate size would not matter and the more aggressive manager would have no fee advantage (although limits to fee arbitrage would have to eventually take effect, otherwise nothing would stop investors from moving into increasingly more aggressive core–satellite investing). It should now be clear that successful core–satellite investing has to solve a variety of problems at the heart of modern pension fund management: how many active investments should a pension fund undertake, ie, what is the proportion of satellites to core?; where (in which regions, asset classes, styles, etc) should a pension fund be active?; how can multiple managers be optimally combined? The following sections demonstrate that all three questions can be solved simultaneously as a straightforward risk budgeting exercise. Risk budgeting issues are also discussed in Scherer (2000 and 2001) and in Winkelmann (2000).

7.1 MATHEMATICS OF MULTIPLE MANAGER ALLOCATION: TWO-MANAGER CASE

Let us go through a simple two-manager example to study how the mechanics of optimal manager allocation work. (See Appendix A for a more general approach.) Active manager risk and return are given by the usual expressions

$$\alpha = w_{\alpha_1} + w_{\alpha_2}$$

$$\sigma_\alpha = \left(w_{\alpha_1}^2 \, \sigma_{\alpha_1}^2 + w_{\alpha_2}^2 \, \sigma_{\alpha_2}^2 + 2 w_{\alpha_1} \, w_{\alpha_2} \, \sigma_{\alpha_1 \alpha_2} \right)^{\frac{1}{2}}$$

where σ_{α_i} (for $i = 1, 2$) denotes the tracking error of manager i, and w_{α_i} is the respective weight. The marginal contribution to active risk (how much active risk – measured in tracking error – changes if we put a small additional amount of the respective manager into the portfolio) can be calculated as the first derivative of the tracking error expression

$$\frac{d\sigma_\alpha}{dw_{\alpha_1}} = \frac{w_{\alpha_1} \, \sigma_{\alpha_1}^2 + w_{\alpha_2} \, \sigma_{\alpha_1 \alpha_2}}{\sigma_\alpha} \tag{7.1}$$

Multiplying this expression by $w_{\alpha_i}/\sigma_\alpha$, we arrive at the percentage risk allocation for each manager:

$$\frac{d\sigma_\alpha}{dw_{\alpha_1}} \frac{w_{\alpha_1}}{\sigma_\alpha} = \frac{w_{\alpha_1}^2 \, \sigma_{\alpha_1}^2 + w_{\alpha_1} \, w_{\alpha_2} \, \sigma_{\alpha_1 \alpha_2}}{\sigma_\alpha^2}$$

The reader might note that this term looks like an elasticity. As already shown in Chapter 6, the sum of these elasticities equals one as the tracking error is linearly homogeneous in terms of weight (ie, doubling weights will double tracking error). For illustrative purposes, this is repeated for the two-manager case:

$$\frac{d\sigma_\alpha}{dw_{\alpha_1}}\frac{w_{\alpha_1}}{\sigma_\alpha} + \frac{d\sigma_\alpha}{dw_{\alpha_2}}\frac{w_{\alpha_2}}{\sigma_\alpha}$$

$$= \frac{w_{\alpha_1}^2 \sigma_{\alpha_1}^2 + w_{\alpha_1} w_{\alpha_2} \sigma_{\alpha_1\alpha_2}}{\sigma_\alpha^2} + \frac{w_{\alpha_2}^2 \sigma_{\alpha_1}^2 + w_{\alpha_1} w_{\alpha_2} \sigma_{\alpha_1\alpha_2}}{\sigma_\alpha^2}$$

$$= \frac{\sigma_\alpha^2}{\sigma_\alpha^2} = 1 \qquad (7.2)$$

The optimal solution for two managers can be found by trying all possible manager combinations, hence "grid searching" for the optimal solution. This involves increasing the weight of manager one (simultaneously decreasing the weight of manager two) over the whole spectrum of weights and calculating the corresponding information ratio (IR)[3] for each weight combination.[4] This allows us not only to find the optimal manager combination but also to find out more about the optimality conditions.

We assume that both managers exhibit a 5% tracking error. Manager one manages to create a 5% alpha while manager two returns an alpha of only 3%. Both managers show a correlation of 0.3. How should we optimally combine both managers? The optimality criterion is to maximise the information ratio. Figure 7.1 (overleaf) visualises the grid search process, plotting information ratio as well as marginal return to marginal risk ratios, as a function of manager one's weight.

The overall information ratio is maximised at a weight of about 75% for manager one and of 25% for manager two. However, Figure 7.1 also shows the ratio of marginal return to marginal risk for both managers. We can see that the optimal manager allocation is characterised by an equal ratio of marginal return to marginal risk across all managers and that this ratio equals the optimal information ratio of the combined portfolio. All lines intersect at the maximum information ratio (see Appendix A for more details). We can therefore write

$$\frac{\alpha_1}{\left(w_{\alpha_1}\sigma_{\alpha_1}^2 + w_{\alpha_2}\sigma_{\alpha_1\alpha_2}\right)\big/\sigma_\alpha} = \frac{\alpha_2}{\left(w_{\alpha_2}\sigma_{\alpha_2}^2 + w_{\alpha_2}\sigma_{\alpha_1\alpha_2}\right)\big/\sigma_\alpha}$$

$$= IR_{total}^* \qquad (7.3)$$

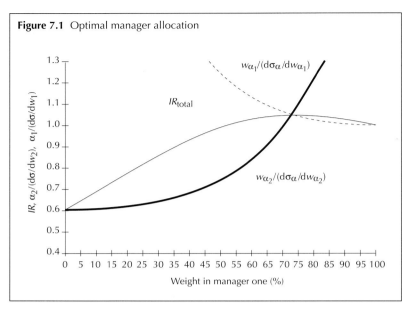

Figure 7.1 Optimal manager allocation

This is the core principle of multiple manager allocation. In fact, it is the core principle of any optimal portfolio decision. We can rewrite the constant relationship between performance and risk contribution by expanding both sides with $w_{\alpha_i}/w_{\alpha_i}$ ($i = 1, 2$) and multiplying both sides by σ_α:

$$\frac{w_{\alpha_1}}{\left(w_{\alpha_1}\sigma^2_{\alpha_1} + w_{\alpha_2}\sigma_{\alpha_1\alpha_2}\right)\Big/\sigma^2_\alpha} = \frac{w_{\alpha_2}}{\left(w_{\alpha_2}\sigma^2_{\alpha_2} + w_{\alpha_2}\sigma_{\alpha_1\alpha_2}\right)\Big/\sigma^2_\alpha}$$

$$\frac{\text{Return contribution}_1}{\text{Risk contribution}_1} = \frac{\text{Return contribution}_2}{\text{Risk contribution}_2} \qquad (7.4)$$

The ratio of return to risk contribution will be the same for both managers provided they have been optimally allocated. We can also use this principle to derive the implied alphas for a given manager allocation:

$$\alpha_1 = IR^*_{total}\frac{d\sigma_\alpha}{dw_{\alpha_1}} = IR^*_{total}\left(w_{\alpha_1}\sigma^2_{\alpha_1} + w_{\alpha_2}\sigma_{\alpha_1\alpha_2}\right)\sigma^{-1}_\alpha$$

The implied alpha rises with tracking error (greater risk), weightings (both directly reflecting conviction about a manager's ability) and covariance (less diversifying) with other managers.

7.2 WHY MULTIPLE MANAGERS?

We have already seen in the previous section that adding a second manager increases the information ratio of the total portfolio. What would adding more managers do to the information ratio? Suppose that we can add uncorrelated managers to our portfolio and suppose for simplicity that those managers show zero correlation between them. How many managers would we add? What would happen to the information ratio? Writing out the expressions for alpha and tracking error, assuming equal weights among managers, we get:

$$IR_{total} = \frac{\sum \frac{1}{n} \alpha_i}{\left(\sum \left(\frac{1}{n} \right)^2 \sigma_{\alpha_i}^2 \right)^{\frac{1}{2}}} = \frac{\overline{\alpha}}{\overline{\sigma}_{\alpha}} n^{\frac{1}{2}} \qquad (7.5)$$

As the number of managers increases, the information ratio will also rise (the increase, however, is itself lessening). Naively, we might think there would be an incentive to add all available managers. What stops this happening in reality? Primarily, the average alpha in the universe is, by definition, negative.[5]

Hence, increasing the number of managers indiscriminately will still diversify active risks, but at the expense of picking up smaller or negative alphas from less capable managers, so the average will converge to zero. Moreover, it will be difficult to find more and more uncorrelated managers (availability issues). In addition, this would increase coordination, selection and monitoring costs arising from a divided manager structure.

The dominant arguments for multiple manager allocation are diversification and specialisation. Specialisation aims at the nominator in Equation (7.5). The idea is that it is unlikely that a balanced manager can provide first quartile information ratios on all decisions taken (on government bonds, credit, currency overlay, equity management, etc). Rather than accepting a diluted information ratio (diluted by less excellent decision areas), specialists should focus on selecting and should raise the average alpha in a multiple manager fund.[6] Consultants (unsurprisingly) favour this argument as it depends mainly on fund selection skills. It rests on the assumption that narrowing down the universe (making fewer prices to forecast) will result in an increased forecasting ability.[7] Specialisation in its purest form only exists if each specialist has a different benchmark reflecting a personalised special skill, appropriate to that specialist, in this particular universe.

In contrast, diversification aims at reducing risk for a given alpha level. It arises from a diversification of signals, ie, different managers create different forecasts and hence perform better, as long as the signals provide value. Forecast diversification tends to create less correlated alphas and hence assists the risk reduction in adding on another manager. In diversification's purest form, different managers are given the same benchmark. Diversification without manager selection skills, however, proves to be counter-productive; active risks would cancel out without alpha left on the table, hence the sponsor gets a passive fund at active costs.

Specialisation and diversification do not exclude each other. There is, and always will be, incentive to diversify among specialists. However, selection, monitoring and coordination costs will again limit the extent of this procedure.

So far in this chapter, it has been established that adding on individual managers can increase the active return per unit of active risk (portfolio return minus benchmark return) and hence the stability of active returns. However, would a plan sponsor choose to hold a multiple manager portfolio if in possession of all the individual managers' information? Does the separation of responsibilities still lead to an overall optimal solution? One approach to solving the problem would be "to replace decentralised management with decentralised prediction making and centralised management".[8] Effectively, this means that asset managers sell their forecasts (hence ceasing to be asset managers) and plan sponsors optimally combine these forecasts to construct a portfolio that is fully compatible with their objectives. This is a multiple adviser, rather than a multiple manager, structure.[9] However, most managers refuse to sell their predictions (not to mention that very often they do not even generate quantitative forecasts). They do so because the marginal costs of reselling their signals are very small and the revealed information is difficult to control. Moreover, they do not want to unbundle their services as a good signal is worth more to an asset manager with more under management and information can then be utilised on a greater asset base and hence earn higher fees. The problem is currently solved either by assuming it away (assuming zero correlation between active returns and asset class returns) or by imposing it away, by forcing managers to create uncorrelated active portfolios. Section 7.9 and Appendix B deal with this in more detail.

7.3 WHY CORE–SATELLITE?

The essence of the fee arbitrage argument supporting core–satellite investing is that partially substituting active funds for passive funds (to generate fee savings) and investing the remaining part of a portfolio into more aggressive funds (high tracking error funds at the same or moderately higher fees) will on balance result in fee savings while performance remains unaffected. High tracking error funds can be generated by the fund manager by taking a low tracking error fund and multiplying the active positions by a multiple greater than one. Alternatively, the investor could invest in an active fund and finance this investment from selling the underlying index, hence isolating the active portfolio. Repeating this several times generates any targeted leverage. However, the paradox remains that no one would buy a low tracking error fund at the same asset-based fee (fees calculated as a percentage of assets given to the manager) if a combination of passive investments and high tracking error funds yields the same active risk budget, but at lower costs. However, continuing fee arbitrage is not an equilibrium situation. If it were, every investor would move into core–satellite, reducing the amount of assets under active management. Even if fees were to rise for active funds, this would not offset the loss in revenues from a reduced amount of funds under active management (as otherwise there would not be an arbitrage situation in the first place).

If mandates were priced as lump sum payments plus performance-based fees (as costs for a given manager are likely to be unrelated to portfolio size or aggressiveness), there would no longer be fee arbitrage. Already there is a tendency towards this model as fees quoted by asset managers are very often based on breakeven dollar amounts. An asset manager will have a breakeven value (based on cost structure and equity return requirements) and scale the asset-based fee accordingly in order to generate (at least) the breakeven income. There is a caveat, however: investment managers point out that high active risk funds require different model portfolios (new model portfolios and therefore non-scalable business) and should hence be quoted at higher fees. This argument is certainly true, but it will only apply to those with active risk requirements higher than the point where the long-only constraint is binding. For all those who are not quite as aggressive, employing aggressive funds at higher costs might be an inefficient way to achieve active risk exposure.

7.4 CORE–SATELLITE: HOW MUCH SHOULD BE ACTIVE?

The answer to any "how much?" question critically relies on assumptions and opinions (how high does the investor rate active managers) as well as on preferences (risk-aversion).[10]

Supposing an investor can allocate funds between a passive portfolio and an active portfolio with a 5% tracking error, this would be a straight-forward calculus problem; maximising the information ratio with respect to w and supposing risk-aversion is 0.2 and the information ratio is 0.5, the optimal tracking error would amount to 1.25%. This solves the first-order condition of the standard utility optimisation problem[11]

$$\frac{dU}{d\sigma_\alpha} = IR - 0.2 \cdot 2 \cdot \sigma_\alpha = 0$$

In order to generate a 1.25% tracking error, we need 25% of a 5% tracking error product. Hence the optimal solution is 25%, as can be seen in Figure 7.2 (overleaf).

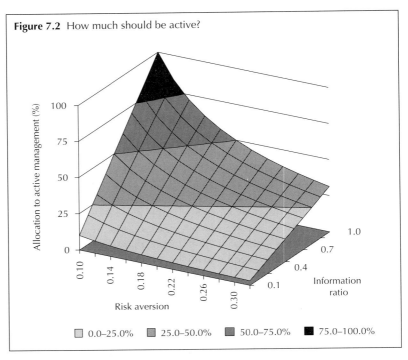

Figure 7.2 How much should be active?

Allocation to active management (%)

100

75

50

25

0

Risk aversion: 0.10, 0.14, 0.18, 0.22, 0.26, 0.30

Information ratio: 1.0, 0.7, 0.4, 0.1

☐ 0.0–25.0% ☐ 25.0–50.0% ☐ 50.0–75.0% ■ 75.0–100.0%

As one would expect, a combination of high IR and low risk-aversion leads to an allocation to active management of about 100%. Observing a plan sponsor's allocation for passive investing and knowing the risk-aversion would then allow us to calculate the implied assessment of the skill (information ratio) of active managers using reverse optimisation (see Appendix A). If satellites become more aggressive (high marginal contribution to risk), core–satellite investing does not necessarily result from a fading belief in active management.

7.5 WHERE TO BE ACTIVE?

The degree to which assets are actively managed is typically decided on a "top down" basis; first choose between active and passive and then decide where active management is employed. More importantly, the optimal manager mix is found by simultaneously choosing between active and passive managers in each region (or alternatively style buckets) of our portfolios. This is a straightforward optimisation problem (see above), where high alpha managers get a bigger allocation (in terms of either weight or tracking error) unless they need too much risk to generate a given outperformance or unless they show high correlations with other managers. In this section we will focus on manager allocation on the basis of allocating weights.[12]

As an example, we will assume that a portfolio is split between two regions (50% each).[13] In each region we can choose between four active managers and one passive manager. We will not allow manager allocation to override regional allocations, ie, we would not concentrate our portfolio in one region purely because there are highly skilled active managers in that particular part of the world (or style bucket). Each manager initially targets a tracking error of 5%. However, their information ratio differs; managers in country one have an information ratio of one while those in country two each have an information ratio of 0.3. Active managers show correlation of active returns of 0.3 within a country and zero otherwise. The objective is to maximise alpha subject to a 1% tracking error constraint.

Given the assumptions above, the solution can be found in Figure 7.2. A considerable part of money in country one would be managed actively while there would be little active management in country two. A fraction of 36% is managed actively. The optimality condition in Equation (7.3), from the previous section, is satisfied as the ratio of marginal excess return to marginal risk contribution is equal to all assets and equals the information ratio of 1.5. This scenario can be likened to an American portfolio where the money is split between the US (a highly efficient market) and Latin America (a less efficient market). The optimal allocations support our pre-understanding that there should be more passive investing where few good managers can be found, and vice versa. As correlations are assumed to be symmetrical, with no difference in information ratio and volatility, we end up with equal weights for active managers within a given market.

Continuing this example, we can assume (holding everything else equal) that manager one in country one runs a tracking error of only 2.5%, which provides a different allocation as in Table 7.1. Most notably, manager one gets a much bigger weight to make up for the small tracking error.

Table 7.1 Optimal manager allocation

Manager	w (%)	IR_i	σ_i (%)	α_i (%)	$d\sigma/dw_i$ (%)	$d\sigma/dw_i\, w_i/\sigma$ (%)	$\alpha_i/(d\sigma/dw_i)$
Country 1, active 1	6.95	1	5	5.0	3.30	22.9	1.5
Country 1, active 2	6.95	1	5	5.0	3.30	22.9	1.5
Country 1, active 3	6.95	1	5	5.0	3.30	22.9	1.5
Country 1, active 4	6.95	1	5	5.0	3.30	22.9	1.5
Country 1, passive	22.20	0	0	0.0	0.00	0.0	–
Country 2, active 1	2.08	0.3	5	1.5	0.99	2.1	1.5
Country 2, active 2	2.08	0.3	5	1.5	0.99	2.1	1.5
Country 2, active 3	2.08	0.3	5	1.5	0.99	2.1	1.5
Country 2, active 4	2.08	0.3	5	1.5	0.99	2.1	1.5
Country 2, passive	41.67	0	0	0.0	0.00	0.0	–
Total	100.00	1.5	1	2	–	100.0	–

Table 7.2 Optimal manager allocation (continued)

Manager	w (%)	IR_i	σ_i (%)	α_i (%)	$d\sigma/dw_i$ (%)	$d\sigma/dw_i\, w_i/\sigma$ (%)	$\alpha_i/(d\sigma/dw_i)$
Country 1, active 2	6.95	1.0	5	5.0	3.30	22.9	1.5
Country 1, active 3	6.95	1.0	5	5.0	3.30	22.9	1.5
Country 1, active 4	6.95	1.0	5	5.0	3.30	22.9	1.5
Country 1, passive	15.26	0.0	0	0.0	0.00	0.0	–
Country 2, active 1	2.08	0.3	5	1.5	0.99	2.1	1.5
Country 2, active 2	2.08	0.3	5	1.5	0.99	2.1	1.5
Country 2, active 3	2.08	0.3	5	1.5	0.99	2.1	1.5
Country 2, active 4	2.08	0.3	5	1.5	0.99	2.1	1.5
Country 2, passive	41.66	0.0	0	0.0	0.00	0.0	–
Total	100.00	1.5	1	2	–	100.0	–

Allocation to manager one will be extended until the relation between marginal contribution to portfolio risk and marginal contribution to excess return equal those of the other managers. Practically, this will mean that competitive pressure will force manager one in country one to lower the asset-based fee.

However, manager allocation in country two remains unchanged as we assumed zero correlations among active returns in different regions.

7.6 RISK ALLOCATION VERSUS MANAGER ALLOCATION

So far, the examples we have used have been of the optimal manager allocation using weights rather than tracking error. This is exactly the problematic scenario in which a retail client might find himself. However, institutional clients could agree with the manager on a new (more or less aggressive) tracking error target, making it possible to leave manager weights constant (weighting them equally within a region and instead choosing between managers on the basis of assigned aggressiveness).

The "Ideal world" noted in Table 7.3, would have no restrictions (no

Table 7.3 Optimal manager allocation based on different choices

	Multiple manager allocation	
	Based on tracking error	Based on weights
Ideal world	Same optimal results	
Constraints on country weights only	Optimal risk allocation	Limited alpha transfer
Binding long-only constraints	Limited leverage (explicit modelling of IR slippage)	No problem

short sales limits, no country limits, etc), and both approaches (choosing either weights or tracking errors) would yield the same results, ie, the same value added. However, reality differs from the idealised world above and hence both approaches will yield different solutions. The first major difference is that there will be no room for (explicit) passive management as soon as variations in tracking error are introduced. Actually passive management will be implicit in the level of tracking error chosen as essentially a low tracking error means that only a small fraction of the fund is managed actively. Instead, all funds will be active funds with varying tracking error targets. Competent managers have a higher tracking error assigned to them while less competent managers are assigned a lower tracking error. Passive management is still present, but it is implicit (amount of dead-weight in total portfolio) rather than explicit. A general side effect of the industry moving to core–satellite is that the figures of passive assets under management are probably inflated as the core–satellite approach itself just makes passive investments explicit rather than implicit.

Assuming that the short sales constraints are not binding, it is easy to see that choosing tracking error allows greater flexibility than using weights as the constraints on physical investments are no longer binding. Suppose all good managers are located in Latin America (LA) and the LA benchmark weight happens to be 10%: choosing weights rather than tracking error restricts the alpha from LA managers as only a maximum of 10% can be invested into LA assets. However, the contribution from LA active risk to the total risk budget could be improved (increased) if the LA bets were leveraged up.

To slightly modify the previous example, assume that country one has a 10% benchmark weighting while country two has one of 90%. All other assumptions remain the same. How would a solution based on tracking error allocation (budgeting of risk) compare with a solution based on weight allocation (manager allocation)? The results can be seen in Tables 7.4 and 7.5 (overleaf).

The optimisation confirms the perception we have built previously. Choosing weights (as depicted in Table 7.4) seriously constrains manager allocation because if the best managers are tied up in a small benchmark allocation, optimality conditions will not be met. While tracking error allocation correctly assigns the biggest part of the risk budget to the best managers, weight allocation fails to do so. In fact, we can see that percentage contributions to risk are equal to those in Table 7.1. This is not surprising as the benchmark does not matter in a world of perfect alpha transfer. While the information ratio for tracking error allocation is about 1.5, it only amounts to 0.9 for weight allocation. This example clearly favours tracking error-based multiple manager allocation. Leveraging investment processes indiscriminately faces some practical restrictions, as the next section contends.

Table 7.4 Optimal manager allocation (weight allocation)

Manager	w (%)	IR_i	σ_i (%)	α_i (%)	$d\sigma/dw_i$ (%)	$d\sigma/dw_i \, w_i/\sigma$ (%)	$\alpha_i/(d\sigma/dw_i)$
Country 1, active 1	2.50	1.0	5	5.0	1.19	3.0	4.2
Country 1, active 2	2.50	1.0	5	5.0	1.19	3.0	4.2
Country 1, active 3	2.50	1.0	5	5.0	1.19	3.0	4.2
Country 1, active 4	2.50	1.0	5	5.0	1.19	3.0	4.2
Country 1, passive	0.00	0.0	0	0.0	0.00	0.0	–
Country 2, active 1	6.81	0.3	5	1.5	3.23	22.0	0.5
Country 2, active 2	6.81	0.3	5	1.5	3.23	22.0	0.5
Country 2, active 3	6.81	0.3	5	1.5	3.23	22.0	0.5
Country 2, active 4	6.81	0.3	5	1.5	3.23	22.0	0.5
Country 2, passive	62.76	0.0	0	0.0	0.00	0.0	–
Total	100.00	0.9	1	1	–	100.0	–

Table 7.5 Optimal manager allocation (risk allocation)

Manager	w (%)	ϕ_i	IR_i	σ_i (%)	α_i (%)	$d\sigma/dw_i$ (%)	$d\sigma/dw_i \, w_i/\sigma$ (%)	$\alpha_i/(d\sigma/dw_i)$
Country 1, active 1	2.50	2.8	1.0	5	13.86	9.15	22.9	1.5
Country 1, active 2	2.50	2.8	1.0	5	13.86	9.15	22.9	1.5
Country 1, active 3	2.50	2.8	1.0	5	13.86	9.15	22.9	1.5
Country 1, active 4	2.50	2.8	1.0	5	13.86	9.15	22.9	1.5
Country 1, passive	0.00	–	0.0	0	0.00	0.00	0.0	–
Country 2, active 1	22.50	0.0	0.3	5	0.14	0.09	2.1	1.5
Country 2, active 2	22.50	0.0	0.3	5	0.14	0.09	2.1	1.5
Country 2, active 3	22.50	0.0	0.3	5	0.14	0.09	2.1	1.5
Country 2, active 4	22.50	0.0	0.3	5	0.14	0.09	2.1	1.5
Country 2, passive	0.00	–	0.0	0	0.00	0.00	0.0	–
Total	100.00	–	1.5	1	2	–	100.0	–

7.7 LIMITATIONS OF CORE–SATELLITE INVESTING

In an ideal world, core–satellite would be 100% indexed, plus a sum of independent market-neutral long-short overlay managers (zero net market exposure with uncorrelated bets that are added on, ie, overlaid to a passive benchmark), thereby disentangling asset and manager allocation. However, this world does not comply with reality as most institutional managers face long-only constraints. We will therefore compare core–satellite investing with a so-called "enhanced indexing" approach,[14] ie, the combination of low tracking error active fund managers.[15] The ability to generate high risk-adjusted returns (high information ratio) drops as portfolios get more concentrated; this relationship is captured in Figure 7.3. Very aggressive satellite portfolios can only be generated with loss in infor-

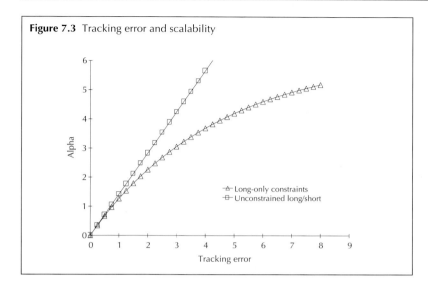

Figure 7.3 Tracking error and scalability

mation ratio, while there is little loss for enhanced indexing (low tracking error active management). In the chosen simulation example (a fairly typical active equity manager situation), there is virtually no loss in information ratio up to about 1% tracking error.[16] More aggressive management, however, must lead to a reduction in information ratio.

Satellites have to be very active in order to generate a target tracking error for 100% of assets while only using x% of total assets. In general, this will not work without loss in information ratio as it forces long-only managers to hold increasingly undiversified active portfolios (in order to create high tracking error). Long–short managers, however, would just scale up their position without loss in information or diversification. The extent to which this argument is true depends on the level of x chosen and the products involved (macro funds find it easier than micro funds to generate higher tracking error without loss in IR). Practical modelling will have to include an estimate for the information ratio slippage (information ratio as function of tracking error). The problem then becomes maximising

$$ IR\left(\sigma_\alpha\right)\sigma_\alpha - f\left(\sigma_\alpha\right) - \lambda\sigma_\alpha^2 \qquad (7.6) $$

with respect to risk, where $f(\sigma)$ denotes fees as a function of tracking error. A necessary condition for optimality is given by

$$ \sigma_\alpha = \left(IR\left(\sigma_\alpha\right) - \frac{\overset{(+)}{\mathrm{d}f\left(\sigma_\alpha\right)}}{\mathrm{d}\sigma_\alpha} \right) \bigg/ \left(2\lambda - \frac{\mathrm{d}IR\left(\sigma_\alpha\right)}{\underset{(-)}{\mathrm{d}\sigma_\alpha}} \right) \qquad (7.7) $$

Bracketed signs indicate the derivative. An increase in tracking error will, for example, lead to a deteriorating information ratio as short sales constraints become binding.

The usual optimality condition $\sigma_\alpha = IR/2\lambda$ will only be obtained if fees, as well as information ratios, are independent of tracking error.

Additionally, investors are likely to create a negative size-bias as over-weights (higher weightings than index weights) increasingly have to be financed from big stocks. Again, this can be seen from a Monte Carlo simulation study of manager behaviour. We choose a 100-stock benchmark with different benchmark concentration levels and also a log concentration model where zero stands for no concentration (ie, equal weighting) and concentration levels rise as the numbers get bigger.[17] Results are summarised in Figure 7.4.

Table 7.6 Core–satellite versus enhanced indexing

	Core–satellite	Enhanced indexing
Ideal world (no constraints)	Fee arbitrage favours core satellite (not a long-term equilibrium situation)	
Allocation	Equally applicable	
Binding short-sale constraint	Loss in IR for high aggressiveness levels	Manager allocation by choosing weights
Short-sale constraint plus concentrated benchmark	Negative size bias	Neutral

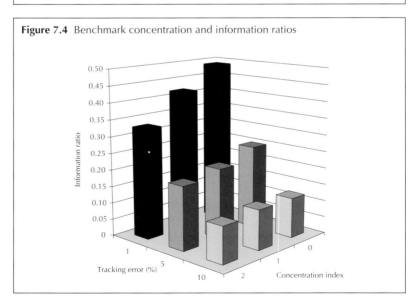

Figure 7.4 Benchmark concentration and information ratios

The effect of increasing benchmark concentration is most pronounced for small tracking errors. For very aggressive portfolios, there is almost no difference as the long-only constraint is already limiting enough. The biggest information ratio can be achieved for unconcentrated benchmarks and small tracking errors.

7.8 INPUT GENERATION

Portfolio optimisation is very sensitive to variations in inputs (see Chapters 3 and 4).[18] Managers with high information ratios are seen to be "attractive", and thus tend to get the highest fraction of the active risk budget. This problem is familiar to those who are involved in multiple manager allocation. Time series data of manager performance are only available in different lengths; hence estimates are prone to different estimation errors. A low information ratio might be statistically significant if there were

Table 7.7 Manager data with different time lengths

Year	Fund 1	Fund 2	Fund 3	Fund 4	Fund 5
1970	0.63	0.33	0.59	n.a.	n.a.
1971	−1.83	−0.34	−1.14	n.a.	n.a.
1972	1.75	2.68	3.31	n.a.	n.a.
1973	2.08	2.81	0.33	n.a.	n.a.
1974	−0.79	1.21	0.81	n.a.	n.a.
1975	3.88	4.21	4.72	n.a.	n.a.
1976	3.88	4.83	4.82	n.a.	n.a.
1977	1.42	0.00	1.42	n.a.	n.a.
1978	2.15	2.00	2.06	n.a.	n.a.
1979	1.85	1.59	2.42	n.a.	n.a.
1980	1.13	−0.72	0.96	n.a.	n.a.
1981	2.95	2.97	2.52	n.a.	n.a.
1982	0.32	−0.71	−0.41	n.a.	n.a.
1983	5.87	6.69	5.43	n.a.	n.a.
1984	1.23	0.32	−0.73	n.a.	n.a.
1985	0.73	1.32	0.71	1.63	2.91
1986	2.63	2.47	2.45	2.88	4.00
1987	0.62	−0.51	0.44	−0.32	−0.21
1988	0.31	−2.26	0.74	−0.80	−1.35
1989	−1.16	−0.90	−1.24	−0.86	−0.64
1990	1.09	−0.24	1.10	−0.07	0.52
1991	−2.17	−0.90	−0.45	−1.63	−1.64
1992	1.93	2.25	2.93	4.23	3.57
1993	3.75	5.13	2.93	4.23	5.67
1994	−0.88	0.10	−0.06	−0.97	−0.56
1995	2.22	1.10	1.79	2.07	1.26
1996	3.01	2.96	1.63	1.72	2.36
1997	−2.69	−3.26	−3.39	−3.71	−2.00
1998	−2.38	−1.83	−0.65	−1.23	−1.87
1999	1.64	1.36	1.25	2.82	0.88

Table 7.8 Estimation results

	Fund 1	Fund 2	Fund 3	Fund 4	Fund 5
		Truncated sample estimator			
α	0.58	0.45	0.68	0.67	0.86
σ	2.03	2.28	1.94	2.32	2.38
IR_i	0.28	0.20	0.35	0.29	0.36
			Maximum likelihood		
α	1.17	1.16	1.24	1.42	1.58
σ	1.93	2.19	1.71	2.49	2.38
IR_i	0.61	0.53	0.73	0.57	0.66
			Bayes		
α	1.17	1.16	1.24	1.42	1.58
σ	2.24	2.55	1.98	2.90	2.78
IR_i	0.52	0.45	0.63	0.49	0.57

enough data, while a high information ratio might not if it were based on a short history. Portfolio optimisers have no way of detecting this and treat both numbers with the same certainty. This section illustrates the estimation error problem and a potential solution.[19]

Suppose you have five potential value specialists in which to invest (see Table 7.7); you would be given annual returns from 1970 to 1999 (30 observations) for three funds but only half the data for two of the five funds.[20] Faced with this problem, it is common practice to truncate all time series and use the data from 1985 onwards. The results (truncated sample estimator) are shown in Table 7.8. It is obvious that this procedure throws away available information on funds one to three. Remember that the level of the information ratio determines the active–passive decision, while the dispersion determines manager allocation. But, can this be improved upon?

Alternatively, one can use maximum likelihood techniques that incorporate the correlation between fund series. For the long series (funds one to three ranging from 1970 to 1999), αs are still found by averaging over the 30-year period. Risks are also calculated using the long data series as these are the maximum likelihood estimates. For the short series, we first compare the αs for the longer time series before and after 1985. The difference is scaled according to the sensitivities (see Chapter 4 on Bayesian methods for a detailed explanation of methodology) found by two multiple regressions of the returns for funds four and five on the remaining funds one to three in Table 7.7. As returns have been different in both periods – higher up to 1985 – information ratios are adjusted upwards.[21]

However, the dispersion of information ratios is still relatively high, and well above the true information ratio of 0.5 each, as estimation error is not accounted for. Using an uninformative prior to reflect estimation error, we get the estimates labelled "Bayes". Taking estimation error into account will not change the means, as means take on the role of expected values and there is no uncertainty about an expected value. However, risks are increased considerably by scaling down information ratios. It is worth noting that risk increases are higher for the short series (higher estimation error). Bayesian adjustment can help in a multiple manager allocation exercise in order to reflect different time series lengths and estimation error, and hence arrive at more realistic active–passive allocation decisions.

7.9 ALLOCATING BETWEEN ALPHA AND BETA BETS

So far, the manager allocation problem has been seen in isolation from the asset allocation problem; we neither took into account the interaction between active returns and asset class returns nor looked at the incentives of an asset manager to engage in structural bets. A structural bet is a position that is designed to collect the long-term (average) risk premium of an asset class. It is designed to stay on the portfolio, irrespective of market conditions and effectively changes a client's benchmark. Suppose an asset manager has got the objective to maximise risk-adjusted active returns, with a tracking error target of 5% (assuming there are no further restrictions), and a market-neutral portfolio construction information ratio of 0.5. The risk premium for taking on equity risk is 7% and equity volatility is 20%. How should the manager then allocate the 5% risk budget to maximise active returns? Introducing the possibility of structural bets, active returns can now be generated by two competing sources. One is to permanently increase equity exposure (structural beta bet); the other is to take market-neutral (beta-neutral) stock bets, so-called "alpha bets". For every unit of active risk created by the structural equity bet, one unit of alpha risk is crowded out for a given risk budget. What would be the optimal allocation of alpha and beta bets for a single manager? Figure 7.5 (overleaf) plots the total information ratio relative to the excess beta (portfolio beta minus one) for the above example.[22]

The information ratio increases in excess beta. However, there is a limit where the active portfolio becomes very concentrated in beta bets and the information ratio falls again. If the excess beta is zero, then we arrive at the information ratio for pure stock picking. In an environment where structural bets are attractive (high risk premium) there is a considerable incentive for the portfolio manager to take on structural risk and crowd out alpha risk. For 7% risk premium, an excess beta of 0.15 would be optimal, as in the example above. Figure 7.5 also shows that the incentive to crowd out alpha bets would be lower in a low risk premium environment. Collecting the risk premium by effectively changing the benchmark would be optimal from the myopic view of a single manager, but what would be the consequence for the correlation between managers and asset classes, and between managers themselves? If two managers take the same struc-

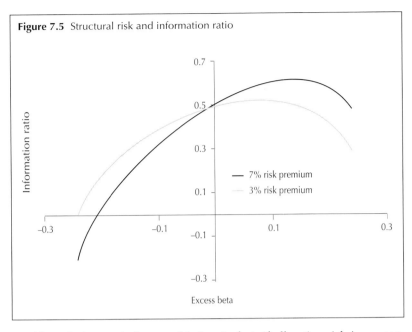

Figure 7.5 Structural risk and information ratio

tural bet, their correlation would rise. In fact, if all active risk is concentrated in the structural bet, it would reach one.[23] The same would happen to the correlation between active returns of any given manager and their benchmark. Increasing correlations have a negative impact on total risk. How would the plan sponsor's total risk exposure change if a manager kept the tracking error limit the same but substituted alpha bets for structural bets? Figure 7.6 plots total risk against excess beta. We can see that taking structural bets effectively changes the sponsor's benchmark (hence violating risk tolerance). Instead of a risk close to 20%, the sponsor might end with 25% total risk even though tracking error remains unchanged.

We have looked at the problem mostly from a single manager view so far, but what would be the consequences in a multiple manager framework? Suppose a plan sponsor has to determine optimal asset allocation (β bets) and multiple manager allocation (α bets). Alpha bets yield active returns, while beta bets yield a risk premium over cash. The combined covariance matrix of asset class risk premia (here indexed by β: $\boldsymbol{\Omega}_{\beta\beta}$) and active manager returns (indexed by α: $\boldsymbol{\Omega}_{\alpha\alpha}$) is given by

$$\boldsymbol{\Omega} = \begin{bmatrix} \boldsymbol{\Omega}_{\beta\beta} & \boldsymbol{\Omega}_{\beta\alpha} \\ \boldsymbol{\Omega}_{\alpha\beta} & \boldsymbol{\Omega}_{\alpha\alpha} \end{bmatrix}$$

We also assume that αs are perfectly transportable and that the sponsor does not face any add-up constraints (neither managers nor asset classes

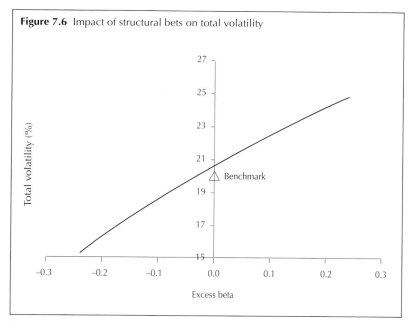

Figure 7.6 Impact of structural bets on total volatility

have to add up to one, short positions in both are allowed). The total problem can then be written down as

$$U = \mathbf{w}'\boldsymbol{\mu} - \frac{1}{2\lambda}\mathbf{w}'\boldsymbol{\Omega}\mathbf{w}$$

$$\mathbf{w}' = \begin{bmatrix} \mathbf{w}_\beta & \mathbf{w}_\alpha \end{bmatrix}, \quad \boldsymbol{\mu}' = \begin{bmatrix} \boldsymbol{\mu}_\beta & \boldsymbol{\mu}_\alpha \end{bmatrix}$$

$$\boldsymbol{\Omega} = \begin{bmatrix} \boldsymbol{\Omega}_{\beta\beta} & \boldsymbol{\Omega}_{\beta\alpha} \\ \boldsymbol{\Omega}_{\alpha\beta} & \boldsymbol{\Omega}_{\alpha\alpha} \end{bmatrix}$$

Expanding this expression we get

$$U = \underbrace{\mathbf{w}'_\alpha \boldsymbol{\mu}_\alpha - \frac{1}{2\lambda}\mathbf{w}'_\alpha \boldsymbol{\Omega}_{\alpha\alpha} \mathbf{w}_\alpha}_{\text{Multiple manager problem}}$$

$$+ \underbrace{\mathbf{w}'_\beta \boldsymbol{\mu}_\beta - \frac{1}{2\lambda}\mathbf{w}'_\beta \boldsymbol{\Omega}_{\beta\beta} \mathbf{w}_\beta}_{\text{Asset allocation problem}}$$

$$\underbrace{- \frac{1}{\lambda}\mathbf{w}'_\beta \boldsymbol{\Omega}_{\alpha\beta} \mathbf{w}_\alpha}_{\text{Interaction term}}$$

Current practice has been to (often implicitly) assume the off-diagonal matrices' correlation to be zero and to solve the problem separately.[24] If this were true, both problems could be separated, and we would ignore the interaction term without losing efficiency. Solutions for separate optimisation are given below (see Appendix for more details):

$$\mathbf{w}^*_{\beta,\,\text{sep}} = \lambda \mathbf{\Omega}^{-1}_{\beta\beta} \mathbf{\mu}_\beta$$

$$\mathbf{w}^*_{\alpha,\,\text{sep}} = \lambda \mathbf{\Omega}^{-1}_{\alpha\alpha} \mathbf{\mu}_\alpha$$

However, it becomes apparent that the same risk-aversion drives beta and alpha bets. Applying different risk-aversions in the separated problems is inconsistent with the total problem and yields a sub-optimal solution.[25]

Alternatively, an asset manager could run a partial optimisation where optimal asset allocation weights are independently derived in a first step and manager weights are calculated in a second step, taking into account cross-correlations between managers and asset classes. The partial optimisation can be shown to lead to

$$\mathbf{w}^*_{\alpha,\,\text{par}} = \lambda \left(\mathbf{\Omega}^{-1}_{\alpha\alpha} - \mathbf{\Omega}^{-1}_{\alpha\alpha}\mathbf{\Omega}_{\alpha\beta}\mathbf{\Omega}^{-1}_{\beta\beta}\mathbf{\mu}_\beta \right)$$

Substituting the solution vectors back into the utility function of the total optimisation problem, we get a positive expression for the loss in utility:

$$U\left(\mathbf{w}^*_{\text{par}}\right) - U\left(\mathbf{w}^*_{\text{sep}}\right) = \frac{\lambda}{2}\mathbf{\mu}^T_\beta \mathbf{\Omega}^{-1}_{\beta\beta}\mathbf{\Omega}_{\beta\alpha}\mathbf{\Omega}^{-1}_{\alpha\alpha}\mathbf{\Omega}_{\alpha\beta}\mathbf{\Omega}^{-1}_{\beta\beta}\mathbf{\mu}_\beta$$

This difference would approach zero if correlations became small. Separate overlays of active managers, ignoring cross-correlations between managers and asset classes, yield to a loss in utility. This is identical to other asset allocation problems (currency management, balanced portfolio management or asset–liability management) where it is also vital not to ignore correlation. However, while correlations between bonds and currencies are given and cannot be changed by the investor, this is not the case in manager allocation exercises. Plan sponsors who impose an orthogonality constraint on active returns do not have to worry about these results.[26]

7.10 CONCLUSIONS

The key factor driving the common move into core–satellite investing is fee arbitrage. As long as fee savings outweigh reduced information ratios, then the core–satellite approach is preferable to enhanced indexing. By definition, arbitrage is not an equilibrium concept. Explicit allocations to passive investments depend on whether investors allocate between managers on the basis of weights or tracking error. Allocations based on tracking error facilitate alpha transfer and hence are in many cases superior to allocations based on choosing manager weights.

Successful core–satellite investing, as a risk budgeting exercise, will have to deal with implementation issues like the incorporation of estimation error and the optimal treatment of time series covering different data periods and lengths. (In line with the arguments raised in Chapter 2, we used an optimisation framework to derive the risk budgets.) Even though core–satellite investing is the route currently favoured by many investors, enhanced indexing should not be overlooked as an alternative. Multiple manager allocations very often follow a two-step process; the first step derives the optimal strategic asset allocation, while the second step allocates across managers given the first-step asset allocations. This procedure will lead to a loss in portfolio efficiency unless sponsors have imposed orthogonality conditions on manager alphas.

APPENDIX A: MULTIPLE MANAGER MATHEMATICS

Any fund can be decomposed into a combination of an index fund (core) and an active portfolio (long–short satellite).[27] As we can see, every benchmarked investor is already investing in a particular core–satellite product, namely one core (benchmark) and one satellite (zero investment long–short portfolio). Scaling up active bets using a scaling factor (ϕ) will not increase the information content of any given portfolio; the difference will be leverage, not information.[28] Measures of skill, like the information ratio, are independent of leverage and will hence show no difference between an aggressive implementation of a particular investment strategy and a less aggressive implementation. Two active portfolios, which only differ in leverage, will have a correlation of one. Let us write down the return (alpha) for a core–satellite product with a total allocation ($w\%$) in active funds (w_i) as

$$\alpha = \sum_i w_i \phi_i \alpha_i = \sum_i w_i \alpha_i, \quad \sum_i w_i = w, \quad w_i \phi_i = w_i, \quad \phi_i \geq 0$$

$$(A1)$$

where α_i denotes the alpha (portfolio minus benchmark return) of the ith manager. A more aggressive implementation of the same strategy will yield a higher expected alpha. Investors have two ways of allocating between multiple managers; they can allocate either on the basis of assigning weights to active managers (weight allocation) or on the basis of aggressiveness, ie, tracking error (risk allocation). Both ways do not necessarily lead to the same results, as we will show later. Risks in a core–satellite approach can be calculated as

$$\sigma_\alpha = \left(\sum_i \sum_j \omega_{\alpha_i} \omega_{\alpha_j} \sigma_{\alpha_i \alpha_j} \right)^{\frac{1}{2}} \qquad (A2)$$

where $\sigma_{\alpha_i \alpha_j}$ denotes the covariance between managers' alphas. As tracking error is linearly homogeneous in either weights or scaling factors, we can use a simple Euler equation approach to decomposing tracking error. The risk budget (percentage of active risk attributed to the ith manager) can then be calculated as a sum of elasticities adding up to one:

$$\varepsilon_i = \frac{\delta\sigma}{\delta\omega_i}\frac{\omega_i}{\sigma}, \quad \sum_i \varepsilon_i = 1$$

Optimising the risk budget and, hence, simultaneously determining the active allocation (how much should be active?) and the allocation between managers (where to be active?) are now a straightforward optimisation exercise.[29] Minimise total portfolio risk subject to an alpha constraint:[30]

$$\text{min: } \bar{\sigma} = \left(\sum_i \sum_j \omega_i \omega_j \sigma_{ij} \right)^{\frac{1}{2}}$$

$$\text{subject to: } \alpha = \sum_i \omega_i \alpha_i \tag{A3}$$

with regard to either w, weight allocation, or ϕ, risk allocation. In order to facilitate the mathematics, we change to a matrix representation of Equation (A3) and write the corresponding Lagrangian together with the first order conditions:

$$L = \boldsymbol{\omega}' \boldsymbol{\Omega}_{\alpha\alpha} \boldsymbol{\omega} - \gamma \left(\boldsymbol{\omega}' \boldsymbol{\alpha} - \alpha_{\text{target}} \right) \tag{A4}$$

$$\frac{dL}{d\boldsymbol{\omega}} = \boldsymbol{\Omega}_{\alpha\alpha} \boldsymbol{\omega} - \gamma \boldsymbol{\alpha} = 0 \tag{A4a}$$

$$\frac{dL}{d\gamma} = \boldsymbol{\omega}' \boldsymbol{\alpha} - \alpha_{\text{target}} = 0 \tag{A4b}$$

where $\boldsymbol{\omega}$ and $\boldsymbol{\alpha}$ are column vectors of manager weights and manager alpha, and $\boldsymbol{\Omega}_{\alpha\alpha}$ denotes the covariance matrix of alphas. From Equation (A4a) we get $\boldsymbol{\omega} = \boldsymbol{\Omega}_{\alpha\alpha}^{-1}\boldsymbol{\alpha}\gamma$. Inserting this into Equation (A4b) yields

$$\gamma = \frac{1}{\boldsymbol{\alpha}'\boldsymbol{\Omega}_{\alpha\alpha}^{-1}\boldsymbol{\alpha}} \alpha_{\text{target}}$$

The optimal weight vector can now be found as

$$\boldsymbol{\omega}^* = \frac{\boldsymbol{\Omega}_{\alpha\alpha}^{-1}\boldsymbol{\alpha}}{\boldsymbol{\alpha}'\boldsymbol{\Omega}_{\alpha\alpha}^{-1}\boldsymbol{\alpha}} \alpha_{\text{target}} \tag{A5}$$

Substituting this into the formula for tracking error variance gives us the expression for the minimal risk level for the given alpha target: $\sigma_\alpha^2 = \left(\boldsymbol{\alpha}'\boldsymbol{\Omega}_{\alpha\alpha}^{-1}\boldsymbol{\alpha} \right)^{-1} \alpha_{\text{target}}^2$. Comparing this with the expression for the Lagrange multiplier, we write $\gamma = \sigma_\alpha^2/\alpha_{\text{target}}$. Hence Equation (A4a) becomes

$$\Omega_{\alpha\alpha}\,\boldsymbol{\omega} = \frac{\sigma_\alpha^2}{\alpha_{\text{target}}}\,\boldsymbol{\alpha}$$

$$\frac{\Omega_{\alpha\alpha}\,\boldsymbol{\omega}}{\sigma_\alpha}\,\frac{\alpha_{\text{target}}}{\sigma_\alpha} = \boldsymbol{\alpha}$$

$$\frac{\Omega_{\alpha\alpha}\,\boldsymbol{\omega}}{\sigma_\alpha}\left(\frac{\alpha_{\text{target}}}{\sigma_\alpha}\right) = \boldsymbol{\alpha}$$

The individual optimality conditions for multiple manager allocation can be read as elements of the above vectors[31]

$$\frac{d\sigma_\alpha}{d\omega_{\alpha_i}}\left(\frac{\alpha_{\text{target}}}{\sigma_\alpha}\right) = \alpha_i \tag{A6}$$

as

$$\frac{d\sigma_\alpha}{d\boldsymbol{\omega}} = \begin{bmatrix} d\sigma_\alpha / d\omega_{\alpha_1} \\ \vdots \\ d\sigma_\alpha / d\omega_{\alpha_n} \end{bmatrix} = \frac{d\left(\boldsymbol{\omega}'\,\Omega_{\alpha\alpha}\,\boldsymbol{\omega}\right)^{\frac{1}{2}}}{d\boldsymbol{\omega}}$$

$$= \frac{1}{2}\left(\boldsymbol{\omega}'\,\Omega_{\alpha\alpha}\,\boldsymbol{\omega}\right)^{-\frac{1}{2}} 2\,\Omega_{\alpha\alpha}\,\boldsymbol{\omega} = \frac{\Omega_{\alpha\alpha}\,\boldsymbol{\omega}}{\sigma_\alpha}$$

It also follows from Equation (A6) that

$$\frac{\alpha_i}{\alpha_j} = \frac{d\sigma}{d\omega_{\alpha_i}}\Big/\frac{d\sigma}{d\omega_{\alpha_j}} \tag{A7}$$

Optimal risk budgeting implies that the ratio of marginal contribution to alpha and marginal contribution to risk equals the information ratio of the total multiple manager portfolio for every single fund (assuming no short-sale constraints).

APPENDIX B: MULTIPLE MANAGER ALLOCATION AND CORRELATION STRUCTURE

Using the same technique as in the currency hedging appendix to Chapter 2, the partial optimisation solution can be found by solving

$$U = \mathbf{w}_\alpha'\,\boldsymbol{\mu}_\alpha - \frac{1}{2\lambda}\,\mathbf{w}_\alpha'\,\Omega_{\alpha\alpha}\,\mathbf{w}_\alpha + \mathbf{w}_\beta'\,\boldsymbol{\mu}_\beta - \frac{1}{2\lambda}\,\overline{\mathbf{w}}_\beta'\,\Omega_{\beta\beta}\,\overline{\mathbf{w}}_\beta + \frac{1}{\lambda}\,\overline{\mathbf{w}}_\beta'\,\Omega_{\alpha\alpha}\,\mathbf{w}_\alpha$$

$$\tag{B1}$$

with respect to $\mathbf{w}_\alpha$ leaving $\overline{\mathbf{w}}_\beta = \lambda \mathbf{\Omega}_{\beta\beta}^{-1} \boldsymbol{\mu}_\beta$ fixed. The result is given

$$\mathbf{w}_{\alpha,\text{par}}^* = \lambda (\mathbf{\Omega}_{\alpha\alpha}^{-1} - \mathbf{\Omega}_{\alpha\alpha}^{-1} \mathbf{\Omega}_{\alpha\beta} \mathbf{\Omega}_{\beta\beta}^{-1} \boldsymbol{\mu}_\beta)$$

Simultaneous optimisation, taking the interaction term into account, yields

$$\mathbf{w}_{\beta,\text{sim}}^* = \lambda \left(\left(\mathbf{\Omega}_{\beta\beta} - \boldsymbol{\theta}\mathbf{\Omega}_{\alpha\alpha}\boldsymbol{\theta}' \right)^{-1} \boldsymbol{\mu}_\beta - \left(\mathbf{\Omega}_{\beta\beta} - \boldsymbol{\theta}\mathbf{\Omega}_{\alpha\alpha}\boldsymbol{\theta}' \right)^{-1} \mathbf{\Omega}_{\alpha\alpha}^{-1}\mathbf{\Omega}_{\alpha\beta} \boldsymbol{\mu}_\alpha \right)$$

(B2a)

$$\mathbf{w}_{\alpha,\text{sim}}^* = \lambda \mathbf{\Omega}_{\alpha\alpha}^{-1} \boldsymbol{\mu}_\alpha - \mathbf{\Omega}_{\alpha\alpha}^{-1} \mathbf{\Omega}_{\alpha\beta} \mathbf{w}_\beta^*$$

(B2b)

Alpha and beta bets are mutually corrected for their communality. Those managers who take structural bets (systematic exposure to marketwide influences also shared by the benchmark) will end up with a lower allocation, as if these would remain undetected. However, in practice, this is rarely done. By moving from the separate to the partial solution, we can now check whether there is an increase in utility. We only have to substitute the solution vectors into the utility function to achieve

$$U(\mathbf{w}^p) - U = (\mathbf{w}^S) = \frac{\lambda}{2} \boldsymbol{\mu}_\beta^T \mathbf{\Omega}_{\beta\beta}^{-1} - \mathbf{\Omega}_{\beta\alpha}\mathbf{\Omega}_{\alpha\alpha}^{-1}\mathbf{\Omega}_{\alpha\beta}\mathbf{\Omega}_{\beta\beta}^{-1} \boldsymbol{\mu}_\beta$$

(B3)

As long as $\mathbf{\Omega}_{\beta\beta}^{-1} - \mathbf{\Omega}_{\beta\alpha}\mathbf{\Omega}_{\alpha\alpha}^{-1}\mathbf{\Omega}_{\alpha\beta}\mathbf{\Omega}_{\beta\beta}^{-1}$ is positive definite, the utility difference (quadratic form) will be positive. We proved that separate optimisation of manager and asset allocation leads (in an otherwise unconstrained context) to a utility loss, as long as manager alpha and asset allocation show non-zero correlation. In the case of zero correlation, all conditional distributions become unconditional and separation of alpha and beta bets will still result in the optimal solution. However, positive correlation between alpha and beta bets might even arise when individual alphas are orthogonal (uncorrelated) with their respective benchmarks. Suppose a manager with a pure government benchmark takes a "diversification bet" into emerging market debt. While the alpha from this structural bet would be roughly orthogonal to the government bond benchmark (low correlation of emerging market debt), there would be a unitary correlation between this bet and the emerging market part of the strategic allocation (beta bet).

1   The availability of very aggressive products in the form of hedge funds might also serve as a catalyst. Sometimes multiple manager allocation is referred to as an additional driving force. However, this can also be achieved in a traditional framework.

2   See Freeman (1997).

3   The information ratio is defined as the ration of active return, ie, portfolio return minus benchmark return. Practitioners misleadingly use active return and alpha synonymously. While this is wrong – the term alpha is reserved for risk-adjusted active returns – we will use this convention until otherwise noted. The reader should keep in mind, though, that the

information ratio as a measure of risk-adjusted out-performance, as defined above, can easily be gained by investing into a riskier asset. The resulting active return would arise from collecting a risk premium rather than from superior information.

4 Grid searching is only feasible for problems with up to three managers (changing weights for two managers and treating the third manager as residual). Higher-order problems can be solved using commercially available optimisers.

5 This follows directly from Sharpe's arithmetic of active management (Sharpe, 1991).

6 However, specialisation does not come without costs. Breaking up a balanced mandate into regional bonds and equity mandates would make timing and asset allocation decisions much more difficult to implement, unless an overlay manager is employed, where this is legally feasible.

7 Examples for specialisation are asset class-specific specialists like currency overlay manager, dedicated fixed-income specialist, value manager, etc.

8 Sharpe (1991), p. 219.

9 See Rosenberg (1977).

10 See Sorensen *et al.* (1998) for a similar approach.

11
$$\max U = IR \cdot \sigma_\alpha - \lambda \sigma_\alpha^2, \frac{dU}{d\sigma_\alpha} = IR - 2\lambda\sigma_\alpha$$

12 See Di Bartolomeo (1999) on issues in multi-manager investing.

13 Regional division might not always be the best division. A plan sponsor will try to save fees in supposedly very efficient markets and will be prepared to employ active managers in less developed asset classes. Hence they might make large stocks the core and invest into active smaller company management. (This could still be done on a capitalisation equivalent basis, so that no discrepancies between the sum actual benchmarks and strategic benchmarks occur.)

14 Enhanced indexing is defined as low tracking error active management. Sometimes the term is used for quantitatively driven products with tight risk controls. A very good treatment of enhanced indexing can be found in Di Bartolomeo (2000).

15 This section draws heavily on the results of Grinold and Kahn (1999, Chapters 14 and 15) and puts them into the context of core–satellite investing.

16 The simulation methodology is directly taken from Grinold and Kahn (1999, p. 419ff). Suppose there is an investment universe of 200 stocks with a residual volatility of 20% each. The stocks are equally weighted in the benchmark. The portfolio manager adjusts his/her return expectation for each stock only once a year. His/her information coefficient (correlation between forecast and realisation) is 0.1. We perform a simulation and obtain a series of alphas for each stock: $\alpha_i = 0.1 \cdot 20\% \cdot \varepsilon_i$, with $\varepsilon_i \sim N(0, 1)$. For each simulation, we construct an optimal portfolio subject to the short-selling restriction.

17 See Grinold and Kahn (1999, pp. 428–30) for a description of the methodology.

18 See Chopra and Ziemba (1993), Michaud (1998), Britten-Jones (2000) and Chapter 3 of this book. Although estimation error is already dealt with in Chapters 3 and 4, it is worthwhile repeating this issue in a multiple manager context.

19 The proposed methodology stems from Stambaugh (1997).

20 The data are generated by drawing random active returns with 2% active risk and 1% expected active return. Correlation is assumed to be 0.8. Hence the true information ratio is 0.5. All return realisations before 1985 for funds four and five are deleted to arrive at the test data set.

21 The underlying assumption is that returns are drawn from a stationary distribution.

22 The graph can be easily constructed by writing the information ratio as a function of excess beta only:

$$IR(\beta) = \frac{(\beta-1)(R-r) + IR\left(\bar{\sigma}^2 - (\beta-1)^2 \sigma_m^2\right)^{\frac{1}{2}}}{\bar{\sigma}_\alpha}$$

where $R - r$ denotes the risk premium on equities, σ_m denotes equity volatility and $\bar{\sigma}_\alpha$ the prefixed tracking error.

23 The correlation between two managers can be calculated as

$$\rho_{ij} = \frac{(\beta_i - 1)(\beta_j - 1)\,\sigma_m^2}{\overline{\sigma}_{\alpha i}\,\overline{\sigma}_{\alpha j}}$$

24 Muralidhar (2001) also stresses the importance of taking into account manager versus manager and manager versus asset class correlation.

25 It is worth noting that this condition is not met in practice. Suppose an investor holds a benchmark with a volatility of 15 and an excess return over cash of three. This results in a marginal rate of substitution (trades off return against variance) of 0.00667. Being 99% invested yields a variance of 220.52 (2.97 risk premium), while a market exposure of 101% yields a variance of 229.52 (3.03 risk premium). Dividing the difference in return by the difference in variance gives the marginal rate of substitution between return and variance. Investing into an active manager with 5% tracking error and 1% alpha (which many would already deem undesirable) reveals a marginal rate of substitution of 0.04, which is many times bigger than the one implied in the asset allocation choice.

26 Orthogonality means that active returns and benchmark returns are uncorrelated. In a CAPM world this can also be obtained by imposing beta-neutrality.

27 Strictly speaking, this is not quite true as the theoretical loss of a zero investment long-short portfolio can become infinite (a short position in a rising stock can theoretically lead to unlimited losses).

28 For the use of scaling factors in asset management, see also Lee (2000, Chapter 4).

29 See Kritzman and Chow (2001), who uses VAR to describe risk budgets. In a normally distributed world, both approaches are equivalent.

30 Baierl and Chen (2000) optimise with more difficult constraints.

31 See Grinold and Kahn (1999, p.134).

BIBLIOGRAPHY

Baierl, G., and P. Chen, 2000, "Choosing Managers and Funds: How to Maximise your Alpha Without Sacrificing your Target", *Journal of Portfolio Management* 26, Autumn, pp. 47–53.

Britten-Jones, M., 1999, "The Sampling Error in Estimates of Mean-Variance Efficient Portfolio Weights", *The Journal of Finance* 54, pp. 655–71.

Chopra, V., and W. Ziemba, 1993, "The Effects of Errors in Means, Variances and Covariances on Optimal Portfolio Choice", *Journal of Portfolio Management* 19, Winter, pp. 6–11.

Di Bartolomeo, D., 1999, "A Radical Proposal for the Operation of Multi-Manager Investment Funds", Northfield Information Services, Inc.

Di Bartolomeo, D., 2000, "The Enhanced Index Fund as an Alternative to Enhanced Index Equity Management", Northfield Information Services, Inc.

Freeman, J., 1997, "Investment Deadweight and the Advantages of Long Short Investment Management", *VBA Journal*, pp. 11–14.

Grinold, R., and R. Kahn, 1999, *Active Portfolio Management*, Second Edition (New York: McGraw Hill).

Kritzmann, M., and G. Chow, 2001, "Risk Budgets", *Journal of Portfolio Management* 27, Winter, pp. 56–60.

Lee, W., 2000, "Theory and Methodology of Tactical Asset Allocation", Fabozzi Associates (Pennsylvania: New Hope).

Michaud, R., 1998, *Efficient Asset Management* (Harvard Business School Press).

Muralidhar, A., 2001, "Optimal Risk Adjusted Portfolios with Multiple Managers", *Journal of Portfolio Management* 27, Spring, pp. 97–104.

Rosenberg, B., 1977, "Institutional Investment with Multiple Portfolio Managers", Proceedings of the Seminar on the Analysis of Security Prices, University of Chicago, pp. 55–160.

Scherer, B., 2000, "Preparing the Best Risk Budget", *Risk* 13, pp. 30–2.

Scherer, B., 2001, "Tracking Error and Funding Assumptions", *Journal of Asset Management* 2, pp. 235–40.

Sharpe, W. F., 1991, "The Arithmetic of Active Management", *The Financial Analysts Journal* 47, pp. 7–9.

Sorensen, E., K. Miller and V. Samak, 1998, "Allocating Between Active and Passive Management", *Financial Analysts Journal* 54, pp. 18–31.

Stambaugh, R., 1997, "Analysing Investments Whose Differences Vary in Length", *Journal of Financial Economics* 45, pp. 285–331.

Winkelmann, K., 2000, "Managing Active Risk at the Total Fund Level", in: L. Rahl, *Risk Budgeting*, pp. 39–64 (London: Risk Books).

Index

heuristic portfolio construction 171
"hill" plot 56
historical covariance, and
   predictive covariance 123
historical data, and asset allocation
   119–20
human capital 31–3

I

illiquid assets, correcting for
   autocorrelation 15–17
implied alphas 200
implied asset movements 179
implied market movements 179
implied position analysis 178–80
implied return forecasts 97
implied returns 141
implied risk and return
   analysis 18–23
      basic risk decomposition 18–20
implied view analysis, reverse
   optimisation 20–22
in-sample optimisation 164
information coefficients 171
information ratios 178, 179, 199,
   209, 210, 211, 213
input generation, and core–satellite
   investing 211–13
input return forecasts 97
integration techniques
   for calculating lower partial
      moments 71–4
      Monte Carlo integration 73–4
      numerical integration 69–71
      software 71
inverse Wishart 132
investment information, applying
   across client portfolios 23
investment process, benefits of
   portfolio construction 170
investment skill xiii
investment universe, and
   clustering techniques 11–15

J

JP Morgan EMBI+ Index 50, 52, 57

K

Kolmogorov–Smirnov statistic 66
kurtosis 50, 51, 56

L

Lagrangian multipliers 3
lambda-associated portfolios
   versus rank-associated portfolios
      100–101
liability-hedging assets 5
life-cycle investing model 31–3
linear regression
   and characteristic portfolios
      99–100
   and portfolio resampling 91–2
lower partial moment calculation
   61
lower partial moments 58–68
   approach using empirical distri-
      bution and single return series
      58–61
   best practice 65–8
   estimation 64–8
   integration techniques for
      calculating 71–4
   and multiple return series 61–3
lower partial moments-based
   method, compared with variance-
   based methods 68–70

M

manager allocation, versus risk
   allocation 206–8
manager alpha, and prior
   information 112
"marginal contribution to risk"
   (MCTR) 18
market movements 179
Markowitz, H. 105
Markowitz optimisation 71